behavioral research

A Series of Books in Psychology

EDITORS

Richard C. Atkinson
Jonathan Freedman
Gardner Lindzey
Richard F. Thompson

lawrence s. meyers
and
neal e. grossen
CALIFORNIA STATE UNIVERSITY, SACRAMENTO

behavioral research

theory, procedure, and design

W. H. FREEMAN AND COMPANY   San Francisco

Library of Congress Cataloging in Publication Data

Meyers, Lawrence S
    Behavioral research: theory, procedure, and design.

    1. Psychological research. I. Grossen, Neal E.,
joint author. II. Title [DNLM: 1. Behavior.
2. Research. BF121 M613b 1974]
BF76.5.M48   150'.7'2   73-16492
ISBN 0-7167-0842-6

Printed in the United States of America

10 9 8 7 6 5 4 3 2

contents

section one
the beginnings of research

section two
the foundation of research

section three
the techniques of research

section four
the communication of research

16   Communication of Research Findings

appendix A
the analysis of research

appendix B
mathematical and statistical tables

preface

This book is intended for students taking their first behavioral research course, introducing them to the concepts, tools, and procedures applicable to the behavioral and social sciences. It is organized around the information used by a researcher from the inception of a project to its completion.

The goal of science is to achieve knowledge about the world, and research is the means to that goal. In Section One, The Beginnings of Research, we discuss the relationship of research to science and scientific knowledge.

Since the immediate task of research is to observe phenomena and collect data, we present the definition of measurement and some properties of data in Section Two, The Foundation of Research.

Entering the laboratory, in Section Three, The Techniques of Research, we examine several scientific methodologies relevant to many diverse settings, from the natural environment, to the classroom, to the formal scientific laboratory.

Following laboratory work, it is often necessary to make statistical calculations in drawing conclusions from the data. A prior familiarity with statistics is not required. We explain some of the basic statistical principles for understanding research design; Appendix A provides a simplified description of some useful calculations for the interested student. We should emphasize, however, that our treatment is no substitute for a study of statistics.

The final step in the research project is to present a summary of findings in a standardized fashion. The writing of reports is discussed in Section Four, The Communication of Research.

We would like to express our appreciation to all those who have contributed their time and energy to this book, but take ultimate responsibility for its contents. We are indebted to the literary executor of the late Sir Ronald A. Fisher, F.R.S., to Dr. Frank Yates, F.R.S., and to Longman Group Ltd., London, for permission to reprint Tables C, D, and F in Appendix B from their book *Statistical Tables for Biological, Agricultural and Medical Research.*

September, 1973

Lawrence S. Meyers

Neal E. Grossen

behavioral research

section one

the beginnings of research

For centuries man has been engaged in scientific pursuits, and the results and applications of his efforts have literally changed the world around us. Science in all its forms (e.g., physical, chemical, behavioral, and so forth) and ramifications (e.g., technology) is a major factor in the development of western civilization. Recently, particularly during the twentieth century, science in and of itself has become the object of study, and this section is an example of such an inquiry.

The question "What is science?" is anything but straight-forward, and because of its generality, it is very difficult to answer. When less general questions—or ones that are more answerable—are asked no one set of answers is given; rather, a variety of answers, many directly antagonistic to each other, may be heard. Our analysis, therefore, is only one of many that have been presented on the nature of science.

The whole research process, in all its detail and complexity, takes place in an environment of three worlds:

1. *The Empirical World.* Scientists begin with the assumption that there is a world external to themselves, and that this world can be interacted with, i.e., measured.

2. *The Theoretical World.* Scientists not only seek to measure the empirical world, but also attempt to understand and explain its workings. That is, scientists believe either that the empirical world is ordered (and that we may come to understand this order) or that they can impose upon the empirical world some ordered schema. This process necessitates the development of a *scientific theory.*

3. *The Human World.* Between the Empirical and Theoretical Worlds lies Man. The empirical world is known to us through our senses or consciousness, and the theoretical world is generated by our intellect.

It is the purpose of the first chapter to suggest some of the ways in which these three worlds interact for people to acquire this most precious gift—knowledge.

the nature of scientific inquiry

Upon enrolling in the first research course in a behavioral science curriculum, you may naturally entertain some preconceived ideas on the nature of the scientific enterprise and the relationship of the nature of science to the activities in which you will be engaged. Science textbooks used in earlier grades, mass media representations of what scientists do, college introductory textbooks (particularly introductory psychology books), and general cultural sophistication have supplied many of you—in addition to most members of society—with a particular conception of science. It is the purpose of this chapter to summarize the aculturated view of science and then to indicate some of the basic problems inherent in such an approach.

A Traditional Description of Science

The concept of science, whether physics, medicine, psychology, or any other science, probably brings to mind a number of images. You might perhaps think of the astronomer staring through his telescope and then writing down his observations; of a biochemist looking through a microscope attempting to add to the understanding of some disease; of a psychologist observing a rat or other animal running through a maze, or of the anthropologist talking to a primitive native on some South Sea island about his or her family relationships. All of these activities generate *data* (the recorded observations) for the particular scientist and serve to further our knowledge about the world in which we live. In principle these data sometimes agree or fail to agree with certain of the conjectures (*hypotheses*) the scientist had previously made.

When the observations made by one scientist are obtained by other scientists under approximately the same conditions, this observational agreement may be summarized by what is called a *factual statement*.

Once a number of factual statements are developed in a science, it may appear to the scientist that certain of these may be related to one another. A statement that relates factual statements to one another is called an *empirical law*.

Ancient man, for example, must have observed the activity of the moon. At some times, there was a large and bright disk in the night sky, at other times, a large and bright crescent was seen, at still other times, a small and bright crescent, and finally, there were times when no portion of the moon was visible. Since these observations were repeatedly made, we have a group of factual statements. Each observation is repeated every 28th day; the observations therefore occur in some ordered sequence. The empirical law that summarizes these ordered relations is: "the lunar cycle repeats itself every 28 days." An empirical law is said to be *empirical* because it has its basis in observations (that is, factual statements that are themselves based on observation), and it is said to be *lawful* in that it summarizes a relationship of certain sets of factual statements to other sets of factual statements.

Scientists, however, usually do not stop with the establishment of empirical laws; they search after an explanation of such laws. Explanation is obtained when a satisfactory *theory* has been developed. Philosophers of science tell us that a theory consists of at least two main components (see Fig. 1.1). The first may be called the abstract calculus, consisting of a series of *postulates* considered to be immutable. These postulates provide the foundation of the theory, and are ideally a set of analytical (logical, mathematical, etc.) statements. All such statements are necessarily universal statements. From the postulates, deductions can be made; these deductions are called *theorems*. The second component of a theory is what may be called *rules of correspondence*. These rules essentially relate some of the theoretical terms used in the postulates to an empirical counterpart. The step from the theorem to an empirical prediction is mediated by a particular *hypothesis* made by the scientists. We may illustrate this transition by the following example:

POSTULATE: The degree of strength with which a response is associated with a stimulus (this association is called learning) is a direct function of the number of reinforcements given immediately after the responses and the magnitude of each of the reinforcements.

THEOREM: All else being equal, the greater the amount of reinforcement following a response, the greater the amount of learning that will occur.

HYPOTHESIS: If the subjects in Group A are given more reinforcement than those in Group B for comparable responses, then the subjects in Group A will learn more than those in Group B.

PREDICTION: The subjects in Group A will receive $r + r'$ amount of reinforcement and will take less time to solve Task X than those in Group B who will receive only r amount of reinforcement.

Note that the postulate is a general (i.e., universal) statement relating learning to reinforcement, and that the theorem considers just one specific line of reasoning from the postulate. The hypothesis is really a specification of the theorem to be studied by the scientist. We are still talking of two as yet hypothetical groups (A and B) that would receive different amounts of reinforcement. Finally, in the prediction, we see that Groups A and B will be run in an experiment, that each will be asked to learn Task X under different conditions, and that we will observe the amount of time taken by the subjects in each group to solve the task. If the prediction is correct, the scientist would probably assume that the hypothesis was likewise correct, and since the hypothesis was derived from the theory, that the theory has in this instance been verified or confirmed.

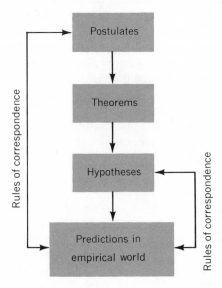

Fig. 1.1 A simplified schematic of a theory.

The scientist uses a theory to organize and explain a range of empirical laws and diverse factual statements. An empirical law is said to be explained when it has been made an integral part of the theory. That is, on the basis of the postulates in the abstract calculus of the theory, logical deductions or theorems are drawn. By means of the correspondence rules, a translation is made from the logical to the empirical statements. On the basis of the empirical statements, it is predicted, from the theory, that if such and such conditions are met, such and such should occur (be observed, measured, etc.). These occurrences, in turn, should be subsumed within the empirical law. In attempting to explain the occurrence of the sunrise, for instance, stating the empirical law "the sun rises in the east every 24 hours" gives an inadequate explanation of the phenomenon in that it does no more than state the observations that the sun does indeed rise every 24 hours. An adequate explanation of the occurrence of the sunrise in the east about 24 hours after yesterday's dawn would invoke various physical theories such as the Theory of Optics, Theory of Mechanics, etc.

A theory can be a powerful tool to the scientist in an understanding of the world. To cite a well-known theory, Sir Isaac Newton, on the basis of relatively few postulates, was able to deduce the laws of both pendulum motion and planetary motion. Both sets of laws were explained by relating each to the concept of gravity. Furthermore, by observing that the orbit of the planet Neptune showed particular variations from that specified by the theory, it was predicted that there must be a sizable gravitational force acting on that planet at an even further distance from the sun. Calculations —again based upon the theory—indicated that the origins of force must be in space. Upon turning their telescopes to that place in the sky, astronomers discovered the existence of the planet Pluto. The prediction of the existence of Pluto could not have been made on the basis of the existing empirical laws, since at that time observations were not complete enough. Only from a sophisticated theory, i.e., a theory that could allow very precise predictions, could such an hypothesis have been derived.

We should mention here that not all sciences, particularly psychology, have reached the point of developing very quantitative theories. In order to maintain continuity in the remainder of this chapter, however, we will refer to even very loosely connected notions as theories.

Some Complications

The encapsulated view of science just presented will probably strike most of you as being basically correct. It should be pointed out, however, that there are a number of vitally important assumptions implicit within this view of science. The traditional scientific framework typically fails to analyze certain of these, and with very good reason; a careful analysis may suggest that many of these assumptions are at best, oversimplified, and at worst, incorrect. The purpose of the remainder of this chapter is to indicate to you the nature and complexity of certain of these assumptions and their implications for traditional science.

Observation

Traditional science assumes a direct "translation" between the physical event and the observation of that event. This suggests that a scientist can accurately observe and record events that occur in the empirical world. We feel, however, that such a translation may not be as direct as many of us assume because man is an information analyzer and processor; as such he actively interprets and structures the stimulus input that he receives. We suggest that processing of information received by the observer may modify the information so that it is more than a photographic picture of the physical world; that is, the information is no longer a direct representation of the real world.

The process of observation is much more complex than many of us realize and it will be instructive to consider the process of observation as two separate functions. Appreciating how arbitrary this separation is, let us call these two aspects of observation *sensation* and *perception*.

Sensation

The act of receiving a stimulus input and the sensory consequence of this input will be called sensation. For most practical purposes we can equate sensation with the physiological effects that arise as a result of the activation of sensory receptors. We assume, for simplicity, that "raw" sensation is a direct physiological representation of the sensory input.* Man, however, translates his sensations into a meaningful organizational pattern by providing structure to the sensation. For examples of this translation we need to consider perception.

Perception

Perception will be treated as the *psychological process* of seeing, hearing, tasting, etc. This process of perception is the result of the decoding of the

---

*For those who disdain simplicity, Lindsay and Norman (1972) present an excellent discussion of information processing at the sensory level.

sensations that arise as a consequence of stimulation of the sensory system. We will maintain that this psychological process, perception, is influenced by prior experience (learning), since it can be shown that the way one processes and translates information can change as a function of experience.

There are many available examples demonstrating the influence of experience on perception. In the following pages we will present a few classic examples of the operation of this process. Generally speaking, these examples fall into one or the other of two categories of perceptual phenomena. The first category we will call *universal*. These perceptual phenomena result from information being processed in similar ways by most observers and thus these experiences depend on learning to a much lesser extent than perceptual phenomena belonging to the second category.

The second and largest category of perceptual phenomena contains those whose translation depends in a large part on the prior experience of the observer. We will call this category of perceptual phenomenon *idiosyncratic*, meaning that not all observers will see the stimulus object(s) in the same way. Instead, the way observers perceive these latter phenomena is a direct result of their knowledge about the stimulus situation.

Universal perceptual phenomena

There is a variety of interesting universal perceptual phenomena with which you may already be familiar. One of these is the classic Müller-Lyer illusion, experienced by almost all human observers. This illusion is presented in Fig. 1.2. The question is: Which line is longer? Most of you will probably judge that Line B is longer. If you measure the lines, however, you will find them to be the same length. But even after you measure them, and in a sense "know" them to be the same length, the line with the outward pointing arrows will still appear to be longer.

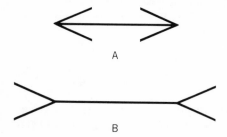

Fig. 1.2 The Müller-Lyer illusion.

Look at Fig. 1.3. Here is a set of several lines. Look at the two horizontal lines. Are they straight and parallel? Most of you will probably see these two lines as having a slight outward curve in the center, but if you place a straight edge along the lines, it will be found that they are in fact straight. If you examine the lines again, however, they will still appear curved even though you know they are straight.

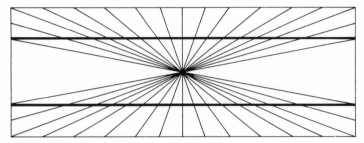

Fig. 1.3 Illusion of curvature.

Let us present one final example of this type of perceptual phenomena. Look at Fig. 1.4.

Fig. 1.4 Spiral or concentric circles? (From Phillips "The Origins of Intellect: Piaget's Theory." W. H. Freeman and Company. Copyright © 1969.)

Place your pencil point in the alley at the top of the figure and do not remove it from the paper. The idea is to follow the alley to the center of the maze as quickly as you can without going out of the alley or breaking any printed lines. Time how long it takes to reach the goal. Did you ever reach the goal? You now know that this figure is really a set of concentric circles. Look at it again. It still looks possible to reach the goal (the center), but in reality, this is an impossible task.

These perceptual phenomena demonstrate that we may translate our sensations into a particular structure and that this structure imposed on the input remains even after we have tested its "reality." These, then, are some examples of where we, as observers, fail to make a direct translation of the empirical world.

Idiosyncratic perceptual phenomena

If you consider the group of black splotches presented in Fig. 1.5, they will probably seem a random array. If you continue to view the collection of black spots you may find that there seems to be a recognizable figure in it—you may begin to see a man on a horse. At this point you have imposed structure on the input (as a function of experience) when there really is none or at least very little. Look at this figure again. Now you most likely will see a man on a horse, and most of you will now have some trouble seeing this figure as anything else. Why? Because your experience with the figure has influenced your perception of it.

Perceive

Fig. 1.5 Prolonged exposure will reveal a man on a horse.

Now let us borrow an example used by Hanson (1958) to illustrate a similar point. Consider the animal drawn in Fig. 1.6. Now consider the

groups of birds drawn in Fig. 1.7. Note that in the lower right hand portion of Fig. 1.7 is the drawing presented to you in isolation in Fig. 1.6.

Fig. 1.6 Bird or antelope?

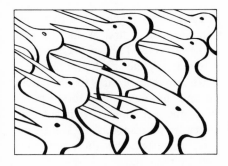

Fig. 1.7 A group of birds.

Was the object in Fig. 1.6 the drawing of a bird? Perhaps it was. Now consider Fig. 1.8 in which is drawn a group of antelope. Again in the lower
right hand portion of Fig. 1.8 is the drawing presented to you in isolation

Fig. 1.8 A group of antelope.

in Fig. 1.6. Was the animal in Fig. 1.6 the drawing of an antelope? Well,
perhaps it was. Most people will probably see the drawing in Fig. 1.6 as
either an antelope or as a bird, depending upon the context (i.e., seen
either in Fig. 1.7 or in Fig. 1.8). Notice, however, that the *same physical
sensation* (or stimulus elements, etc.) of Fig. 1.6 may be *seen* (perceived)
differently. Observation, then, may depend upon more than simply the

physical stimulus. The physical stimulus gives rise to a sensation which, in combination with the general context, then results in a perception.

Consider another example based on an experiment by Bruner and Minturn (1955). Read the following line of letters aloud:

X   C   J   B   N   T

Since that was such an easy task, how about reading the following line of numbers aloud this time:

74   39   82   B   65   27

You have perhaps noticed that the fourth stimulus in each of the two lines is physically identical but that you probably read it first as the letter B and second as the number 13. Bruner and Minturn used very short exposure durations (well under a second) in order to magnify the effect, and reported that most of the experimental subjects who were expecting to see letters reported the ambiguous stimulus as a B and those expecting to see numbers reported it as 13. The explanation of these findings is that subjects were psychologically *set* (i.e., prepared, ready, predisposed) to see an instance of a *particular* class of events, and, therefore, saw the ambiguous stimulus through the framework imposed by their set.

Another, even more dramatic demonstration of the same sort of phenomenon, is reported by Bruner and Postman (1949). These investigators asked subjects to recognize playing cards which were presented for very short durations. Bruner and Postman used five different playing cards in which one card *had the color of the suit reversed*, (e.g., spades were red and hearts were black). They presented these "trick" cards with normal cards in different orders to the various subjects. The question was how long would be required for recognition of the proper suit to take place. Fig. 1.9 shows the number of correct identifications of the playing cards as a function of exposure time. Notice that at all exposure times used, there is a much higher identification percentage for the normal cards. Some subjects failed to ever correctly identify the trick cards. The investigators also found that once the subject "caught on" to the trick cards he could identify them almost as well as the normal ones. One subject, who had trouble with the recognition of the trick cards, is quoted as saying "I don't know what the hell it is now, not even sure it's a playing card."

The conclusion to be drawn again is that prior experience with playing cards prepared the subjects to see them in a certain way and when the physical properties of these cards did not meet with expectations, subjects had some difficulty identifying them correctly.

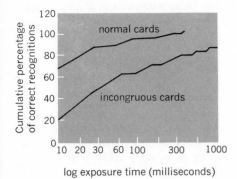

log exposure time (milliseconds)

Fig. 1.9 Cumulative percentage of normal and incongruous playing cards correctly recognized as a function of increasing exposure time.

As a final example of experience influencing our observation, let us borrow another of Hanson's (1958) examples. If a physicist were shown Fig. 1.10, he or she would see an X-ray tube viewed from the cathode.

> Would Sir Lawrence Bragg and an Eskimo baby see the same thing when looking at an X-ray tube? Yes, and no. Yes—they are visually aware of the same object. No—the ways in which they are visually aware are profoundly different. Seeing is not only the having of a visual experience . . .

> I can make nothing of the Arab word for *cat*, though my purely visual impressions may be indistingisuhable from those of an Arab who can. I must learn Arabic before I can see what he does. The layman must learn physics before he can see what the physicist sees. (Hanson, 1958, pp. 15–16.)

Fig. 1.10 An X-ray tube viewed from the cathode.

Observation, then, depends to a large degree upon prior knowledge. In Hanson's (1958) terminology

> . . . seeing is a 'theory-laden' undertaking. Observation of x is shaped by prior knowledge of x. [p. 19.]

That is,

> what is to see boxes, staircases, birds, antelopes, bears, goblets, X-ray tubes? It is (at least) to have knowledge of certain sorts. (. . . electric eyes are blind . . . cameras cannot see.) It is to see that, were certain things done to objects before our eyes, other things would result. . . . To see an X-ray tube is at least to see that, were it dropped on stone, it would smash. To see a goblet is to see something with concave interior. [pp. 20–21.]

Cameras and electric eyes are blind even though they can "sense" what is "out there." People, not cameras, perceive, and what we as people see depends not only upon the physical object but also on the processing of the sensation by our nervous system. Perception, or what we see, encompasses sensation plus meaning. This meaning, because it is applied by our individual processing of the input information, is unique to us as individuals. Only to the extent that our genetic makeup or memory systems supply a similar kind of meaning to given sensations can we say that we see the same things.

By now you should realize that observation is not as direct a translation of the empirical world as scientists may wish. The notion of objectivity is also tied up with the notion of direct translation. Recall that objectivity is defined by traditional science as consensual agreement. The visual illusions presented earlier are excellent examples of the problem of consensual agreement. An illusion, by definition, indicates the absence of a one to one correspondence of the empirical world to observation. Although almost everyone sees two lines of different lengths (Müller-Lyer illusion) or two bent lines (see Fig. 1.3), does it follow that the two lines *are* of different lengths or *are* bent? And what of the effects of experience upon observation? What shall we see when presented with the ambiguous stimulus of Bruner and Minturn? It appears necessary, then, to examine the notion of objectivity in some detail.

Objectivity

As a student you may have encountered the question of objectivity in the course of taking examinations. For most purposes, examinations can be classed into two types—multiple choice or essay examinations. We usually class multiple guess examinations as "objective" and essay examinations as "subjective." Why? Because your grade on an essay test depends on the instructor's idiosyncratic response (much to your chagrin) to your answer. We all know that different instructors may grade the same essay answer in completely different ways. These same instructors, however, would assign identical grades had the exam been multiple guess simply because any scorer, including a machine, can score the exam given the answer key.

The concepts of subjective and objective, at least as they are used in traditional science, come fairly close to the usage given by people with regard to the two types of examinations. Objectivity indicates that people in general would agree upon the event in question: that is, if you were to observe a rat turning to the left in a maze, this would be considered objective in the sense that any observer in your place would also report that the rat had made a lefthand turn. Subjectivity indicates that people in general may not agree upon the event in question. Whereas one observer might believe that the rat turned left because it "knew" that some cheese was to be found there, another might believe that the rat was simply "curious" about the left portion of the maze. Beliefs, differing as they may among observers, may be difficult to agree upon, and would tend to be labeled as subjective.

Although scientists generally accept the meaning of objectivity as given in the preceding paragraph, there are a number of problems in the concept itself. The traditional notion of objectivity rests upon agreement of several observers. However, this consensual or public meaning of objectivity, *provides only for agreement.* Could not the majority in some sense be wrong as in our illusion examples? The pygmies in Africa live in a dense jungle area. There is generally very little open space, and consequently, pygmies have little opportunity to learn about the relative size of objects when great distances are involved. Let us say that you go into the jungles of Africa, locate a pygmy and with his permission bring him out onto some of the plains of that continent. You now point to something very far in the distance grazing on top of a hill and identify that animal as an elephant.

The pygmy looks at that animal and says, "My, what a small animal. I can hold it in the palm of my hand."

You look at him amazed and say, "No, you don't understand. That elephant is very large, much larger than you or I, but he is seen at so great a distance that he appears to be small."

The pygmy looks at you and says, "No, you are incorrect. That is a very small elephant; it's a miniature elephant, and I can hold him in the palm of my hand. Look at him, he is not more than half an inch long to begin with. How can you possibly say this animal is huge?"

You may decide that you can convince the pygmy of the incorrectness of his position and you ask the pygmy to walk with you toward that elephant, who, we will assume, remains happily grazing on the top of the hill. As you walk toward the elephant, it of course appears to become larger and larger. The pygmy looks at this phenomenon and says, "My heavens, that is indeed a strange animal, who can grow at so rapid a rate as what we see here."

Exasperated, again you say, "No, you are incorrect; the elephant is the same size. What we are doing is moving closer to him and because we are moving closer to him, he appears to be larger."

The pygmy looks at you and says, "No, you are incorrect, the elephant is indeed growing before our very eyes. Look at him, he is much larger now than he was five minutes ago when we started to walk."

Now you and the pygmy can argue back and forth, but it is very unlikely that one will convince the other of the incorrectness of his position. Is the pygmy being subjective while you are objective? Well, of course, he is; then again, from the pygmy's point of view, he is being quite objective and it is you who are being rather subjective. The pygmy can bring other pygmies into the conversation and they will probably all agree with the first that the elephant is very, very small when looked at from afar and tends to grow when you walk toward him. You, of course, can bring other people from your introductory psychology class and try to convince each of the pygmies that as you approach a distant object, it will appear to be larger because of certain relationships between the size and the distance of the objects that you are looking upon. Who is right? Well, perhaps you are right, but *if* you are, it is *not* because you can bring *more* people to agree with you than the pygmy can bring to agree with him, *it is because you have more knowledge than the pygmy*. It is not, however, who is right and who is wrong; we all in one sense know that the pygmy is incorrect. The point is that it is not a matter of who has more votes. The pygmy, of course, has fewer votes, but that, in and of itself, does not make him wrong. You have more votes, but that, in and of itself, does not make you right.

If objectivity is restricted to the notion of consensual agreement, then that observation called objective will be the one obtaining "more votes." When the pygmy brings other members of his tribe, he has more votes, and so would be correct in stating that the elephant grows at a very rapid rate. When the other members of your introductory psychology class arrive, you might have more votes, and it would then be correct to state that the elephant has remained the same size. Obviously, it is at best cumbersome and at worst meaningless to link the concept of objectivity to consensual validation. Intuitively, what is objective must not readily change back and forth, or must not be subject to the immediate circumstances of the example; that which may readily change is generally what is meant by subjectivity.

If objectivity is not to be defined in terms of consensual agreement, how may it otherwise be defined? The answer is complicated, but we may say, at this stage of our inquiry, that it is related to what you believe is true, and the extent to which you can substantiate this truth. If the pygmy believes that the elephant grows rapidly, he has bought a general framework from which he would be forced (logically) to make a number of other predictions: for example, that the elephant should increase in weight, eat more food, etc. (note that we did this in our illusion examples). These predictions, in turn, would not be borne out. On the other hand, *you* could logically deduce other (opposite) hypotheses from the framework out of which you claim that the elephant remains the same size, and to the extent that your predictions would be confirmed, you would have confidence in your original assessment of the situation. Thus, the judgment of the objectivity of a statement is made not so much by examining the statement itself, but rather by examining inferences derived from the entire conceptual framework (context) from which a statement follows. Thus, it is the invocation of a general framework (i.e., theory) that is used to judge the degree of objectivity, the same general framework, by the way, that influenced our translation of the empirical world to observation in the first place.

Factual Statements

It is often said that science is the accumulation of facts. Indeed, we have been learning facts throughout our entire school history. Let us list two examples of factual statements.

1. A dropped object will have a velocity of 96 ft/sec at the end of three seconds of fall.
2. The population of New York City totals 8,134,761 persons.

These factual statements have certain properties in common. The most obvious, perhaps, is that they represent observations. These observations are generally agreed upon as being accurate and, to the extent that we believe they are accurate, we will call them facts.

Now we should recognize that there are certain problems inherent in treating the concept of fact. One problem, of course, is that facts are themselves based upon observations and all the limitations operating upon the concept of observation must of necessity be operative also in dealing with facts.

There are other problems as well. The actual speed of the falling object in the first example depends upon a number of circumstances: the shape of the object, the barometric pressure, the humidity, etc. If we were to try to determine the actual speed of the object after three seconds, we would take measurements of the speed. What we might find if we were to take these measurements is given below.

Observation number	Observed speed (in ft/sec)
1	95.85
2	96.03
3	96.21
4	95.97
5	96.01

How fast was the object falling after three seconds? You have your choice of which measurement to believe. Scientists, of course, would say that the best estimate of the velocity would be the average of a large number of measurements (probably more than five). That is, the average of those observations would be the scientist's best guess. Under no circumstances, however, can the scientist say "for a fact" that the speed of the object after three seconds was such and such. Limitations of technology and limitations of the human organism itself are such that it is almost impossible to reproduce the exact observation recorded previously. The point is that it is very difficult to specify what the "fact of the matter" is. The speed of the object can only be estimated, although these estimations can, under certain laboratory conditions, be very precise.

It is often said that factual statements can be verified by observation. Although we have seen that perfect verifiability is often not possible, the scientist can, on the basis of many observations, describe the degree to which his observations approximate the conditions of the factual statement. If the approximation is "close" (it is possible to set up a definition of "close" in terms of some statistical principles to be discussed in later chapters), the scientist will accept the observations as verifying the factual statement.

The second factual statement referred to the population of New York City. What is the exact population of New York City? Well, again this will vary a great deal. People are born and people die every few seconds within the city limits. It would be virtually impossible to keep track of the number of births and deaths from instant to instant, but even if this were possible, we could only specify the population of New York City at a given time. Because it fluctuates, it is very difficult to make a precise factual statement about the population of New York City. Again, scientists *and* laymen will generally settle for an estimate rather than forcing someone to tell us the precise population at a given moment in time.

We say "the car is red." This is a factual statement, and we can roughly *verify* this (or presumably any) factual statement by looking at (observing) the particular car in question. Now ask an Arab who speaks no English about the color of this car and he will answer (because of the structure of the Arabic language) that "the car reddens" (Hanson, 1958). This may be a factual statement for the Arab, but you might think twice about agreeing with him. You might say "the diamond sparkles, the star twinkles, and in a sense, the apple reddens, but does the car redden? If he means that the car is red, we'll agree; if he means that the car reddens, in the same way as we mean the star twinkles, then we're not so sure that we agree."

If the Arab is permitted to make the factual statement "the car reddens" and we are permitted to make the factual statement "the car is red" the first problem we have is to determine whether these two statements agree with one another or whether they actually refer to different observations. Now this might be rather difficult to accomplish in that we would need to have a means of determining what it is that the Arab sees. It is conceivable, for example, that the Arab *can* literally see the red emanating from the car, whereas we might simply see the color red as a relatively passive property of the car. The problems involved with language are not new to our analysis, but have been a constant thorn in the side of many thinkers. The problem is that different languages might express slightly different concepts and might even permit people to see the same "objective" event in a slightly different way.

This is not a case of 'say it how you please, it all means the same.' Kant remarked: '. . . they [who philosophize in Latin] have only two words in this connexion, while we [Germans] have three, hence they lack a concept we possess. . . .' This is not merely to speak differently and to think in the same way. Discursive thought and speech have the same logic. How could the two differ? . . . Speaking with colour-words as verbs just is to think of colours as activities and of things as colouring agents.

What if information about colours were expressed adverbially? We would then say 'The sun glows yellowly,' 'The grass glitters greenly,' 'The chapel twinkles greyly.' If everyone spoke thus how could one insist on its being a fact that the sun is yellow, that grass is green, or that the chapel is grey? Could such 'facts' be articulated at all? (Hanson, 1958, p. 33)

If we accept Kant's analysis of the difference in concepts that may be imposed by a particular language system, then we are faced with the problem of an identical objective event being described by different and perhaps almost contradictory factual statements. Isn't a fact in some sense, true, unchangeable, and constant? Can a fact exist for one person and not for another? A person who is color blind may see no difference among the colors that we see. For us, our report of the color of the sun at sunset, of the grass, of the sky, of the ocean, are factual statements. Can these also be facts for the person who is color blind? Perhaps he could take an instrument and measure the wave lengths of the light emanating from these events and observe that each of these events gives rise to somewhat different wave lengths, and perhaps he could even learn to label these wave lengths appropriately as blue, green, red, etc. Is that the same as our statement that reports red, blue, or green? Can the color blind person ever fully comprehend our meaning when we say blue, green, and red? Can we ever express the fact about the car the way in which the Arab may? Which fact is true, which is unchangeable?

By now we should be aware of the need to re-examine our conception of fact. Observation has been treated as being too simple, facts have been treated as being too plain and obvious. Each is itself more complicated; science is many times more complicated still.

Empirical Laws

Empirical laws, sometimes called experimental laws (Nagel, 1961), summarize, as we have mentioned previously, relationships among sets of facts. That is, on the basis of a large number of facts, a general statement is constructed. This experimental law functions to integrate many separate observations. Because they are essentially generalizations from the facts, empirical laws constitute an *inductive* step in reasoning. Induction simply means to extrapolate from that already observed to a more general statement. For example, on the basis of having seen innumerable swans, all of which were white, you might be led to maintain that *all* swans are white. It would be said that you have arrived at that general statement through inductive reasoning. Empirical laws, we maintain, are subject to limitations of fact and fact is subject to the limitations we discussed in terms of observation. Therefore, empirical laws are subject to all the limitations applying to both observation and fact. Besides the aforementioned, empirical laws suffer from some problems of their own. One problem is their general nature. Inductive reasoning, although used by many of us and also by scientists, nevertheless constitutes in some respects an act of faith. To maintain, for example, that many swans are white on the basis of having seen many swans, might seem reasonable to you. To say, however, that *all* swans are white is going well beyond the data. Science, of course, is properly concerned with the general statement, and is only incidentally concerned about particulars. When considering something in general, we must of necessity make a considerable sacrifice, namely, that of relative certainty. In other words, experimental laws must be treated as being less certain than the facts upon which they are based. Scientists, therefore, must treat the empirical law as reflecting a possible, or probable, state of affairs. For this reason, science can never provide any "final," "absolute," or "perfectly correct" answers to most of the questions posed by the scientist.

We are now led to the second problem with regard to empirical laws. This problem is more a matter of the scientist doing science than of the general logical framework within which the scientific statement is made. *Empirical laws*, for all their bases in observation and for all the agreement that has presumably occurred before the statement was made, *may still be wrong*. There are many examples of empirical laws being held as relatively correct for some period of time, and yet, after additional research, were proved to be incorrect. Empirical laws are, at best, hypotheses, that is, conjectures, and should be treated as such. Do not be misled by the word law, which might suggest something true and everlasting; law as used in this sense means only a general relationship and that relationship is one that is believed to be correct. That belief may turn out to be wrong and one should in principle be as prepared to accept the incorrectness of an empirical law as rapidly as one is able to accept its correctness.

The problem, however, goes even deeper than this, for when an empirical law is stated, it identifies relationships among things believed to be operating in the situation. Once those factors are identified, research will tend to attempt to refine our knowledge of the posited relationship. It must be remembered, however, that empirical laws are a product of the historical milieu in which the law itself was constructed. Factors conceived as being important during that time find their way into empirical laws. This is not a fault of science, but is rather simply a product of human inquiry. We must be on our guard to identify such circumstances and be very careful in our interpretation and use of empirical laws in our own research. We will have more to say about the relationship between theory and empirical laws later in the chapter when we discuss the uses to which theory may be put.

Cause

Science consists of more than the making of observations and the recording of facts; it seeks to explain events and phenomena. Tied up with explanation is the concept of cause. The layman wants to know why—i.e., what caused—the apple to fall when dropped, the person to become so sick, the murderer to kill his victim. Although not all explanation is concerned with causality, much of it is, and a large proportion of research attempts to determine causal relationships. It will be useful, then, to examine the concept of cause.

Let us take an uncomplicated example of cause and effect. A rocket is propelled through space. The forward movement of the rocket was presumably caused by the jet of hot gas propelled from its tail. This is an example of an application of Newton's third law of motion which states that for every action there is an equal and opposite reaction and appears to be straight forward enough. Or is it?

How do you know that the expulsion of a jet of hot gas caused the rocket to move forward? One answer might be that the expulsion of gas was followed by the movement of the rocket. If, at the moment you dropped your pen, you heard a clap of thunder, would you say that your pen had caused the thunder? Hardly. It was just a coincidence. If you dropped your pen again, the chances are there would not be another clap of thunder. If another jet of hot gas was expulsed from the rocket, the rocket would move forward again. To demonstrate a causal relationship, therefore, the cause must precede the effect, and this relationship must be reliable.

Is that all? Every time you look at the clock in the kitchen the second hand moves. Did your looking at the clock cause the movement of the second hand? Even though your looking at the clock preceded the observed movement of the second hand, and even though this may be highly reliable, we would be foolish to claim a causal relationship. Why? Obviously, the second hand moves whether or not you look at the clock. To be classified as a cause, the effect should not occur unless the cause is present.

A cause must therefore be both necessary—if you remove the cause, the effect will not occur—and sufficient in a given context for the effect for if you present the cause, the effect should occur. An experiment attempts to determine the necessary and sufficient conditions for the establishment of a causal relationship. If x is suggested to be the cause of y, x is presented and withheld in some systematic way. With everything else constant, (1) removal of x should prevent the occurrence of y, and (2) presentation of x should result in the occurrence of y. The first operation demonstrates the necessity of x, usually called a control group in the experiment, and the second operation demonstrates the sufficiency of x, usually called the experimental group in an experiment.

Is this what we mean by cause? We have established that the cause must precede the effect, and that to be a cause, an event must meet both the necessary and sufficient conditions with respect to the effect. Now, to state that x is the cause of y says not only has x been the cause of y, *but that it always will be*. To lay that kind of claim on the future constitutes a gigantic amount of faith. This is not to say that it should not be done; we merely point out that there is a risk involved. David Hume, the brilliant British philosopher, pointed out long ago that although the sun has risen every morning for millions of years, we still cannot say with certainty that it will rise again tomorrow. We may live our lives today on the assumption that the sun will again rise, but we can never be sure. To say that x is the cause of y suggests a certainty that transcends our experience.

A causal statement, then, speaks of universals, and universals transcend our experience (observation). When we make a statement of causality, we therefore go beyond our "hard data." It must be realized, then, that we tend to admit the universal statement into our knowledge system. And we must further understand that a causal statement because of its universal or general nature can never be wholly verified by our experience. The best that our experience can provide is an increment in our belief of the correctness of the causal statement.

A cause must logically precede the effect. The hot gas must be expelled from the rocket for the rocket to move forward, x must occur before y, etc. Are we therefore correct in concluding, as ancient man probably did, that *the light in the east causes the sun to rise?* Shall we examine this? The light in the east does indeed precede the dawn. Is the light in the east both necessary and sufficient to cause the rising of the sun? Since we cannot perform a laboratory experiment, we must rely upon our observations of "natural" events. (Experimentation is not a prerequisite for science. Astronomers do not conduct experiments.) The light in the east might be sufficient, in that every time ancient man saw the light the sun has always followed. It might even be necessary (we would be willing to bet that if there were no light in the east, as at night, the sun will not rise). Ancient man probably did believe, at one time at least, that the light in the east really caused the sun to rise. How is it that our evaluation of the situation has changed over the centuries? That is, everyone during this century unconditionally holds that the sun caused the light in the east. Why? You might answer: "Look, since the earth rotates on its axis, any given place on the earth is 'moving toward' the sun. Since the light emitted by the sun is scattered by the atmosphere, we will see this scattered light before actually seeing the sun." You might add, quite correctly: "Don't believe everything you see."

Notice the quality of the explanation just proposed. You, in your explanation of the light preceding the dawn, have just refuted all our observations about the light in the east and the dawn. You have told us, in not so many words, that *we cannot identify a causal relationship solely on the basis of our observations.* In fact, the "true" causal relationship may be exactly opposite to that which we have seen. To explain this "true" relationship, you have (albeit implicitly) employed theories of physics, geometry, biology, and psychology. And you trust these theories over our observations! This, then, is the key: *The postulation of causality is a theoretical statement.* In other words, since our very observations cannot be totally relied upon, we know of causality only through our theories. And because causality is a theoretical statement, it must have the property, as do other theoretical statements, of universality.

Many great thinkers have grappled with the concept of causality. Hume suggested that what we label as causal is merely the reliable occurrence of two events in close succession, nothing more, nothing less. This, in turn, places causality in the experience (observation) of individuals. Kant refuted Hume's analysis of causality by proposing that we can never "experience" (observe) causality. Rather, we have a "native predisposition" to categorize particular occurrences as cause and effect. In neither Hume's nor Kant's analysis, however, can we deduce that the sun causes the light in the east, since neither philosopher claimed that we are born with knowledge of planetary movements. It is only through some kind of physical theory that that we can specify the "true" causal relationship. What of the original example of the rocket ship? Our argument still holds. Since we have learned that our observations cannot, in a sense, be trusted, in order to specify that the expulsion of a jet of hot gas caused the rocket ship to move also requires the postulation of a physical theory. The third law of Newtonian mechanics, a part of Newton's major theory, served this function well.

Theory

We expect that you have received the impression, thus far, that theory is an important aspect of science. Actually, it is probably *the* most important aspect, and, as we have seen and shall see again, it bears upon all other scientific enterprises. Even those scientists who claim to be doing non-theoretical research, we will suggest, are in practice still operating from within a theoretical framework. This will be made clear in a moment.

One interesting question that can be asked is how theories affect the behavior of scientists. One major thing that theories accomplish is to provide knowledge. Knowledge, we would maintain, does *not* consist of the accumulation of a variety of observations and facts. Rather, knowledge is of a more general nature and provides for relationships among various observations and continuity among various phenomena. The fact that a dog in one of Pavlov's investigations might have secreted one drop of saliva at one time, three drops of saliva at another time, five later on, etc., are observations that are not yet contributing to knowledge, for unless we understand that these observations are in some way linked, i.e., through the postulation of conditioning, for example, then all they remain are separate and discrete observations. Until one imposes this general framework upon the observations, the observations are in one sense not meaningful.

Acquisition of general (theoretical) knowledge is not only very useful, but also very important. One function that a theory serves is to explain certain observed phenomena and predict as yet unobserved relationships. Another function, implicit in the first, but important enough to mention, is to structure the conduct of the science. To the extent that the theory has reached a sophisticated level of development, it tells the student as well as the scientist what kind of entities exist in the world, and what things do not; it tells what is possible, and what is not possible; it tells what are important and powerful effects, and what are unimportant and weak; it tells what is subjective and what is objective; it tells what should be cause and what should be effect; it tells what is to be observed, and what is not to be observed; in short, it tells what is or should be, and what is not or should not be.

That is a lot of knowledge, and it finds its way into most scientific activities. Recall, for example, the passing mention of the experiment in connection with our discussion of causality. The theory, we finally concluded later, tells us that x is the cause of y. It is through the experiment that we attempt to verify this prediction. The purpose of performing an experiment, then, is intimately connected with a larger theory. And what is it that the experimenter shall observe, that is, which of the infinite number of events taking place during an experiment shall the experimenter choose to measure? Again, the theory—whether highly formalized as in physics or extremely rudimentary as in psychology and other social sciences—provides the answer. A psychologist tests a rat on a maze problem because he believes he will learn something about the learning process. His belief is based upon (or may even originally constitute) his theory. He may measure the speed of the rat in locomoting the maze, the number of errors made, etc., rather than the number of times the rat wiggles his ears, because learning (a theoretical concept) is linked by means of correspondence rules, to speed, errors, etc. instead of ear wiggling. Is its ear wiggling important? It is if you have a reason (a theory) to believe it is; then you would measure it.

An examination of the history of science reveals many examples of the influence of theory on the design of experiments and of observations taken during the experiment. A particular laboratory apparatus or procedure employed by a researcher is as theory-involved as the interpretation of data. Thomas Kuhn (1970) describes this very well in the following excerpt.

> In short, consciously or not, the decision to employ a particular piece of apparatus and to use it in a particular way carries an assumption that only certain sorts of circumstances will arise. There are instrumental as well as theoretical expectations, and they have often played a decisive role in scientific development. One such expectation is, for example, part of the story of oxygen's belated discovery. Using a standard test for "the goodness of air," both Priestly and Lavoisier mixed two volumes of their gas with one volume of nitric oxide, shook the mixture over water, and measured the volume of the gaseous residue. The previous experience from which this standard procedure had evolved assured them that with atmospheric air the residue would be one volume and that for any other gas . . . it would be greater. In the Oxygen experiments both found a residue close to one volume and identified the gas accordingly. Only much later and in part through an accident did Priestly renounce the standard procedure and try mixing nitric oxide with his gas in other proportions. He then found that with quadruple the volume of nitric oxide there was almost no residue at all. His commitment to the original test procedure . . . *had been simultaneously a commitment to the nonexistence of gases that could behave as oxygen did.* (pp. 59–60, italics added)

Laboratory apparatus and procedure are constructed to find something out and implicit in the assumption is that something can be discovered. Since the chemical theories of their time told Priestly and Lavoisier that something like oxygen could not exist, there was hardly need to test for it. And even when standard laboratory practice was abandoned, it took both men years to believe what their data told them. Priestly, himself, never fully grasped what he had found. Lavoisier announced in 1777 not so much the discovery of oxygen, *but rather a new theory of combustion* (Kuhn, 1970). To conceptualize oxygen, a new theory (one that told of the existence of such a gas) had to be presented. Even then, some scientists—including Priestly—could not accept the new theory. We may go so far, in fact, to suggest that oxygen could not be conceived (nor even "seen") until a new theory of combustion was developed. To "see" oxygen, the reader should now realize, is to know what it is and how it works.

We have thus come full cycle. An experiment is designed with the intent of determining a relationship (usually causal) among events. The events that are to be thus examined (observed) are theoretically believed to be important in understanding some larger phenomenon. That which is measured, and the way in which it is measured, is believed (theoretically) to reflect on these events. That which is to be controlled is also of importance and is dictated by the theory. The conclusions we may draw from an experiment can go only so far as current theory allows. For example, in their first studies, neither Priestly nor Lavoisier concluded that they had discovered oxygen. From beginning to end, the scientific activity is a theoretical activity, and observation, procedure, facts, and the like are conceived in terms of feedback to the theory.

A Choice of Theories

If you were asked on an examination "What is the truth value of theories?" the correct answer would probably be "Theories, or rather, the abstract calculus of theories, are neither right nor wrong, neither true nor false; they are analytical or non-empirical inventions by man to be used or discarded as he sees fit." This answer—even the question, for that matter—is more sophisticated than the view of science implying that scientific theories are heading (straight as an arrow, by the way) toward *Final Truth*—or an accurate description of the "real" state of the Universe. The answer, too, is basically correct, but far more difficult to arrive at than you might expect at this point.

What happens to observations inconsistent with or even contradictory to the major theory? No theory in the history of science has been able to absorb all existing data in the field. If unfavorable evidence were grounds for discarding theories, there would be no theory in existence today. What happens to unfavorable data? There are a number of possibilities: (1) they may be ignored entirely; (2) they may be declared as unreliable, suggesting the experimenter may not have performed the experiment properly; (3) they may be recognized as unfavorable, but reflecting on trivial matters anyway; (4) they may be recognized as unfavorable and to be kept in mind in the development of the theory; (5) they may, if important enough, lead to the development of another theory that can then explain them. Actually, all five methods are frequently used by scientists.

Do scientists really disregard unfavorable data? The history of science is filled with examples. In 1633, the Spanish Inquisition—many of the most respected astronomers were members of the church—found Galileo guilty of heresy for supporting Copernicus' heliocentric view of the solar system, despite Galileo's telescopic observations of craters on the moon, phases of Venus, moons of Jupiter, *etc.*—all data strongly in support of Copernican Theory. It is difficult for the scientist, working within the context of one theory, to accept a new theory. Contrary to popular belief, scientists, with respect to their theories at least, are often dogmatic, irrational, and even stubborn. We quote Kuhn (1970, pp. 150–151) in this connection:

How, then are scientists brought to make this transposition [to abandon one theory and choose another]? Part of the answer is that they are very often not. Copernicanism made few converts for almost a century after Copernicus' death. Newton's work was not generally accepted, particularly on the continent, for more than half a century after the *Principia* appeared. Priestly never accepted the oxygen theory nor Lord Kelvin the electro-magnetic theory, and so on. The difficulties of conversion have often been noted by scientists themselves. Darwin, in a particularly perceptive passage at the end of his *Origin of Species*, wrote "Although I am fully convinced of the truth of the views given in this volume . . . , I by no means expect to convince experienced naturalists whose minds are stocked with a multitude of facts all viewed, during a long course of years, from a point of view directly opposite to mine. . . . [B]ut I look with confidence to the future,—to young and rising naturalists, who will be able to view both sides of the question with impartiality." And Max Planck, surveying his own career in his *Scientific Autobiography*, sadly remarked that "a new scientific truth does not triumph by convincing its opponents and making them see the light, but rather because its opponents eventually die, . . .

Truth is told by theory, and theory is made by man. When one theory is discarded, one set of truths is discarded as well. When another theory is adopted, a new set of truths is created. Scientists do not search for truth, they search for theories. Is it true that the universe is finite? Aristotle claimed that it was, and an Aristotelian universe was true until Newton's *Principia* was accepted. Newton, of course, held that the universe was infinite and man lived in a Newtonian universe until early in this century when Einstein introduced his theory of relativity. An Einsteinian universe is, like that of Aristotle, bounded. What then is the true nature of our universe? For the scientist the query itself contains little meaning. Any theory is a *working truth,* providing the framework for observation, research technique, and understanding. But theories are constantly developing into new working truths, or are giving way to new and different theories. Were we to distinguish between absolute truth and heuristic or working truth, only the latter would be appropriate to the domain of science.

section two

the foundation of research

From the previous chapter, and presumably as a result of your cumulative education, you probably recognize that science provides no absolute answers—neither long nor short term. Long term answers have to do with universal statements relating one or more classes of phenomena to other classes of phenomena. Theories change, and as a consequence, so do these relational statements.

In the short run, as well, no absolute answers may be found. The results of any one experiment, no matter how clear-cut, may not at all depict the actual situation under study. The best that can be said of any set of results is that there is *some chance* that the data are, indeed, valid.

The purpose of Section II is to acquaint you with some of the tools that should be used in evaluating these short term situations. Without understanding how these tools can be used, it would be difficult to appreciate the intricacies of the scientific methodologies to be presented in Section III.

The present section will take the following organization: we will begin with the concept of measurement, then present the outcome of the measurement operation, continue with methods of describing data, and end in how these tools may be applied to data collected in an experiment.

chapter two

some basics about data

Types of Data

The collection of data usually involves *measuring* the behavior of a subject in some specified manner. Exactly what is measured varies from one study to another and is a function of the type of question the scientist has asked and the availability of appropriate measuring instruments. The results of a measurement operation produce data and these data, in turn, supply the scientist with particular kinds of information. As it turns out, different measurement operations yield different amounts of information, and we will be concerned, at this point, with this information component.

The Concept of Scales of Measurement

The information contained in data may be analyzed by considering the mathematical scale upon which a given measurement is based. The mathematical concepts with which we will deal here are relatively straightforward. Yet the endpoint of our discussion is extremely important, for in order to use data to answer any question, we need to know what kind of information is contained in the data itself.

The first thing to be made clear is the definition of measurement. Most generally, **measurement consists of the assigning of numbers to "things"** (events, objects, characteristics, responses, etc.) **according to some rule or rules.** Now, the rules may vary somewhat from one situation to another, so—as a word to the wise—we had better know the ground rules before playing the game. Conveniently, there are only four different sets of rules having wide application, and these are known as *scales*. Thus, we may say for present purposes that there are four *scales of measurement*. These scales are:

1. A *nominal* scale.
2. An *ordinal* scale.
3. An *interval* scale.
4. A *ratio* scale.

The scale of measurement or set of rules used by the scientist will directly determine the type of information obtained from the data, and we will treat each scale of measurement in turn.

The nominal scale

A nominal scale, as the term implies, is simply a naming or classification rule. We can refer to differences in categories measured on a nominal scale as being qualitative differences. In using this scale, numbers (or labels in general) are assigned to differentiate (name, classify) different things. An experimenter, in order to keep his records straight, might label this subject as Rat #1, that one as Rat #2, another as Rat #3, and so on. He might just as easily give his rats letters (A, B, C, etc.), names (Abe, George, Herman, etc.), nicknames (Speedy, Fatso, Stinker, etc.), or the like. **In a nominal scale of measurement, the numbers** (or labels) **serve no other function, and supply no further information, than to differentiate** groups of events.

Let us carry this point further. At times, many "things" will be classified in the same way. *Within a nominal scale of measurement, those "things" similarly classified will receive the same label.* Specifically, we single out only one attribute of events, and classify according to this attribute. You should note, of course, that even though two events are placed into the same category, they may differ completely in many other ways. Consider a simple political poll, looking at the political party with which male and female sophomore college students affiliate themselves. A hypothetical set of these data is presented below. Every student has been classified as either

Sex	Republican	Democrat	Other	Total
Male	17	27	12	56
Female	20	24	9	53

a Republican, Democrat, or Other. Thus, 17 males were given the same label (i.e., Republican), 9 females the same label (i.e., Other), etc. The data presented above are therefore nominal data, in that a nominal scale of measurement was used in collecting these data. That is, the "rule" that was used was: "place the student into the appropriate category."

The ordinal scale

An ordinal scale is somewhat more complex than a nominal scale, since the ordinal scale has essentially two rules whereas the nominal scale has only one. The first rule is the same as the one for the nominal scale:

1. **Different numbers reflect different things.**

The second rule is new:

2. **The things that are measured may be ordered or ranked along some dimension.**

Once we have measurements along a dimension we can think of differences as being quantitative rather than qualitative. Thus, any scale depending in part on this second rule enables us to speak of quantitative differences. We have all frequently used an ordinal scale in the course of our everyday lives. Have you ever watched (or been involved in) young boys "choosing up" for a game of stick-ball or football? The group agrees to designate two "captains." These captains are not necessarily the best players, but they must be of equal ability (i.e., of equal rank). The captains then choose who gets "first pick"; picking then alternates between the two captains until all players are chosen. These young captains, in choosing their team, have ranked the entire group of boys in terms of ability and "picked" accordingly. That is, they have *measured* the ability of the boys on an ordinal scale.

Let us point out some aspects of ordinal measurement. Ordering is the application of the mathematical operation of greater than or less than. To order things is to say that one thing has more of a particular characteristic than another—one boy or girl has more ability than another, one person is taller than another, etc. How much more ability, how much taller, asks for information *not* contained in the scale, and this represents a limitation of ordinal data. Consider the two examples presented in Fig. 2.1. Grant, for the sake of discussion, that we as on-lookers have some scale of absolute ability. Each example represents different boys playing at different times. In Example 1, Boy A is the best and Boy F is the worst. Consider two "adjacent" ranks. Boy D is the fourth best and Boy E is fifth best. How much better is D than E? An ordinal scale of measurement cannot give us this answer. Look at Boys C and D. Boy C is third best, Boy D, fourth best. Our ranking procedure, however, cannot tell us that C is substantially better than D whereas D is only slightly better than E. Such information is simply not available. The concept of *how much more* cannot be given by ordinal data; only the concept of *more* is given in such a scale.

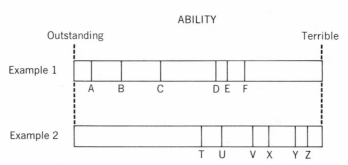

Fig. 2.1 The ranking of two separate groups of boys in terms of playing ability.

Can we compare the boys in Example 1 to those in Example 2? Not really. Boy T is the best in Example 2 but may not be among the best if playing with the boys in Example 1. The ranking procedure again fails to provide this information. Ranks are entirely dependent upon the particular context, and comparisons across two independently ranked groups are completely meaningless.

Ordinal data, then, does provide useful information (rankings), and much of the data collected by behavioral scientists are based upon an ordinal scale. Opinion questionnaires, for example, frequently employ a

Likert type of scale for measuring attitudes. Statements, such as "my most important life goal is to be successful," are presented to individuals and then rated be means of the Likert scale. This scale consists of seven points ranging from "strongly agree" to "strongly disagree," and an example of this scale is given below. One of the features of this scale is that it allows us to rank order subjects' responses. We can assume that the response of "strongly agree" represents more agreement than the response "agree," whereas the response "agree" represents more agreement than the response "slightly agree," and so forth. One thing we cannot rell from this type of scale, though, is how far apart the responses on the scale are. In other words, we cannot tell how much more agreement "strongly agree" represents over "agree." We can only state that it represents *more* agreement.

Strongly agree	Agree	Slightly agree	Neither agree nor disagree	Slightly disagree	Disagree	Strongly disagree
3	2	1	0	−1	−2	−3

The interval scale

An interval scale is somewhat more complex than an ordinal scale, since there are essentially three rules defining the measurement operation. We have already encountered two of these rules in the context of nominal and ordinal scales. These are:

1. **Different numbers reflect different things** (nominal measurement);

2. **The things measured may be ordered or ranked along some dimension** (ordinal measurement).

We may now introduce the third rule of measurement involved in the interval scale:

3. **The intervals between adjacent points of the scale are of equal value.**

Recall the example in which the boys were ranked on their athletic ability. Although they were ranked 1, 2, 3, 4, 5, and 6, Boy C (ranked 3) was highly superior to Boy D (ranked 4) whereas Boy D was only slightly better than Boy E (ranked 5). The intervals (or "distances") between any two ranks varies haphazardly in an ordinal scale. An interval scale sets the points "equi-distant" from one another.

Temperature is a good example of an interval scale. Consider the range of temperatures below and let us apply the three measurement rules to this scale.

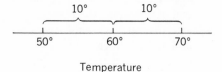

Temperature

1. The scale has a nominal characteristic, in that each number represents a different temperature.

2. The scale has an ordinal characteristic, in that 60° is warmer than 50°.

3. The scale has an interval property in that the difference between 50° and 60° (i.e., 10°) is equal to the difference between 60° and 70° (i.e., 10°). To state this in another way, the same amount of heat needed to raise an object from 50° to 60° will raise it from 60° to 70°.

An interval scale thus provides more information than either nominal or ordinal scales, since we can properly speak of the intervals between measurement points. You should recognize, however, that there are still limitations placed upon the information contained in interval measurement. The primary limitation is that we cannot say that 100° is *twice* as warm as 50° or that 35° is *half* as warm as 70°. These are *ratio* statements and cannot be made on interval data.

To avoid confusion later on, we should mention here that in an interval scale, there is no fixed (or absolute) zero point. That is, although we may label a point as zero, it is an arbitrary label only. For example, 0° F. does not represent "no temperature"; it simply designates a particular temperature. On the centigrade scale, 0° C. is the point that water freezes, and again is equally arbitrary. We will elaborate on this issue in the next section on ratio scales.

The ratio scale

A ratio scale is the most complex or informative of the four scales of measurement considered here, in that it is governed by the most (i.e., four) rules. We have already encountered three of these rules and list them as follows:

1. **Different numbers reflect different things** (nominal measurement);

2. **The things measured may be ordered or ranked along some dimension** (ordinal measurement);

3. **The intervals between adjacent points of the scale are of equal value** (interval measurement).

The fourth rule which must be added to this list to complete the definition of a ratio scale is:

4. **There is an absolute or fixed zero point.**

By including this fixed zero point in the definition, we are now permitted to make ratio judgments.

Examples of ratio scales are time, distance, mass, and various combinations of these. Speed, for example, is distance divided by time. The concept of a fixed zero point should be clear. Logically, it is possible to talk of zero time as the absence of time, zero distance as no distance, zero speed as standing still, *etc.* Because of this fixed zero point, we may also say that 10 miles/hour is *twice as fast* (ratio judgment) as 5 miles/hour, 3 hours *half as long* as 6 hours, and so forth. On no other scale can such ratio statements be legitimately made.

Relevance of Different Scales

We have spent some time and effort outlining the properties of these various scales of measurement. It therefore seems appropriate to add why such a consideration is important. The main point to bear in mind is that different types of information may be derived from each of these scales, and that this information is limited by the rules used to create each scale. Pragmatically, this means that you had better play by the rules or else suffer the consequences. By these rules, you cannot make interval statements on ordinal data, you cannot make ratio statements on interval data, and so on. Therefore, you must know beforehand what kind of scale you are using in your measurement.

A common example of "reading in" more information than is actually contained in data may be drawn from politics. We know that there are more registered Democrats than Republicans in America, and some people (usually Democrats) on the basis of these data, are prone to say that the Democratic Party is in some sense "better than" the Republican Party. Such a statement is, of course, in logical error. The assignment of people to either the Democratic or Republican Parties is a nominal measurement operation, whereas the "better than" statement can be made only on ordinal, interval, or ratio data.

Another example of erroneously drawing information from numbers can be seen as follows: If yesterday's temperature was 40°, and if today's temperature is 80°, then today was twice as warm as yestereday. This statement is incorrect because temperature is an interval scale, and the judgment "twice as warm" can be made only upon ratio measurement.

In summary, then, remember that when collecting data, you must be aware of the scale of measurement that has been employed; any conclusions you may draw from your data are limited by this. Contrawise, if you need to draw certain kinds of conclusions, such as ratio judgments, you must use an appropriate scale of measurement—that is a ratio scale—in your study.

chapter three

the graphing of data

During the course of doing research the scientist needs a medium to represent his observations. Usually the scientist will resort to numbers as representatives of the responses he observes within his experiment. This collection of numbers we call *data*. Since the amount of data that the scientist collects can be voluminous, he needs a convenient way to condense these data so that he can gain some insight into their "meaning."* There are two general methods employed by behavioral scientists to condense large quantities of data in a simple way:

1. *Graphing* or "picturing" the data.
2. Applying some simple *statistical procedures* to the data to generate a few "summarizing numbers."

This chapter is concerned with supplying the basics of the first procedure; the following chapter will deal with the second set of procedures.

---

*"Meaning" is used here to indicate that the knowledge these data convey is theory-bound.

Plotting Frequency Distributions

A distribution is a collection of scores. To have a distribution of test scores means that we have a collection or list of scores from a test, a distribution of heights means that we have a listing of the heights of certain people, and so forth. **A frequency distribution is a collection of scores organized by their order of magnitude and accompanied by an indication of their frequency,** that is, how many of each score we have.

An example of a frequency distribution that may be familiar to you is given below.

Test score range	Number of people falling within this range (frequency)
90—100	7
80—89	15
70—79	40
60—69	70
50—59	50
40—49	25
30—39	10

These data can also be presented pictorially. Such a pictorial representation of the frequency data given above is plotted in Fig. 3.1. This type of graphical representation of a frequency distribution is called a *frequency polygon*. Notice that the test scores are listed on the horizontal (x) axis; the smaller scores are to the left of the x-axis; the frequency of occurrence is scaled on the vertical (y) axis. The frequency polygon, particularly when there are a great deal of data involved, provides a clear and convenient summary of the data, and is to be recommended as an aid to summarizing data. Note that all data points in Fig. 3.1 are connected by straight lines. Only "schematic" or theoretical curves (such as Figs. 3.3 and 3.4) are smooth.

It is sometimes more appropriate to plot the relative frequency rather than the absolute frequency of scores on the y-axis. The reason for this is that by plotting relative frequency it becomes possible to compare two frequency polygons that would ordinarily not be comparable (owing to differences in the overall absolute frequency of the scores). To convert absolute frequency to relative frequency we simply convert the frequencies of each range of scores given on the x-axis to percents. A relative frequency polygon of the frequency polygon given in Fig. 3.1 is given in Fig. 3.2.

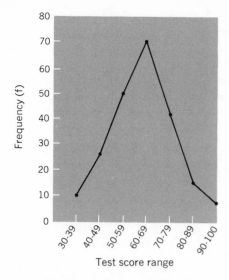

Fig. 3.1 A frequency polygon of the scores given in the text.

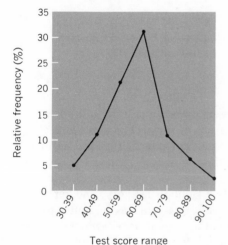

Fig. 3.2 A relative frequency polygon of the scores given in Fig. 3.1.

Frequency distributions are often encountered in behavioral science, and it is important that you are able to deal with them. All frequency distributions share this feature: **frequency is always plotted on the y axis, and the "event" being counted is always plotted on the x axis.** What kinds of "events" might be counted? The answer is anything. In Fig. 3.1, we counted the number of scores made by students falling into each of the test score ranges. We might just as well have plotted each of the test scores (as opposed to grouping them), and the resulting graph of these might resemble that given in Fig. 3.3. In Fig. 3.3, the plot of individual scores is not the true distribution, but rather the distribution we might expect theoretically. Hence, the curve is smooth rather than a set of several points connected by straight lines. As a point of information, smooth curves will be drawn elsewhere in this book and represent an idealized (theoretical) distribution of scores. Smooth curves are constructed by plotting points according to the mathematical equation of the distribution, rather than using data that is actually collected in research.

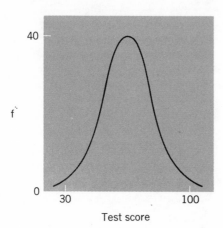

Fig. 3.3 Plot of a frequency distribution of test scores.

We may get even "fancier" if we choose. Later in this book we will introduce a statistical procedure (analysis of variance) which results in the calculation of a number designated as F. For simplicity, suppose that we program a computer to generate a distribution of randomly (e.g., every number has an equal chance of being chosen) chosen numbers, calculate a mathematical value called F, store this value in memory, and repeat this process several times. After a few minutes, we tell the computer to stop, and print out a frequency distribution of all the values of F it has just calculated. Were we to plot this distribution, it would probably look something like that presented in Fig. 3.4. We would say that we have plotted a frequency distribution of the F statistic or that we have plotted an F distribution. Again, notice that Fig. 3.4 is a smooth curve and is therefore a theoretical approximation of the distribution of F-values we would expect the computer to generate.

Other Kinds of Plots

A great deal of the data collected in behavioral research can be plotted in ways other than those mentioned above. Suppose that a researcher wished

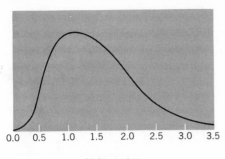

Fig. 3.4 An F distribution.

Values of F

to determine the effect of the number of hours a student studied on the score of a mid-semester exam. The details of conducting such an investigation will be covered in a later chapter. For now, let us assume that the results came out as listed below. Assume, for the sake of the example, that each group of students is of equal academic ability. The data below have been graphed in Fig. 3.5.

Number of study hours	Average exam score
0	40
1	42
2	50
4	60
6	85
10	96
15	98

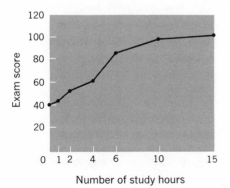

Fig. 3.5 Exam score as a function of number of study hours.

You should note the following about Fig. 3.5.

1. Each group has studied a given number of hours for the exam. The number of hours studied are scaled on the x axis.

2. The researcher measured the effects of studying by means of exam scores. These are scaled on the y axis.

3. As a general rule, that which is measured is always scaled on the y axis; that which reflects the methodology used in an investigation is usually represented on the x axis.

From Fig. 3.5, it is clear that even with no formal studying, some points may be scored on the exam. One, two, or even four hours of study, however, do not substantially produce higher grades than no studying at all in our example, but somewhere between four and six hours of study results in dramatic improvement in scores. However, this effect levels off after ten hours, i.e., it does not, in our example, pay to study fifteen hours—you can afford to stop after ten without worry.

Very often, research is conducted in such a way that more than one curve is drawn on the same set of axes. Suppose that we wished to examine the effectiveness of two teaching techniques (discussion vs. lecture). Let us take two comparable classes of an introductory history course, choose two comparable instructors, and have one instructor use a discussion technique and the other a lecture technique. Further, let us monitor the success of each technique by administering the same weekly exams to each class. The hypothetical results of such an enterprise are presented in Fig. 3.6. Note that each technique is represented by a solid or broken line, and that a "key" is presented in the body of the graph. On the basis of these data, we would conclude that although both techniques eventually produced comparable results, the discussion technique produced its effects much more rapidly.

Consider one last example. A coffee manufacturer wants to learn about some of the factors contributing to coffee drinking. An appropriate study

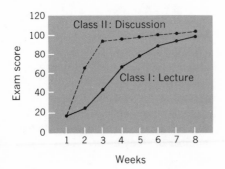

Fig. 3.6 The effectiveness of two teaching methods over an eight-week period.

is conducted to determine what happens to coffee intake as a function of the stress which people may be under and if men show different patterns of coffee intake than women. We have constructed a set of hypothetical results below. The plotting of these data is a little trickier than any of the

Sex	Amount of stress	
	Little stress	Much stress
Male	2.5	4.3
Female	1.1	1.8

previous examples. As always, that which is measured is scaled on the y axis. But what goes on the x axis; do we put stress, or sex, or both? First, we *cannot* put both on the same axis. Which *one* do we put on the x axis? Generally, you pick the one that seems *more* continuous. In this case, amount of stress seems more continuous than sex.* Hence, we would plot stress on the x axis and then use a separate line on the graph for men and women. One line in Fig. 3.7, then, describes the number of cups of coffee consumed by men under different levels of stress, whereas the second line does the same for women. On the basis of Fig. 3.7, we would conclude

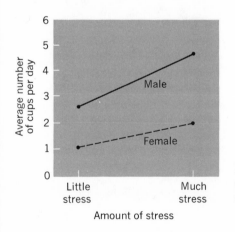

Fig. 3.7 Average number of cups of coffee as a function of stress for males and females.

*The notion of "continuous" may be thought of as something which can take on *any* value within given limits. For example, length is continuous in the sense that you can theoretically specify the *exact* length of an object, that is, there are an infinite number of lengths and the object you are measuring must (by definition) be equal to one of them. Continuous is usually contrasted to "discrete," in which something can take on only *certain* values. For example, the amount of money in a bank is discrete (non-continuous) in the sense that you can specify only certain values ($.01, $.05, $1.17, $1,327.26, etc.) rather than an infinite number of values (you cannot have fractions of a cent).

that men generally drink more coffee than women. Furthermore, stress raises the coffee intake of men much more than it raises the coffee intake of women.

The data plots that have been presented in this chapter are fairly common in behavioral science literature. Frequency polygons are especially common in textbooks, but plots such as Fig. 3.7 are very common in both textbooks and technical journals.

chapter four

measures of central tendency and variability

Measures of Central Tendency

Many of you are already familiar with at least one measure of central tendency. This is the average or mean. The average is often used to refer to your overall average grade point, the average score on an exam you have just taken, or the average man in the street. The average is simply a way of conveniently summing up a large amount of information so that we can talk about what "typically" happens. Numbers that are "typical" of a group of other numbers are called measures of central tendency. The average or mean is only one of several measures of central tendency. The purpose of this chapter will be to review a few of these measures of central tendency along with some measures of variability.

The mean

The *mean* as mentioned above is an equivalent term for that which you typically call an average. The method for determining the mean or average of a group of numbers is already well known to most of you and consists of adding up all the scores and dividing by the total number of scores. We can define this procedure in more precise mathematical terms, but before we do, you need to be familiar with some notation we will have occasion to use from time to time.

X is used to stand for a particular score in a series of scores.

$\bar{X}$ (read X-bar) stands for the mean of the distribution of numbers.

N is the total number of measures in a particular set.

Σ is the Greek capital letter sigma. It is used to stand for the mathematical operation of summing and is called a summation sign.

i is a subscript that is used to refer to particular scores in a set of scores. For example, the set of X scores would look something like this: $X_1, X_2, \ldots, X_i, \ldots, X_N$. We use this subscript, then, to define the location of a particular score in an array of numbers (set of numbers).

We can now define the procedure for calculating the mean $(\bar{X})$ in mathematical terms.

$$\bar{X} = \frac{\sum_{i=1}^{N} X_i}{N}$$

Written in English, this formula says: The mean is equal to the sum of all the scores divided by the total number of scores. Specifically, the notation in the above formula indicates that in order to calculate $\bar{X}$ (the mean) you first add up all the scores (X_i) starting with the first one $(i = 1)$ and ending with the last (Nth) one. Once this sum has been calculated, it is divided by N to obtain the mean $(\bar{X})$.

The mode

The mode is defined as the score that occurs most frequently, and can be calculated from "raw" data simply by counting which score occurs most frequently. If a distribution has two scores that occur most frequently, then there are two modes, and it is called a bimodal distribution. In theory, it is possible to have a large number of modes. An example of a bimodal distribution is given in Fig. 4.1.

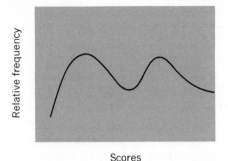

Scores

Fig. 4.1 An example of a frequency polygon which has two modes (bimodal).

The median

The median is the middle score in a set of scores ordered from lowest to highest. In other words, the median is the score having the same number of scores on either side of it. If there is an even number of scores, the median is half-way between the middle two scores, i.e., the average of these two scores. Consider the following seven scores:

$$2 \quad 7 \quad 8 \quad 9 \quad 14 \quad 16 \quad 17$$

The middle score (the median) would be the fourth from either end or the number 9.

$$2 \quad 7 \quad 8 \quad 9 \quad 14 \quad 16 \quad 17 \quad 20$$

Eight scores are given above but now there really is no middle score; rather 9 and 14 are both middle scores. Here the median would be $(9 + 14)/2$. Thus, the median for this latter set of scores would be 11.5 or a score half-way between the two middle scores, 9 and 14.

Measures of Variability

We have seen that it is possible to partially summarize data by one number reflecting the central tendency of a distribution. We may rephrase this point as follows: since scores in a distribution are typically not all the same (i.e., they vary from one another), it is useful to have a number to characterize all those in the distribution. It is also true, however, that if we have a measure of central tendency, by definition we have no indication of how much the scores in the distribution differed or varied from one another.

As it turns out, knowledge of the variability of the data is an extremely important consideration. For the purpose of this section we will not be concerned with the reasons for the scores being different from one another; our primary concern will be with simply describing this variability.

Consider the two frequency plots depicted in Fig. 4.2. These two plots have similar means, but are the scores in the two frequency distributions similar? Your response to this should be no, that in Distribution B scores more frequently occur at greater distances from the mean than in A. This is equivalent to saying the scores in B are more variable than the scores in A. Consequently, even though two groups of scores have similar means, it is possible that they differ in other ways, such as in variability.

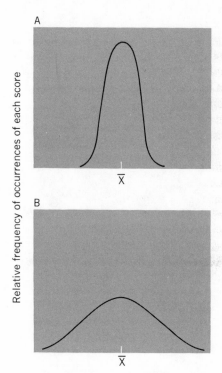

Fig. 4.2 Two frequency polygons showing (A) low variability and (B) high variability of scores.

Range

One of the simplest measures of variability is the *range*. **The range is defined as the highest score minus the lowest score.** The range is only a rough estimate of variability since it only considers information about the two extreme scores in the distribution and gives no information about the relative number of scores that are at variance with the mean of the distribution.

For example, Fig. 4.3 depicts two distributions having the same range (100 − 5 = 95). What of the variability? Distribution B is obviously more variable since it contains more scores farther from the mean.

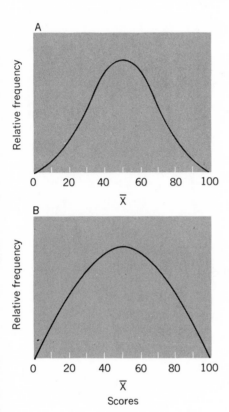

Fig. 4.3 Example of two frequency distributions with the same range but differing in variability.

4.3

Variance

The variance of a distribution gives a mathematical summary of how much the scores deviate or are at variance with the mean. For example, Distribution B in Fig. 4.3 would have a larger variance than Distribution A. A small variance indicates that most of the scores in the distribution lie close to the mean; a large variance indicates that most of the scores are relatively far from the mean. The variance of a distribution is proportional to the sum of the squared deviations around the mean and is calculated as follows:

$$\text{Variance} = \frac{\sum_{i=1}^{N}(X_i - \overline{X})^2}{N - 1}$$

An example of this calculation is given in Table 4.1.

Table 4.1   Example of Calculating the Variance from a Set of Scores

Name	Score	$X - \overline{X}$	$(X - \overline{X})^2$
X_1	4	-12	144
X_2	10	-6	36
X_3	11	-5	25
X_4	14	-2	4
X_5	15	-1	1
X_6	15	-1	1
X_7	16	0	0
X_8	16	0	0
X_9	17	$+1$	1
X_{10}	17	$+1$	1
X_{11}	19	$+3$	9
X_{12}	20	$+4$	16
X_{13}	20	$+4$	16
X_{14}	20	$+4$	16
X_{15}	21	$+5$	25
X_{16}	21	$+5$	25

$N = 16$ $\Sigma X_i = 256$ $\Sigma (X - \overline{X}_i)^2 = 320$

$\overline{X} = 16$

$$\text{Variance} = \frac{\sum_{i=1}^{N}(X_i - \overline{X})^2}{N - 1}$$

$$\text{Variance} = \frac{320}{16 - 1} = 21.33$$

The above method of calculation of the variance may in some cases result in excessive round-off error. An alternative method of doing this calculation, which minimizes rounding error, is given below. An example of calculating the variance using this recommended procedure is given in Table 4.2.

$$\frac{N\sum_{i=1}^{N}X_i^2 - \left(\sum_{i=1}^{N}X_i\right)^2}{N(N-1)}$$

Variance is a very useful method for summarizing the variability. In addition, one of the most powerful statistics that can be used to evaluate quantitative data (the Analysis of Variance) is based on an analysis of the variability of the scores about the means of the various groups which you have run in your experiment.

Table 4.2   Alternative Method of Calculating the Variance

Subject	Score (X_i)	X_i^2
X_1	4	16
X_2	10	100
X_3	11	121
X_4	14	196
X_5	15	225
X_6	15	225
X_7	16	256
X_8	16	256
X_9	17	289
X_{10}	17	289
X_{11}	19	361
X_{12}	20	400
X_{13}	20	400
X_{14}	20	400
X_{15}	21	441
X_{16}	21	441
	$\Sigma X_i = 256$	$\Sigma X_i^2 = 4416$

$$\text{Variance} = \frac{N\sum_{i=1}^{N}X_i^2 - (\sum_{i=1}^{N}X_i)^2}{N(N-1)}$$

$$= \frac{(16)(4416) - (256)^2}{(16)(16-1)}$$

$$= 21.33$$

Standard deviation

A third measure of variability is the standard deviation, symbolized as SD. The SD is defined as the square root of the variance:

$$SD = \sqrt{\text{Variance}}$$

The standard deviation is a very useful statistic, and we will deal with some of its uses in the next chapter.

chapter five

the normal curve

Of the many theoretical distributions encountered in behavioral research, by far the most common is the *normal distribution*. This distribution is frequently approximated by data collected in the course of research and consequently, knowledge of its properties can be a valuable research tool. A normal distribution is presented in Fig. 5.1.

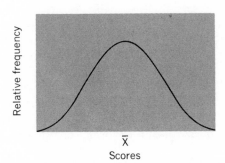

Fig. 5.1 A normal distribution of scores.

Notice that the curve drawn in Fig. 5.1 is smooth (i.e., no data points are given) and so should indicate to you that the curve is *theoretical*. That is, the normal distribution is defined and therefore drawn according to a specific equation. No empirical distribution will conform *exactly* to this curve, but some will come fairly close to normality.

It will be convenient to refer to the *inflexion* points of the normal curve. An inflexion point is the place where a curve changes (with respect to the *x* axis) from bow-shaped "upwards" (convex) to bow-shaped "downwards" (concave). We indicate each of the two inflexion points on the normal curve in Fig. 5.2.

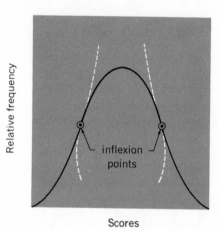

Fig. 5.2 The inflexion point is where the curve changes from concave to convex with respect to the *x* axis.

Since we have a distribution of scores (which in this case are distributed normally) we may speak of a mean (μ) and a standard deviation (σ) on the scores.* Let us assume that:

$$\mu = 100$$
$$\sigma = 10$$

We may now go one step further. Since the distribution is normal, *we can now*, after these two calculations, *fill out the entire x axis!* This is done in Fig. 5.3. Now, we used no magical potions in this process—simply a couple of pieces of information. First of all, in a normal distribution, Mean equals Median equals Mode. We therefore place the score of 100 at the exact middle of the distribution. The score of 110 is exactly one "σ unit" above the mean (100 + 10 = 110) and 90 is exactly one "σ unit" below the mean (100 − 10 = 90). It happens that in a normal distribution those scores

*We are dealing with a theoretical distribution, and the symbols of $\overline{X}$ for mean and SD for standard deviation are technically inappropriate because these symbols are used to describe collected sets of scores. The symbols used in the text, μ (read as mu) and σ (sigma) represent the *theoretical* (based on an infinite number of scores) mean and standard deviation, respectively.

lying 1 σ unit away from the mean are located at the two points of inflexion. Once you know where scores 90 and 110 go, you also know where every other number goes. For convenience we will henceforth use σ units as the scale of the *x* axis, and this scale will now be called a *z* scale.

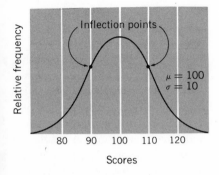

Fig. 5.3 Normal distribution with *x* axis filled in from knowledge of $\overline{X}$ and SD.

Some Uses of *z* Scores

We have just seen that we can discuss the normal distribution in terms of raw scores, such that the mean of 100 is located at the center of the distribution, and 110 is located at the inflexion point, and in terms of σ units, with the mean located at zero sigma unit and +1 σ unit located at the right inflexion point and −1 σ unit located at the left inflexion point. The mean, in this sense, is the reference point and represents zero σ units. We may, then, redraw the distribution using σ units on the *x* axis; this is demonstrated in Fig. 5.4. When we use σ units, we are referring to a *z* scale. We may, in fact, say that −1 σ equals a *z* score of −1, +2 σ equals a *z* score of +2, etc.

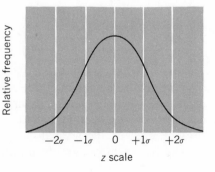

Fig. 5.4 The normal distribution in terms of σ units.

Notice that although we have two "languages," there is a "translation" from one to the other. This "translation" takes the following form:

$$z = \frac{X - \mu}{\sigma}$$

where X = any raw score
 μ = theoretical mean
 σ = theoretical standard deviation

What do you suppose the value is of speaking in terms of z scores rather than in terms of raw (actual) scores? There are two major gains we make in the z score language. The first is that we may compare raw scores which were beforehand not comparable, assuming the two distributions of scores have similar shapes. Consider that your score on a recent mid-term exam was 45, while an acquaintance of yours in another section taking a different exam earned a 75. Who did better? For this, you need to know the mean for each exam. Assuming that the mean for your exam was 30 (with an SD of 5) and for your friend's exam was 80 (with an SD of 10), it should be clear that you "did better" than your friend. How much better? The best way to answer this is to convert each test score to a z score:

You	Friend
Score = 45	Score = 75
Mean = 30	Mean = 80
Standard Deviation = 5	Standard Deviation = 10

$z = \dfrac{\text{Score} - \text{Mean}}{\text{Standard Deviation}}$	$z = \dfrac{\text{Score} - \text{Mean}}{\text{Standard Deviation}}$
$z = \dfrac{45 - 30}{5}$	$z = \dfrac{75 - 80}{10}$
$z = \dfrac{15}{5}$	$z = \dfrac{-5}{10}$
$z = +3.0$	$z = -0.5$

Your z score is equal to 3 while your friend obtained a z score of -0.5 (the minus sign indicates that the score was below the mean). If we assume for the sake of discussion that the scores on the exams were normally distributed, we may interpret these z scores by drawing the normal curve. As can be seen in Fig. 5.5., your friend scored just slightly under the mean, but should still earn a "C" grade on the test. Your z score is literally "out of sight" since z scores as high as that occur very infrequently, i.e., z scores as high as three have a low frequency of occurrence. Your grade should be at least "A+."

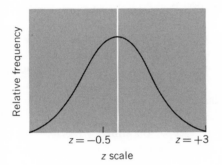

Fig. 5.5 The normal curve with $z = +3$ and $z = -0.5$ marked on the x axis.

This brings us to the second major gain in using the z score language, namely, the use of z scores in speaking of probability, e.g., the likelihood of the occurrence of a particular score. We treat this next.

Areas Under the Normal Curve

The shape of the normal distribution is such that most of the scores are relatively close to the mean; the further away you go from the mean, the less likely it is for a score to occur. We may illustrate this by considering how much area under the curve is represented at various points. Some points are drawn in Fig. 5.6. About .68 of the area lies between -1.0 and

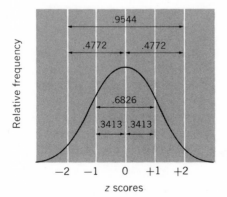

Fig. 5.6 Some areas under the normal curve.

+1.0. We get this value by referring to Table A in Appendix B. Note that when z equals 1.00, the corresponding area (the area between the z score and μ) is given as about 34%. The chances of arbitrarily picking a score from a normal distribution of z equals ± 1.0 is about 68%, or about .68. The chances of that score lying between z equals ± 2.0 is .9544. What we have done is use the area between two points as an indicant of the chance of obtaining a particular score.

Let us return to you and your friend and the results of your mid-semester exams. With respect to your friend, the percentage of the area under the curve exceeding his score is about 69; in other words, the chance is about 69% of obtaining his score or better on the exam. With respect to you, approximately 50% of the right half of the curve is behind you (see Table A, Appendix B) and therefore somewhat less than 1/10 of 1% of the area lies above your score; in other words, the chance of obtaining your score or better is about one out of one thousand, an unusual event indeed.

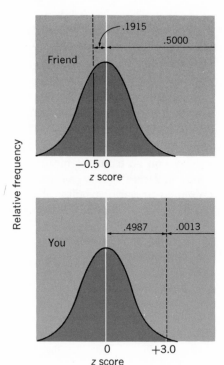

Fig. 5.7 Proportion of area above the exam scores of you and your friend.

The Importance of the Normal Distribution

We have examined the normal curve and some of its properties because this curve is of considerable importance to the behavioral scientist. Much of the data collected in behavioral research tends to be roughly distributed in a normal manner. The scientist may, under such circumstances, intentionally overlook departures from normality and treat the measures as though they were normal. Thus, he may meaningfully compare two or more groups of scores by transforming his data into z scores. Probability statements, deriving from normal curve statistics, may also be imposed on collected data that approach normality. Furthermore, some of the statistical analyses referred to throughout this book rest on the assumption that groups of measures are distributed in a normal manner. In short, a knowledge of some of the properties of the normal curve, together with a few key assumptions by the scientist regarding his data, is a valuable aid in doing behavioral research.

chapter six

sampling procedures

We remarked in the first chapter that scientists tend to develop and work with general or universal statements, often based on an induction from certain particular instances. That is, universals are not observable in the empirical world —at best, only particular examples are available through observation.

Although all scientific theories are comprised of a network of universal statements, the content of the statements and the particulars upon which the statements are based generally differ from one science to another. Thus, a chemist may neutralize a particular acid solution with a particular basic solution with the intent of learning about compound combination *in general*, while a behavioral scientist asks a volunteer to learn a list of words with the intent of learning about memory processes *in general*.

The road from the particular to the universal is fraught with philosophical obstacles, some of which we have already touched upon. The road is also fraught with scientific obstacles, and it is these considerations that occupy us in this chapter.

A scientist may go from particular to universal if three conditions are satisfied:

1. The movement from the particular to the universal must be logically correct. To *induce* that all swans are white when the scientist has observed several purple swans is a breach of the rules of logic.

2. The data collected in a study must be reliable. If one group in an experiment performed better than another, we need to know if this will usually happen under the same experimental circumstances, or if it was simply a "quirk" (this will be discussed in the following chapter).

3. The subjects for the research project should be representative of the group to be used in the universal statement. It would be inadvisable to study how people interact with one another by using a group of catatonic schizophrenic patients from a nearby state hospital. Although these patients may reveal much about catatonic schizophrenics, the scientist's aim to generalize his findings to *all* people would certainly not be met.

To summarize, then, if we wish to formulate an empirical law about, say, our perceptual abilities, we may conduct an experiment on a handful of subjects, but we want to generalize the results to all human beings. To properly infer from the small group of subjects (our sample) to all human beings (our population) requires an understanding of *populations and samples*.

Samples and Populations

A population is a clearly defined group of events, objects, individuals, and so forth. Used in this way, we can identify as many different populations as we wish. We list below a few possible populations with which scientists may be concerned:

all humans	all values
all smokers	all electricity
all oak trees	all hospitals
all solar systems	all women
all atoms	all energy

As you can see from the above, the population refers to *all* members therein although populations may be of considerably different sizes.

Research is conducted within populations. When the population is very small, for example, All Members of the School Football Team, it may be possible to tap *all* members of that population. When, as is more often the case, the population in which you are interested is very large, for example, all humans, it is not possible to survey all of its members; hence, we can deal with only a *sample* of that population.

Types of Samples

A sample is a portion of a population chosen by some clearly defined set of procedures. A sample, therefore, is *always* a portion of some population. Usually, we will want to make statements regarding the population on the basis of the characteristics of the sample. In other words, *we usually wish to infer the nature of the population from the data collected on the sample.* You can easily see, then, that to fulfill the purpose of inference, the sample should reflect (be representative of) the general population. There are a number of procedures available, however, to select those members of the population who are to be sampled.

The random and independent sample

This type of sample may be defined by the use of two procedures:

1. That every individual in the population has an equal chance of being chosen. This is what is meant by *random*.

2. The selection of any one individual in no way affects the selection of any other. This is what is meant by *independent*.

Random and independent samples form the basis of all sampling procedures and the procedure is itself a very popular sampling technique. As we shall soon see, however, the bulk of behavioral research does not employ random and independent samples.

The stratified sample

Of all the sampling procedures, the stratified sample is probably the best known to the general public, since the major political polls, made public via the news media, employ stratified sampling. A set of three procedures defines the stratified sample:

1. *The entire population is classified according to some schema.* Thus, in a political poll, we may have urban or rural dwellers, the various geographical regions, socio-economic level, religion, and so forth.

2. *The number of people sampled in each category should conform to the proportion of that group in the entire population.* Thus, if 50% of the population live in big cities, 35% in small towns, and 15% on farms, then those same proportions should be maintained in your sample.

3. Having decided on the categories and proportions that will be used, *the individuals to be chosen within these constraints should be randomly and independently sampled.* Thus, if you plan to survey big city, middle class, Democratic, Roman Catholic women, you should randomly and independently sample *all* those who conform to this classification.

The importance of maintaining proportionality in a stratified sample can readily be shown. Suppose one of the issues in a college election is the banning of sororities and fraternities from the school. Upon sampling 25 Greek letter people and 25 non-Greek letter people, you discover that all those belonging to such societies oppose the ban and all those not belonging favor the ban. On the basis of this small poll, things look fairly evenly divided. But further suppose that in the whole school there were 127 Greek letter people and 436 non-affiliates. A proportional division of the categories would clearly reveal overwhelming support of the banning of the sororities and fraternities. The proportionality principle therefore permits you to keep things in perspective.

Useful information regarding the sample—and therefore the population —can be obtained by stratifying the sample on the basis of factors *potentially relevant* to the particular problem. This potential relevancy factor is extremely important when using stratification. If some of the levels of the stratification are not relevant to the problem (*i.e.*, some levels give comparable results to each other), you have lost nothing but a little effort and have achieved the knowledge of these sub-groups being comparable. Blood type of individuals responding to a political poll, for instance, would probably not be a relevant consideration. But it is also possible that certain classifications have *not* been used in the sample that may turn out to be crucial in accurately describing the population. Religion of respondents, for example, should not be omitted from the stratification.

The contrasting sample

The contrasting sample is really a variant of the stratified sample in that the proportionality procedure is now somewhat modified in the following manner: *certain categories in the stratification are intentionally oversampled.* By "oversample" is meant that *more* than the proportion of people in one or more categories required by the stratification procedure are incorporated into the sample. The reason that you might wish to oversample certain sub-groups in the entire population is that the particular issue is, for one reason or another, more relevant to these groups than others. For example, many school boards requiring additional funds must submit the monetary request to a vote of the entire community. If there is one sub-group in the community whose vote is crucial to the issue (i.e., upper-middle class couples with no children), you might wish to oversample these people to accurately gauge the best publicity strategy. Of course, if you are using a contrasting sample rather than a stratified sample, you need to clearly define the to-be-oversampled groups and have an adequate reason for placing more weight on these sub-groups rather than others.

The purposeful sample

Every now and then some news publication digs through its records and comes up with some astonishing statistics. There are some towns, for instance, that during a national election, have *always* given the majority of their votes to the candidate who became President of the United States. In fact, there has been at least one movie made of just such an occurrence with reporters, politicians, and tourists converging on the town once the voting record was known. This town, at least before it became a national point of interest, could have comprised a purposeful sample. *Purposeful sampling is randomly and independently sampling a particular sub-group within the population that is—for whatever reason—representative of the entire population.* Whenever you employ a purposeful sample, you must make the assumption that this sub-group is *still representative* at the time you take your measurements.

The incidental sample

The incidental sample is one of the most important of all the sampling procedures mentioned because it is the most typical sampling procedure used in behavioral research. *Incidental sampling is randomly and independently sampling a particular sub-group within the population because that sub-group is highly convenient and/or available.* This differs from a contrasting sample in that, here, the sub-group is not more relevant—it is simply available. It also differs from a purposeful sample in that there is usually no data base to suggest that the sub-group in question is representative of the total population.

An incidental sampling procedure is not *necessarily* a "bad" technique, but the following assumption needs to be made: *the incidental sample is representative of the total population.* Unfortunately, most researchers all too flippantly make this very serious assumption, and the greatest violators are the "academic, basic researchers." These scientists—and we do not exclude ourselves—use a carefully inbred strain of rats (bearing only a morphological similarity to wild rats) for animal research and usually employ college freshmen and sophomores who are taking introductory psychology for human research. Whether the rat research can ever be generalized beyond the laboratory rat, or the freshmen research beyond the freshmen, is a question that has been considered but not yet been satisfactorily answered in most cases.

Closing Remarks

While a knowledge of sampling procedures is important for most scientists, behavioral scientists appear to run greater risks in their research than some of those practicing the "hard" sciences (e.g., physics, chemistry, etc.). A nuclear physicist generally assumes that, under certain conditions of measurement, one electron is similar to another, i.e., that they will behave comparably in a given situation. A behavioral scientist cannot make an assumption that is analogous to two humans. It seems safe to say that humans differ in many more ways from one another than electrons, and to the extent that individual differences are encountered, the importance of proper sampling procedures is increased. Although we may seriously question the generality of research on college freshmen, the physicist would not question the generality of his research to all electrons. We therefore urge you to concern yourself seriously with sampling procedures in behavioral research.

chapter seven

drawing conclusions from experimental data

A scientist performs research so that he can gain more knowledge about the world. To achieve this, it is often possible to make some very precise changes in the environment and then measure the changes that occur in behavior. Furthermore, it is typical for the scientist to use numbers (usually based on one of the scales of measurement discussed earlier) to represent the behavior in question. It will also be recalled that an experiment consists of at least two conditions, the Experimental Condition and the Control Condition.* At the completion of an experiment, then, the researcher has one list of numbers representing the behavior of subjects in the Experimental condition and another set of numbers representing the behavior of Control subjects.

You may recall from our discussion of scientific inquiry in Chapter 1 that research is not conducted in a vacuum; rather, the scientist is operating from within some theoretical framework and the experiment is intimately related to the theoretical structure. Thus, the experimenter usually has certain expectations of how the two conditions should differ at

*We will expand upon the notion of Experimental Condition and Control Condition in Chapters 9 and 10. For now, these terms are being used to represent different groups.

the end of a study, and these expectations are termed the *experimental hypothesis*. The scientist usually expects that the experimental hypothesis will be confirmed by the research, and our task in this chapter is to outline how a scientist can tell from the measurements he has made (data) whether or not he has succeeded in confirming his hypothesis.

Much of the research conducted by behavioral scientists usually involves measuring many subjects or groups under each of the conditions in an experiment. The reasons why many subjects are exposed to each condition or treatment will be discussed in later chapters. For now, we only wish to point out that the scientist, if he has made a prediction, will usually talk about the *means* of his groups. That is, he will predict that the mean performance measure of subjects in the Experimental condition will be greater than (or less than) that for subjects in the Control condition.

Of course, in most instances, the mean of the Experimental conditions would, indeed, differ from the mean of the Control; in fact, you should probably consider it remarkable if the two means corresponded *precisely*. The issue, therefore, is not whether the two means have different values; rather, the vital concern is whether or not any observed difference between the means is "real." That is, if the Experimental group performed at a different level than the Control group in your particular study, what you want to know is: **If the study were repeated over and over, would the two conditions usually result in similar differences?** This is the vital question of the **reliability of the obtained differences** between the means of your two groups, which must be considered after the completion of an experiment. Assume for example that the mean of the Experimental condition was greater than the mean of the Control. If the experiment were repeated several times, and each time the Experimental mean exceeded that of the Control condition, the scientist should eventually be convinced that the originally observed difference was reliable. If, however, experimental repetition produced no consistent results, it would be judged that the originally observed difference was not terribly reliable.

The reliability question can be approached in one of two ways:

1. You may repeat the experiment sufficiently often to satisfactorily answer the question. Of course, most researchers do not have the time, money, patience, and interest for such a task. Additionally, the terms "sufficiently" and "satisfactorily" may be very difficult to agree upon from one scientist to another. Generally, scientists do not use this repetition procedure to answer the reliability question.

2. An alternative method is to make use of the information contained in the data of the experiment by employing particular statistical procedures to *estimate*, or *infer*, what would *probably happen* if we followed the repetition procedure. This is the alternative chosen by scientists themselves, and

the remainder of the present chapter will attempt to illustrate the concepts upon which some of the more commonly used statistical procedures are based.

Some Information in Data

Central tendency

We said in the previous chapter that—assuming a proper sampling procedure—we can infer characteristics of the population on the basis of a representative sample. We also mentioned that information in the data may be used to answer the reliability question. Let us see some of the information contained in a set of data. Suppose that we wish to deal with the average height of the American female. Since it would be a near-hopeless task to measure the entire population, we choose a random and independent sample, measure the height of each of the sampled females, and then . . . ? Our estimate of the population mean would be the mean height of those women in our sample. Being that we have only an estimate, it is possible that we are, in small or large degree, wrong. Nevertheless, *the mean of our sample is the most accurate* (albeit, only) *estimate of the mean of the population.*

Our estimate of the population mean may be improved in one of two ways. First, as the number of sampled individuals increases, our estimate should become more precise. That is, the closer we get to sampling the entire population, the better will the sample mean approximate the population mean. Second, we may repeatedly sample the population, each time drawing randomly and independently. Assuming, for simplicity, that the samples are of equal size, the average of these sample means would be the best estimate of the mean of the population.

Variability

Thus far, we are referring to a measure of central tendency, i.e., the mean, as estimating characteristics of a population. An equally important aspect of the data is its variability, and we may illustrate some similar principles with the aid of the following three samples:

Sample A	Sample B	Sample C
98	70	160
101	80	100
102	120	10
99	100	40
100	130	190
$\overline{X}_A = 100$	$\overline{X}_B = 100$	$\overline{X}_C = 100$
$\mathrm{Var}_A = 2.50$	$\mathrm{Var}_B = 650.00$	$\mathrm{Var}_C = 5850.00$

Although each of the sample means is 100, it should be clear that other characteristics of these samples (and, thus, we may assume, the populations) differ markedly. The variability within each group, i.e., *within-group variability*, increases from A to B to C as either inspection of the data or a look at the calculated variances easily shows. We may in fact say that, despite the small number of scores, the variance of each sample is our best estimate of the respective population variance. Furthermore, as was true in our discussion of the mean, increasing sample size or taking the average variance of many samples (of equal size) drawn randomly and independently from the population will give us a better estimate of the population variance.

On the basis of the sample variance, however, we may go one step further. Let us draw (or measure) a single score rather than a sample from Populations A, B, and C. Of the three drawings, which score or measure is likely to be *closest* to our estimated mean of each population? In answering this question, you need look no further than the within-group variability, since this describes the "spread" of scores about the mean. Hence, the draw from Population A will probably be the closest to 100, the draw from Population C the furthest from 100, and the draw from Population B in between the other two.

The implications of this simple example are far-reaching, and will be developed in the following sections. For now, think back to the question of reliability: If a study were repeatedly conducted, would there be similar differences between the experimental and control conditions? We stated that the answer can be approached statistically. Notice that we are beginning to answer it now. The outcome of repeated sampling can be inferred on the basis of sample statistics. That is, we can infer that repeated sampling from Population A will result in scores fairly close to 100, whereas repeated sampling from Population C should result in a larger spread of scores.

We may summarize what we have said in this section as follows:

1. The calculated characteristic of the sample (mean, variance, or anything else) is the best estimate of that characteristic of the population from which it was drawn.

2. As the sample size increases, its characteristics become an increasingly better estimate of the respective characteristics of the population.

3. The average of equal-sized samples is the best estimate of the respective population characteristics. *

4. Certain results of continued sampling may be predicted by the sample within-group variability.

The Reliability of Mean Differences

We may now return to the reliability question and examine it in somewhat greater detail. It happens that this question is asked many times throughout a research enterprise and in a slightly different way each time. It is important to understand each of the questions and each of the types of answers that are given. The first question, asked after the data are summarized is:

What are the chances of finding the same mean differences were the same experiment repeated several times?

We have seen that of the two alternative ways of answering this question, actually repeating the study many times or applying statistical techniques to the data, the latter procedure is somewhat easier to execute.

In applying statistical principles to the data, however, the question needs to be rephrased:

Do the mean differences reflect sampling from two distinctive populations?

The scientist, now acting as a statistician, attempts to determine, through statistical operations, the answer to the above question. Essentially, he assumes that, at the outset of his statistical work, the two samples were drawn from the same population.† After he completes his statistical work, he must then decide the answer to the question.

---

*If the samples are of unequal size, a *weighted* average should be calculated.

†He must make this statistical assumption, called the Null Hypothesis, in order to use his statistics. It is a result of his role as statistician that the assumption is made; as the researcher, he does not have to believe it.

The decision on the above question is made by the researcher, not the statistician, but since there is another role change, the question is again rephrased:

Does the mean difference reflect a SIGNIFICANT mean difference?

In a sense, the results of the statistics are laid out before the researcher in the form of numbers; a decision as to how to treat those numbers remains to be made. The problem is essentially this: Since the means and variances of two samples will almost always be different, there is always the possibility that two distinctive populations were sampled. How "real" or "remote" the possibility is must be decided on the basis of criteria agreed upon by the scientific community. To indicate that he is speaking of probability and not of certainty, the researcher speaks of "significant" differences. Thus, if two means are said to be *significantly different*, the researcher is betting that, in all likelihood,

1. the mean differences probably reflect sampling from two distinctive populations, and

2. that, therefore, were the study repeated several times under the same conditions, the relationship of one mean to the other would be upheld.

A case in point

We may integrate and expand on what we have covered so far by referring to a hypothetical example. Consider the results of three experiments, conducted at different times and for different purposes. Our intent is to use an intuitive approach to understand further the notion of "significant difference."

The data collected in Experiment 1 are these:

Group E	Group C
20	90
10	50
80	10
90	30
60	5
15	15
5	10
$\overline{X}_\text{E} = 40$	$\overline{X}_\text{C} = 30$

The range of scores in Group E is from 5 to 90, and the range of scores in Group C, is from 5 to 90. Furthermore, the scores in each group appear to be haphazardly distributed, such that a score between 5 and 90 could end up in either Group E or Group C. This virtually complete overlap of the two distributions is schematically represented below. The shaded areas depict the within-group variability associated with each sample.

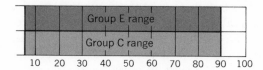

Are the two means significantly different? Most assuredly not. Compared to the huge variability within the two groups, the group differences are practically negligible. It would be fairly safe to say that, were Experiment 1 repeated, it would be anyone's guess as to which group would have the higher mean.

This comparison, then, between within-groups variability and the obtained mean difference, is a useful index for evaluating the question of how reliable a difference may be between two groups.* Were we, in fact, to examine the ratio of mean difference to within-groups variability, we would find the ratio to have a value of well below one. That is:

$$\text{ratio value} = \frac{\text{mean difference}}{\text{within-groups variability}}$$
$$= \frac{\text{relatively small}}{\text{huge}}$$
$$= \text{less than one}$$

The data collected in Experiment 2 are these:

Group E	Group C
42	30
37	33
41	28
38	29
43	32
39	27
40	31
$\bar{X}_E = 40$	$\bar{X}_C = 30$

*We should point out that this argument is substantially weakened with very large sample sizes.

Experiment 2 presents just the reverse of that given in Experiment 1. The range of scores in the C Group is from 27 to 33, whereas the range in Group E is from 37 to 43. The samples in this example do not at all overlap; the numbers do not appear to be arranged haphazardly between the groups and the schema below reflects this lack of overlap.

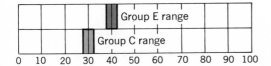

Although the mean difference is identical to that obtained in Experiment 1, the small amount of within-groups variability tends to make us judge the mean difference as a huge one. We might, therefore, construct the following ratio:

$$\text{ratio value} = \frac{\text{mean difference}}{\text{within-groups variability}}$$
$$= \frac{\text{relatively huge}}{\text{tiny}}$$
$$= \text{much, much greater than one}$$

Is there a significant difference between the two groups in Experiment 2? Most likely, in that a repeat of the study should closely replicate the original findings.

The data collected in Experiment 3 are these:

Group E	Group C
45	22
50	24
35	38
30	30
48	36
32	40
40	20
$\overline{X}_E = 40$	$\overline{X}_C = 30$

Experiment 3 lies between the two extreme examples just mentioned. It is, of course, the most ambiguous of the three. The two distributions overlap, but not completely; the scores do not appear to be haphazardly distributed, but they are certainly not as well placed as those in Experiment 2.

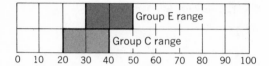

Is there a significant difference between the groups in Experiment 3? Maybe yes, and maybe no. Only the use of the appropriate statistical procedure will tell us for sure.

Sources of Variance

Although we frequently refer to within-groups variance, you should not get the impression that all variance in a study is within-group variance. Generally, in a two-group study, there are two gross reasons for scores to differ from one another. One reason is that the scores were taken under different experimental conditions (Experimental vs. Control condition), and this reason reflects *between-groups variance*; the other reason for scores to differ results from other factors subsumed under *within-groups variability*. We treat each in turn.

Between-groups variance

As we will see in Section III, the Experimental condition differs in specific ways from the Control condition in an experiment. That is, the former may receive one dosage of a drug, the latter another dosage level; the former may be exposed to one teaching method, the latter another, etc. Typically, the researcher expects his measurements to be different (between his groups) *because* of differences in drug dosage, teaching method, etc. The difference or variance of group means reflects in part the effectiveness of the manipulation. Statistically, *between-groups variance* reflects the differences of group means from the overall or grand mean.

Within-groups variance

Within each group, the scores themselves will probably differ to some extent. That is what we have previously called within-groups variability, and may be identified by the difference between each score from its respective group mean. The reasons for *within-group variance* are many. One reason is that the experimental treatment might have been slightly but unintentionally different for each measurement (owing to time of day of testing, experimenter fatigue, etc.). Another reason is that organisms, even under the "same" experimental treatment, will still differ from individual to individual. A third reason is that the measuring instrument might be somewhat unreliable, variable, or not sufficiently sensitive. These reasons, and others that you might think of, can be classified as "experimental error," a rather broad catch-all category. Thus, "within-groups variance" is often used synonomously with "error variance."

If between- and within-groups variance together account for all the variance of a study, we may logically write the following:

$$\text{Variance}_{\text{Total}} = \text{Variance}_{\text{Bet}} + \text{Variance}_{\text{within}}$$

Statistically, total variance reflects the difference between each score and the overall mean (the mean of all the scores in the experiment). This does, in a strong sense, deal with all the differences among all the scores in all groups of an experiment.

Degrees of Freedom

We will be working with the notion of degrees of freedom (df) often throughout the book, and it will be convenient to at least introduce the concept here. *Df* are summarized by a number representing the number of numbers that are *free to vary* given certain constraints. Given the constraints (1) that a distribution contains exactly four scores, and (2) that the mean of the distribution is exactly 10, how many of those four scores are free to vary (i.e., how many can you arbitrarily fill in with any number your heart desires)? If you think about it, you will realize that three of the four numbers can take on any value at all. The fourth one, however, is then determined (the fourth number has to be THE number that will produce a mean of exactly 10). One, and only one number, can fill the fourth slot. For example, if we arbitrarily fill in three of the slots with the numbers 20, 55, and 1, the fourth number must be -36 in order to produce a mean of exactly 10. You may wish to try this with any given group of numbers, even fractions, but you will find that you may still choose exactly three numbers completely at random before the last number is totally determined. We say, therefore, that there are *three df* for that situation. If there are five numbers involved, four of them are free to vary (there would be four *df*); with six numbers in total, there are five *df*, etc. Generally,

$$df = \text{number of cases considered} - 1$$

For each source of variance, the appropriate number of df can be calculated. Since the Total Variance is based upon the difference of each observation from the overall mean, the df associated with Variance$_{\text{Total}}$ equals the total number of observations in the experiment minus one:

$$df_{\text{Total}} = N - 1 \quad \text{Where N is the total number of observations.}$$

Since the between-groups variance is based upon the difference between each group mean from the overall mean, the df associated with this source of variance equals the number of groups in the experiment minus one:

$$df_{\text{Bet}} = g - 1 \quad \text{Where g is the number of groups.}$$

Since the within-groups source of variance is based upon the difference between each score from its own group mean, the df associated with this source of variance equals the sum of all the df associated with each group. It will be more convenient, however, to calculate this value indirectly by first calculating the total df and the df associated with the between-groups variance and subtracting:

$$df_{\text{Within}} = df_{\text{Total}} - df_{\text{Bet}}$$

An example of this computation is given in Table 7.1.

Table 7.1 Sources of Variance and df for a Hypothetical Experiment

Group 1 scores	Group 2 scores	Group 3 scores	Group 4 scores
3	12	20	50
6	10	18	42
5	12	17	45
4	15	25	
7		22	
		19	
		16	
		14	

Source	df
Between Groups	3
Within Groups (error)	16
Total	19

$df_{\text{Tot}} = N - 1 = 5 + 4 + 8 + 3 - 1 = 20 - 1 = 19$
$df_{\text{Bet}} = g - 1 = 4 - 1 = 3$
$df_{\text{error}} = df_{\text{Tot}} - df_{\text{Bet}} = 19 - 3 = 16$

F-ratio

We stated earlier than in order to judge whether or not a given mean difference was significant, a useful aid would be the following ratio:

$$\frac{\text{mean difference}}{\text{within-groups variability}}$$

We may now amend this ratio slightly in the present context by dealing in terms of variance for both the numerator and the denominator, and set this amended ratio equal to *F*.*

$$F = \frac{\text{Variance}_{\text{Between groups}}}{\text{Variance}_{\text{Within groups}}}$$

The value of *F* is simply a number summarizing the ratio of the between-groups variance to the within-groups variance. If we drew two samples from the same population, the means of these samples should not differ significantly. This would be reflected by a small *F*-ratio (Experiment 1, p. 77). A small *F*-ratio is considered to be one which has a value of approximately 1 or less. As the value of *F* increases, that is, as the between-groups variance becomes increasingly larger than the within-groups variance, it becomes increasingly probable that the obtained mean difference is reliable (Experiment 2, p. 79).

The Concept of Significant Difference

The value of *F* is the ratio of between-groups variance to within-groups variance, and such a ratio, as we have already seen, is a useful aid in determining the reliability of the observed mean difference obtained in an experiment. The determination of the reliability of mean differences is made on the basis of the *F* distribution. This *F*-distribution may be generated by a computer by randomly taking a fixed number of observations from the same population, calculating the *F*-ratio, storing the *F*-ratio, and accumulating all of the *F*-ratios. What the computer is doing is repeatedly sampling many groups from some given population. We further know, therefore, that if two sets of scores are drawn from the same population, there should be quite a bit of overlap between the two distributions of numbers. Thus, we would expect that the *F*-ratio should be around one most of the time.

---

*The letter *F* was chosen as a tribute to the brilliant statistician R. A. Fisher who developed the analysis of variance techniques, so important to research design and analysis. See Chapter 12.

This expectation is generally confirmed, as can be seen by the typical sampling distribution of the *F*-ratio presented in Fig. 7.1. The bulk of the scores fall between 0.5 and 1.5. It may also be seen in Fig. 7.1, however, that the computer has generated, albeit occasionally, very large *F* values. An *F* value, for example, of 35.98 would occur every now and then over a long period of time, but it is relatively rare.

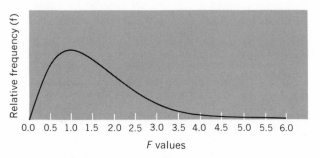

Fig. 7.1 *F* distribution with 3 and 17 *df.*

We have seen that the larger the *F*-ratio, the greater the chances that the observed mean difference is reliable. Looking at the *F* distribution, we can also see, logically enough, that large *F*-ratios are not very likely to occur on the basis of chance. What we need to do, then, is select an *F*-ratio of large enough size that does not occur by chance very often, and use that as a cutoff to establish a reliable mean difference.

The obvious question arises: How often does an *F* value have to occur by chance before we say it occurs relatively often? Psychologists have answered this question as follows:

> Although we know that this is an arbitrary judgment, we will say that an *F* score occurring 5% or less of the time, *i.e.*, one that has a chance of occurrence of less than .05, is a relatively rare occurrence.

If we impose this criterion upon the *F* distribution presented in Fig. 7.1, we might get the situation depicted in Fig. 7.2. The heavy vertical line labeled as the α (read as "alpha," the first letter in the Greek alphabet) level cuts the *F* distribution into two portions, a small portion in which $p < .05$ (read as the probability of an *F* score occurring in this area is less than 5%) and a large portion in which $p > .05$ (read as a probability greater than .05). We say, then, that our α level is set at .05, and that our cutoff point on the *F* distribution is, in our example, $F = 3.20$. An *F* score of 3.20 or greater will be taken as reflecting a significant mean difference, *i.e.*, it occurs less than 5 out of 100 times, or conversely, that only 5 times out of 100 would we probably get an F score of 3.20 or larger if our differences were not due to chance.

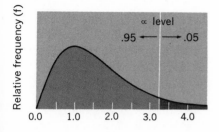

Fig. 7.2 F distribution (3 and 17 df) with $\alpha = .05$.

Significant Differences in an Experiment

The researcher is typically looking for a significant difference between the mean of the Experimental and Control conditions, and to determine if the obtained mean difference is reliable, he calculates an F-ratio. As we said before, the experimental hypothesis usually involves the specification of a significant mean difference. Statistically, however, you are really testing another hypothesis, namely, that *the two groups of numbers come from the same population*, or, if you will, that *the mean difference obtained in the study does not differ significantly from zero*. That is to say, if the mean difference is not a reliable one, then the difference is negligible. Quantitatively, a negligible difference is one that does not differ significantly from a mean difference of zero. This statistical hypothesis, called the *Null Hypothesis*, must be made implicitly in working with the F-ratio since the sampling distribution of F is itself based upon *repeated sampling from the same population* (remember that the computer randomly generates its own numbers).

Clearly, the researcher hopes to reject the Null Hypothesis. He hopes that if he calculates (from his experimental data) a *large enough F* value, i.e., one that the computer would be unlikely to generate *randomly*, then something "nonrandom" must have been going on to "cause" that large a ratio. What is this something? Presumably, it was the effects of his own intervention in the environment of his experimental subjects, i.e., the experimental treatment. What is a "large enough" F value? One that would occur *by chance* 5% or less of the time. **If the scientist obtains a large enough F ratio, he rejects the Null Hypothesis and accepts his experimental hypothesis.** If the scientist does not obtain a large enough F ratio, he fails to reject* the

---

*We say "fails to reject" rather than "accept" the Null Hypothesis since, logically, it is impossible to accept the notion of zero difference (presumably, all things in nature differ somewhat).

Null Hypothesis and does not publicly claim support for his experimental hypothesis.

Technically, the scientist should specify *in advance of the collection of his data* the α level that he will be using in specifying an F-ratio that is "large enough." For most purposes, however, the 5% level is conventionally used. Under some circumstances (see pp. 87 to 88) other levels may be chosen, but again, they should be specified in advance.

Levels of significance

In the earlier example, an F score greater than 3.20 was said to reflect a significant mean difference, in that such a score would occur by chance less than 5% of the time; a score occurring 5% of the time is considered to be sufficiently improbable to indicate a significant mean difference. Note that a score of greater than 3.20 can occur even from samples drawn from the same population, however, so that we have no absolute guarantee that the mean difference is certainly reliable. The best we have, and the best we can ever hope for, is a knowledge of the chances of our being wrong in claiming that the difference between means is reliable. Those chances are clearly less than 5 in 100 of being mistaken.

Now suppose we calculated an F score of 7.38. Since 7.38 is greater than 3.20, its probability of occurrence is less than 5% (i.e., $p < .05$). As Fig. 7.3 indicates, however, the chances of an F-ratio of 7.38 occurring on the basis of chance is not only less than .05, it is even less than .01, that is, less than one time in 100. We know this because when the α level is at .01 (the cutoff point dividing the curve 99% and 1%), the critical F-ratio is about 5.2 in our example. Our calculated value of 7.38 lies even above this point on the curve, and so we may say that the probability of its occurrence is less than 1 in 100 (i.e., $p < .01$).

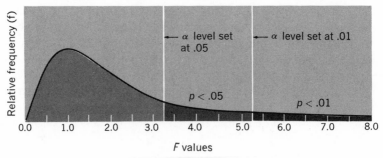

Fig. 7.3 F distribution (3 and 17 df) with $\alpha = .05$ and $\alpha = .01$.

One speaks of levels of significant differences when one states, in a general way, what the possibilities are of obtaining a particular F-ratio by chance. We would say, then, that an F-ratio of 3.51 is (on the basis of Fig. 7.3) significant at the .05 level, and 7.38 significant at the .01 level.

Using the notion of "levels of significance" easily lends itself to falling into the nasty trap of claiming that one F-ratio is "more significant" (has a lower alpha level) than another or that an F-ratio is "highly" significant. We feel, of course, that these claims are nonsense. The vital concern of the scientist should be the likelihood of making certain errors of inference. These considerations, two of which are treated below, should be made before undertaking research.

Type I and Type II Errors

When we report $F = 3.35, p < .05$, and conclude that we obtained a significant mean difference, we indicate that although the computer does generate (randomly) a few 3.35s, they occur less than 5% of the time. It is therefore a sufficiently rare occurrence to reflect a reliable mean difference. Remember, though, that 3.35 *can* occur by chance. Therefore, every now and then (5 times in 100) you will be wrong in claiming a significant difference. This is called a Type I error.

What is the likelihood of making a Type I error? It is equal to your α level. When you report $F = 3.35, p < .05$ and believe you have a significant difference, you stand the chance of being wrong (Type I error) 5 times in 100 (if you look at the bright side, the chances of not making a Type I error here are 95 times in 100). When you report $F = 6.17, p < .005$ and believe you have a significant difference, you stand the chance of being wrong only 5 times in 1,000, since 6.17 tends to occur by chance less that 5 times in 1,000.

The reverse of this may also occur. When you report $F = 3.18, p > .05$, and conclude that the difference is not reliable, you may again be wrong (a Type II error). That is, there might "really be" a difference between the conditions employed, but your experiment, by chance, did not show it.

You should always be aware of the possibility of making one of these errors in an experiment. There are certain times, however, when you should sit down and ponder the consequences of each of these errors.

If you make a Type I error, you are falsely believing that an effect is indeed working. Most of the time no major tragedy will occur because you falsely conclude the reality of an effect, but there may be occasions where such an error could be costly (in terms of future research, time, funds, and so forth). If the cost of making a Type I error is potentially great, and you definitely want to reduce the possibility of making one, you may, under these circumstances, strengthen your α level to .01 or even .001.

The reverse is sometimes true in that Type II errors create the false belief that no effect of the experimental treatment is occurring. Yet there is always the possibility that the "true" effect is masked for one reason or another. If you believe that such masking is likely to occur in your study, and that you do not want to be "led astray," you may weaken your α level to .10 or even .20.

A word of caution

Now that you are aware of Type I and Type II errors, do not run off and start changing your α level as the times for worry are few and far between. By far, in most behavioral research, the .05 α level is appropriate. This level represents a compromise between too loose and too stringent a significance level; it is agreed upon and used by most researchers and most journal editors. You will find much reluctance on the part of other researchers to accept a different level of α in your research.

Above all, once you decide beforehand what chances you want to run in making Type I and Type II errors (by setting the appropriate α level), you then statistically test the Null Hypothesis by calculating an F-ratio and either reject or fail to reject it. No matter how large an F value you obtain, it either exceeds or fails to exceed your prescribed level. Post-hoc "toying" with α is not an especially meaningful activity.

The F Table

Two points need to be made:

1. The actual distribution of F-ratios varies somewhat as a function of df.

2. Rather than ask a computer to construct a sampling distribution of F-ratios each time you run a study, it will be much more convenient for you to simply consult an already prepared table. Such a table summarizes the F values and gives you the various cutoff points at the various significance levels (usually .05 and .01) for many different df.

We have supplied you with a relatively complete Table of F values in Table F of Appendix B. A small portion of it is reproduced in Table 7.2.

Table 7.2   Section of *F* Table with 3 and 17 *df*

*df*den	α level	*df*num 3
	.001	8.73
	.005	6.16
	.01	5.18
17	.025	4.01
	.05	3.20
	.10	2.44
	.20	1.72

Recall that

$$F = \frac{\text{Variance}_{\text{Between groups}}}{\text{Variance}_{\text{Within groups}}}$$

Each source of variance has a certain number of *df* associated with it. Assume that the *df* associated with the numerator is 3 (that is, that there are four groups in the experiment and since $df_{\text{Bet}} = g - 1$, df_{Bet} therefore equals 3) and the *df* associated with the denominator is 17 (that is, in this experiment there were a total of 21 observations in 4 groups. df_{Total} equals $N - 1$ equals $21 - 1$ equals 20. $df_{\text{Within groups}}$ equals $df_{\text{Total}} - df_{\text{Bet}}$; therefore $df_{\text{Within groups}}$ equals $20 - 3$ equals 17). Entering the *F* Table with the specified *df*, you will find the appropriate cutoff for a variety of α levels. Using the example for 3 and 17 *df*, we find that an *F*-ratio of 3.20 or greater is significant at the .05 level, an *F*-ratio of 4.01 or greater is significant at the .025 level, *etc.*

Reporting the *F*-ratio

You may be concerned with communicating statistics to others and, furthermore, in reading the journal literature you will encounter many reports of *F*-ratios. It is therefore important that you be familiar with the standard form of presenting *F*-ratios. For example, if your *F*-ratio is 3.21 with 3 and 17 *df*, and your α level was set at the .05 level, you would report it as follows:

$$F(3, 17) = 3.21, p < .05.$$

Table 7.3 presents a whole range of examples of potential F-ratios and how to report each. We have used 3 and 17 df throughout so that you may readily refer to Table 7.2 for clarification.

Table 7.3   Journal Form of Various F-Ratios

Example	Calculated F-ratio	α level	Reported in literature as
a	3.21	.05	$F(3, 17) = 3.21, p < .05$
b	3.21	.01	$F(3, 17) = 3.21, p > .01$
c	3.20	.05	$F(3, 17) = 3.20, p = .05$
d	.52	.05	$F < 1$
e	1.01	.001	$F(3, 17) = 1.01, p > .001$
f	5.17	.01	$F(3, 17) = 5.17, p > .01$

A few things appearing in Table 7.3 should be specially noted:

1. In Example a, the obtained F value exceeds the tabled value for $\alpha = .05$. A significant difference is therefore said to be found.

2. In Example b, the obtained F value, while equal to that in Example a, does not exceed the specified α level of .01. It must therefore be said that a significant difference was not found.

3. In Example c, we see the rare occurrence of the calculated F-ratio being equal to the tabled value.

4. In Example d, the obtained F-ratio is less than 1. Since no F-ratio of less than 1 is significant at any α level, it is sufficient to report $F < 1$.

5. In Example e, the obtained F-ratio is greater than 1, although just barely. Nevertheless, the entire expression as given in the right-most column must be reported.

6. In Example f, you just missed the tabled value appropriate to your set α level. Although the mean difference must be stated to be nonsignificant, researchers are rarely the kind totally to give up on data. We have seen statements like the following in such cases:

   a. '. . . although the results failed to achieve an acceptable level of significance . . .'

   b. 'There was a strong tendency for Group X to be better than Group Y . . .'

Do not condemn such statements. When your pet hypothesis comes that close to significance, do not be surprised when you find yourself trying to make the most of your data.

section three

the techniques of research

The heart of this book is contained in this section and it may seem that we have brought you to this point by a somewhat indirect route. But you must remember that entering the laboratory without any preparation could be dazzling. You now know what it means to take measurements, to summarize data, to attempt to observe significant differences between groups in an experiment, and so forth.

Given this knowledge, you may still be amazed at the diversity of behaviors that are classified as research. This diversity of behaviors arises out of the diversity of problems with which a behavioral scientist may be concerned. Each class of problems poses its own unique set of questions, and each demands its own unique set of procedures to supply appropriate solutions. Although these methods share a universal base of attempting to derive unambiguous answers, each has its own way of achieving that result.

A Note on Scientific Methods

The term "scientific method" has undoubtedly appeared throughout your readings in many courses. Perhaps you assocate the term with Sir Francis Bacon, a brilliant 16th-17th century scholar, and author of *The Advancement of Learning*, a classic treatise on scientific method. The term "scientific method" is slightly inaccurate, however, for many methodologies are considered to be "scientific." As used today, "scientific method" refers more to a general orientation than to one specified methodology. This implies that observations are made under carefully noted circumstances that make it possible to reproduce the observations should the occasion warrant. Scientific observations can be made in almost any setting ranging from an open field (a natural environment in which the animal under observation is going about his everyday business) to a highly structured laboratory. For the purposes of this book, we identify three general types of scientific methodologies.

1. *Naturalistic observation.* With this methodology observation of organisms takes place with no interference on the

part of the observer. If we were simply to observe the behavior of a squirrel in the field, note the type of activities in which he is engaged and the conditions under which these activities are observed, we would be doing naturalistic observation. Sometimes it is more convenient to bring the animals in from the field and observe them in the laboratory within an environment that is designed to simulate their natural environment. The conditions of observation in such environments can be controlled more precisely and thus offer some advantages over field observations. We still label this activity naturalistic observation since all we are doing is observing what the animal does.

2. *Field Research.* This methodology suggests the observation of an organism in its natural setting with the additional constraint that some sort of intervention on the part of the scientist has taken place prior to the observation. Suppose we wished to observe the squirrel's response to a predator. Instead of waiting for a predator to enter the squirrel's environmental niche—it might take days or even weeks—we might want to introduce a natural predator (such as a weasel or a hawk) into the environment and record the behavior of the squirrel. Since we have actively intervened with the natural occurrence of events, but are still taking observations on the behavior of the squirrel in his home environment, we label this type of activity as field research or naturalistic experimentation. The same sort of experiment done in environments in the laboratory designed to mimic the animals natural environment is also classed as a naturalistic experiment.

3. *Laboratory experimentation.* This methodology implies removing the animal physically from his natural environment and observing him under highly controlled conditions constructed within the laboratory of the scientist.

We begin this section with the most basic of all the research techniques—naturalistic observation. We then spend five detailed chapters on experimentation, in terms of both techniques of conducting an experiment and the overall design of the study. We finally bring to bear both naturalistic observation and experimental techniques in the last two chapters on field research.

chapter eight

scientific methods I: naturalistic observation

The Definition of Naturalistic Observation

Naturalistic observation has two general characteristics:

1. Observation is made of naturally occurring phenomena; that is, observation is made of organisms within their free-ranging environment, or an environment that is very similar to their natural free-ranging environment.

2. The natural occurrence of events is not interfered with or directly manipulated by the observer.

Note carefully that in the criteria of naturalistic observation is the constraint that the observer does not himself influence those organisms under observation. If a subject notices that he is being observed, the chances are that his behavior will be quite different from that that would occur if he did not notice the observer's presence.

Some features of naturalistic observation

We next list some features of naturalistic observation to suggest the type of questions asked using this particular methodology.

1. Perhaps the most obvious feature of naturalistic observation is that it can provide a direct answer to the question of what an animal or human does. If, for example, you want to find out what an elephant does all day, the best thing to do is to watch one.

2. Another feature of naturalistic observation is that it can provide a stepping stone to future research either of the field research or the laboratory experimentation type. In the course of observing an elephant over a period of a day or two, you will find that the elephant will occasionally put his trunk in some sand and spray himself. You may be interested to know why the elephant does this, but it is unlikely that simple naturalistic observation will be able to yield this type of information. To determine why the elephant engages in such behavior, you would have to know the conditions under which that behavior is taking place. Within a naturalistic setting, that behavior is taking place under a multitude of conditions any one of which might be the crucial one. Additional research is required to determine which of those particular conditions are necessary and sufficient to induce the animal to spray himself with sand. Such an inquiry, however, would force the experimenter to intervene in order to answer such a question. This intervention might take the following form: according to the protocol (a list of observations) we have seen the elephant douse himself with sand under conditions a, b, c, d, e, f, and g. We would now want to present condition a independently of b, c, d, e, f, and g and observe whether or not the elephant douses himself with sand. We would then want to present condition b, with a, c, d, e, f, and g constant and so forth, until each of the conditions has been presented separately and in all possible combinations. We would then be in a position to answer the question of the necessary and sufficient conditions for the elephant dousing himself with sand. When we begin to do the systematic manipulations mentioned above, we have, of course, moved into the realm of experimentation.

3. Because of the various restraints operating in a laboratory situation, naturalistic observation may, at times, offer the only feasible means for studying a particular subject. If you are interested in the study of suicide, for example, it would be highly unethical, if not impossible, to study your subject within a laboratory situation. In order to study suicide in a laboratory situation you would most likely have to induce your subject to commit suicide, proceed to study his behavior as he went into the process of committing suicide, observe him as he committed suicide, and report the final outcome of the attempt. The only reasonable way of obtaining data on a

suicide is to attempt to investigate the instances after they occurred, perhaps by means of interviewing those who had known the person.

4. Another feature of naturalistic observation, although not a primary concern of scientists, should nevertheless be mentioned. That is, naturalistic observation can be done with a minimum of equipment although seasoned researchers generally use quite sophisticated equipment. Usually the minimal apparatus required is a stop watch, a pencil, some paper, and perhaps a pair of good binoculars. With this equipment and sufficient training, an individual can accomplish naturalistic observation. Do not get the impression, however, that because of the minimum amount of technological assistance needed to perform naturalistic observation that it would be simple to do. On the contrary, naturalistic observation done well requires a great deal of skill and students attempting this for the first time will rapidly discover that it is indeed a difficult endeavor.

Conditions of Observation I: Natural Environments

If you wish to observe behavior as it occurs in the "real world" then you should observe a species under conditions natural to that species. Observation under natural conditions is exceedingly difficult for at least three major reasons. The first is the difficulty of observing without interference; the second is the difficulty of telling various members of the observed species apart. These two problems are technical in nature, and can be easily overcome. Telephoto lenses and infrared film can solve the first problem, and various dyes, radio signal collars, and the like can deal with the second. The third and most difficult problem to overcome is one that involves the human factor. We must decide what should be observed in the first place and must then communicate the description of the observation.

Observation without interference

There is a variety of considerations to insure that your presence will not interfere with the animal under observation. Among these are the sensory capacities and habitat of the animal. If you are going to observe diurnal animals (those active during the day) then you will need a good pair of binoculars or a spotting scope to observe the animals from afar. You should take the precaution of establishing a watching point that will not interfere with the activities of the subjects. This can often be accomplished by building a blind and then entering or leaving the blind only when the observed subject is absent from its locality. If it is impossible or not feasible to build a blind, then a second, less desirable alternative is to spend a great deal of time in the area in which you wish to observe the animals. This will allow them—it is hoped—to adapt to you so that they will interact "normally" in your presence.

For example, suppose you wanted to observe nursery school children in the natural setting of the schoolroom. How would you go about your observation so that you would be relatively certain that you, as an observer, were not influencing their behavior? You coud just sit in the back of the room and observe without taking part in activities. Your very presence, however, *may* alter the behavior observed and therefore what you would observe is *not* what naturally occurs among these children. Rather, you are observing what naturally occurs among these children when there is a stranger in the corner of the room observing them. Therefore, a better strategy is to observe the subjects from afar or undetected, i.e., by using a one-way mirror, a closed circuit TV system, or some other hidden device.

The problem of identity

Usually in the course of doing a naturalistic observation you will be interested in observing several members of the same species. Consequently, you will want to be able to tell one member from another. With humans and many other species of primates, you will find that you can identify various individuals through bodily and facial characteristics. Under these circumstances, you can assign names to various members of the species and keep track of your observations through visual discrimination.

Unfortunately, species of animals whose members we can readily distinguish are relatively few and although some highly trained observers can make this distinction, the majority of us cannot. Where the discrimination cannot be made, it is necessary to employ some artificial technique to identify members of a species. One identification procedure for mammals is to mark them with dye. The dye should be permanent but not harmful. This is a complex task requiring the live trapping of animals and introducing them to a dying solution—a procedure we do not recommend for a novice. Another simpler but somewhat messy procedure is to peroxide the animals' fur. You should bear in mind, however, that interfering even with the natural color of an animal may affect the behavior that you specifically want to observe. For example, some communities of wild rats will not accept a member of its group dyed by the scientist. This fellow rat may be ostracized or sometimes even killed. The reason for this is that rats have an excellent sense of smell and they use this sense to recognize other rats that belong to their group. Unfortunately, dyes that to us may have no odor may nevertheless change the natural body odor of those animals so marked, sometimes with undesirable consequences.

A second—but somewhat less successsful—marking technique is to clip the fur or the ears of the animal. Each animal would be assigned a different marking. For example, investigators occasionally make small clips on the ears of small mammals. By choosing to clip either one or two ears either one or more times, a larger number of separate "numbers" can be used to identify subjects. One disadvantage of ear clipping is that such marks should obviously be small (to prevent damage to the organism) and may therefore be somewhat indistinct at even small distances. Fur clipping is even less desirable a method, since these marks are usually difficult to see in the first place and are useful for short-term purposes only as the fur grows back rather quickly. Other types of animals can be marked using a variety of procedures. Birds can be marked with color-coded leg bands or dye, fish with small tags clipped to the fins or by making small clips in the fins. Reptiles and amphibians can also be marked by small tags, leg bands, small bits of plastic, or alterations in the scale patterns. For other marking methods, see Short and Woodnott (1969).

The problem of what to observe

Before engaging in naturalistic observation you should give careful consideration to the purposes of your investigation, and precisely what it is that you are going to observe. A careful reading of the literature available on the subject species will be most useful in this context. This will acquaint you with information gathered by other observers on the same species and will enable you to profit from their experience. One thing that you will notice immediately is that observations have been classified by the observer along a number of dimensions. A classification schema is necessary in order to accumulate observations in both a meaningful and organized fashion. The employment of an already successfully used classification schema will make your task that much easier. Intuitively, it makes sense to use some sort of classification in recording your observations. Behavior is emitted by organisms at a fairly steady and often rapid rate. You certainly know from experience that it may be hard to take accurate notes in a lecture course if an instructor packs his talk with too much information. Think of how hard it would be to describe the rapid movements of a rabbit being chased by a hound, or of one child interacting with another.

There are a number of ways to circumvent some of the problems raised above, although at times the circumvention itself may produce other problems. Ideally, the best record would be a film of the entire sequence of reactions taking place during the period of observation. Even assuming that you had the financial support for purchasing the necessary equipment, and adequate conditions were available for the filming, you would still have to transcribe the film record to a written record. Using a tape recorder for narrating the observed behavior provides more complications, for besides having to be thoroughly trained to maintain a clear and constant narration, you can only pay attention to certain aspects of that which is being observed.

Many investigators have resolved some observation problems by designing what essentially is a "shorthand" system. Unlike that used by the stenographer, however, the one of the scientist is simpler. The scientist, you see, has an advantage over the stenographer in knowing precisely what to look for and so requires only a "checklist." This "checklist" essentially comprises the classification schema. A number of categories, such as eating, drinking, sleeping, mating, eliminating, social behavior, and so on are listed and defined on a sheet of paper. Each time a particular behavior occurs, you could simply put a mark next to that category. At the end of some designated time period, the data would provide a good indication of the relative frequency with which each of the responses took place. Such a data sheet is illustrated below.

Activity	Occurrences
Eating	X X X X X X X
Sleeping	X X X X X
Drinking	X X X X X X X X
Mating	—
Eliminating	X X X
Social Behavior	—

It would be possible to achieve even greater precision by incorporating into your record an allowance for the passage of time. Not only would you then know the total frequency with which an activity occurred, but also have some information regarding the sequence in which they were seen. This is illustrated below.

	Occurrences over time				
Activity	1-5 min.	6-10 min.	11-15 min.	16-20 min.	Total
Eating	XXX		XXX	X	7
Sleeping		XXX		XX	5
Drinking	XX		XXX	XX	7
Mating					0
Eliminating		XX		X	3
Social Behavior					0

A variation on the aforementioned procedure is to take samples of behavior across time. This *time sampling* is done by making observations periodically—rather than continuously—and recording what the subject is doing at that time. One advantage of this is that the observer need not be continuously present and observing. The main disadvantage is that it may result in an incomplete record of the behavior, and, in effect misrepresent the full behavior range. To obtain a representative sample of behavior, observations should be made at reasonably short intervals (i.e., every minute, every 3 minutes, etc.) within the total available observation period.

The development of a good classificactory schema is one of the prerequisites to doing naturalistic observation. Categories in a good classification schema are *jointly exhaustive* and *mutually exclusive*. To be jointly exhaustive, the categories must encompass all possible behaviors exhibited by the animal. To be mutually exclusive, a behavior should be placed in only *one* of the categories. This latter requirement is often impossible to meet since some types of activities (e.g., grooming) may occur in a variety of different contexts. An example of this is in the rat. Here we may observe grooming when the rat is in a stressful situation, during sexual encounters, during eating, and in the course of exploratory behavior. Yet, grooming does not distinctly appear to be *just* a part of any one of these contexts. Often it is the experience or talent of the observer that determines how these situations are handled. These categories should be clearly enough defined so that many observers looking at the same animal would be able to identify the category to which each of the behaviors was to be assigned. Listed in Table 8.1 are the major behavioral systems that are evident in most animals. The examples employed in Table 8.1 are those specific behavior patterns observed in dogs—all of which, by the way, are also present in humans.

The particular set of behavioral categories outlined in Table 8.1 are organized in terms of function. That is, the behaviors in any one category serve similar functions. It is also possible to organize behavioral categories along other dimensions, although for most purposes this breakdown will suffice. You should note that many animals do not exhibit all of the major behavioral patterns given in Table 8.1 and many other animals display only some of these behavior patterns in relatively specific instances. For example, most animals display only care-giving behavior patterns towards their own offspring whereas many other animals have no organized behavioral patterns associated with the eliminative behavioral system. Nevertheless, the observer who uses the set of behavioral categories presented in Table 8.1 will find these generally adequate for use in most species of animals. Even if your subject fails to display behaviors belonging to many of the categories, it will be possible to place the observed behaviors in one of the categories listed in the table.

Table 8.1 The Major Behavioral Systems and Examples of Behavior Patterns as Observed in Dogs (Scott, 1968)

System	Function	Examples of behavior patterns
Ingestive	Intake of nutritive substances	Gnawing, lapping
Shelter seeking	Maintaining bodily comfort	Lying in sun, puppies lying together
Investigative	Sensory inspection of environment	Following scent trail
Sexual	Fertilization of eggs	Mounting, clasping
Epimeletic (care giving)	Care-giving nurturance	Licking puppies
Et-epimeletic (care soliciting)	Calling or signaling for care	Whining, yelping
Agonistic	Adaptation to conflict	Biting, running away
Allelomimetic	Coordinarion of movement among individuals	Running together in pack
Eliminative	Disposal of feces and urine	Leg lifting in males

While the categories presented in Table 8.1 represent many possible behaviors an organism may exhibit, your primary concern may be with only one particular category. You will find it necessary under these conditions to refine your classification schema such that the entire table should be comprised of, for example, sexual behaviors. Within the table, the various types of behavior that you have classified as sexual would all be listed.

We may illustrate the type of data obtained from a sophisticated classification schema by referring to the sexual behavior of the male mallard duck. This duck exhibits a number of stereotyped behaviors—or fixed action patterns—during the courtship period. These behaviors, all associated with mating, are called displays and vary from one species of duck to another. The apparent function of specific displays associated with specific species is to prevent interbreeding (Dobzhansky, 1951).

Displays of the male mallard usually follow a specific sequence, lead to a predictable outcome, and are relatively interesting to observe. The male actively courts the female, fights with other males, copulates, at times engages in group sexual behavior, has his own circle of friends, and in general shows a number of behaviors familiar to many of you.

The first step in doing a naturalistic observation on the male mallard is to find a pond with a relatively stable mallard duck population: that is, where the same mallards frequent the same territory for prolonged periods of time. The second thing is to make sure that you observe your subjects very early in the morning, preferably in the first hour following sunrise, as this is the time that they most often engage in courtship activities. Later in the day ducks are more concerned with such mundane activities as eating, sleeping, grooming, and just plain swimming around. Also, more people come around later on in the day and this can interfere with the ducks reproductive behavior. The third thing to consider in observing ducks, as in any naturalistic observation, is to be as unobtrusive as possible by watching the ducks from afar with a pair of good binoculars. If you walk out where you can observe the ducks with the naked eye you will encounter a number of difficulties—the major one being that of inhibited natural behavior.

Fortunately the behaviors that the mallard goes through during courtship have already been extensively studied. This particular duck spends most of its life living in groups. Most of its displays are communal and not directed at any one female, although there is some indication that these communal displays play a role in the hen's selection of the drake. The initial displays usually do not depend on a hen being present although displays can sometimes be elicited by the female performing a nod-swimming response as shown in Fig. 8.1(a).

Usually when the drakes and hens begin to gather together to engage in display behavior, they first have greeting ceremonies. The predominant greeting response is called mock-preening and is shown in Fig. 8.1(b). The bill of the duck during this response is drawn along the underside of the wing resulting in a soft noise and is often preceded by a flock ceremony of drinking.

One of the first displays in which the male mallard engages is called preliminary shaking and is shown in Fig. 8.1(c). This display can be divided into two parts—high swimming and thrusting. High swimming is the most intense part of this display and consists of the male swimming high on the water with his head pulled back. This part of the display is very prolonged, often lasting several minutes, and is followed by the second part consisting of several forward thrusts of the head. It in turn is followed by any one of three other displays and other drakes often reply with still another. These displays are the "grunt-whistle," "head-up, tail-up," and the "down-up." They are shown in Figs. 8.1(d), 8.1(e), and 8.1(f). Two of the displays are preceded by distinctive communicative calls. The name grunt-whistle is derived from the way the call sounds, while the head-up, tail-up is preceded by a distinctively loud whistle. The third display, the down-up, is followed by a whistle and a two-syllable quack which is the same as the flock greeting note.

Fig. 8.1 The courtship behaviors of the mallard duck. (A) Initial displays.
(B) Mock-preening behavior. (C) Preliminary shaking. (D) "Grunt-whistle"
behavior. (E) "Head-up, tail-up" behavior. (F) "Down-up" behavior.
(G) Pumping response. (From Lorenz, "Evolution of Behavior."
Copyright © 1958 by Scientific American, Inc. All rights reserved.)

The main display associated with coitus follows a period of pairing and
usually peaks in early spring. This display begins by the female engaging
in a pumping response shown in Fig. 8.1(g). The male responds out of
phase with the female (when his head is up, hers is down). Following several
minutes of this display, the male swims around the hen and mates with her.

This example represents only a very brief description of the displays of the male mallard duck and should serve to illustrate the complexity of the behaviors of a simple animal. You can well imagine, then, the level of complexity that human behavior may achieve, although these same procedures, with appropriate considerations for the subject, can be applied to both child and adult humans.

Conditions of Observation II: Simulated Natural Environments

The problem of observation

The study of the behavior within the free-ranging or natural environment of the animal has many built-in restraints. That is, there are certain questions that cannot be answered by simply observing the animal within his natural environment. For this reason, scientists have been turning more toward the setting up of artificial natural environments within a laboratory situation. This contrived environment is generally known as an Etho-Box or artificial habitat.

Within the Etho-Box objects and environmental circumstances are arranged such that the animal's natural habitat is as best represented as possible. After constructing the Etho-Box, you proceed to capture live, wild animals of the species for which you have contrived your environment, place these animals in this environment, and allow them to live "naturally" with the exception that they are now usually dependent upon you for their food and water supply. It is worthwhile, in addition, to try to provide natural sources of food and water inside the Etho-Box, although this may be difficult to accomplish at times.

Because the Etho-Box is constructed by the scientist, he must be very careful in making interpretations of the behavior observed within the box. The animals are provided with an artificial environment which may in some subtle or obvious way alter their behaviors from those exhibited in a natural free-ranging situation. Notice, however, that it would be reasonably easy for you to check the validity of your observations by going into the field. If there is a major discrepancy between the behaviors exhibited in the Etho-Box and those exhibited in the free-ranging environment, you should be able to detect these differences through your observations. The major advantage of using the Etho-Box is that certain observations that are otherwise impossible in the free-ranging environment may be accomplished in the Etho-Box. In using the Etho-Box, give your animals a period of adaptation, that is, a period during which they learn about the box, make themselves at home, and generally get used to this artificial environment. You may then begin to observe their behavior.

The problem of identity

The problem of identification of a species within an Etho-Box is somewhat simpler than it is in the wild. Since the animals are observed at short ranges in an Etho-Box, we can avoid the use of dying techniques and use one of the simpler techniques such as ear clipping or tags.

The problem of what to observe

The problems of what to observe are similar to those present in natural environments. The main difference is that in the Etho-Box we have more flexibility of what we can observe than is possible in natural environments.

Suppose that you wanted to examine the burrowing behavior of a rodent. You could construct the Etho-Box in such a way that the rodent could burrow only in a place by the glass wall so that you can observe him both under and above the ground. In this way, you can see the complex tunneling arrangement constructed by some animals, the way in which some rodents hoard food, etc. Additionally, while it would be almost impossible to observe the nocturnal behavior of rodents in the natural free-ranging environment, all you need to do for the Etho-Box is to employ red illumination. Rodents cannot see into the red end of the spectrum and so, if this is the only illumination present in the room, the rodent would behave as though it were nighttime and would presumably emit a variety of nocturnal behaviors. You, as an observer, can see in the red light (although admittedly not very well) and would be able to observe and accurately record the nocturnal behaviors.

Conditions of Observation III: Artificial Environments

The problem of observation

In the constraints of an artificial environment, e.g., the laboratory, zoo, etc., the problem of observing a species of animal is of somewhat less concern than it is in natural environments. The reason is that with artificial environments arrangements can usually be made to suit a specific need. In addition, often when naturalistic observation is done in artificial environments, the observer may be viewed by the animal as being either somewhat irrelevant or as an object that is simply part of the environment.

Introducing an animal into an artificial environment may alter several of his behavior patterns, since there may be a drastic change of circumstances for the animal. For example, monkeys in the zoo show some behavior patterns their wild brothers do not, and their wild brothers show some behavior patterns that they lack. This change in behavior induced by man in captive animals often has many unfortunate consequences, some of which are exemplified by the book *Born Free* (Adamson, 1960).

The problem of identity

Since the animals to be observed are captives, the problem of identity is greatly reduced. In captive animals we can conveniently use the simpler ways of marking them, such as fur clipping, ear marking, or leg bands, since observation of these animals usually takes place under circumstances where seeing these markings is not a major problem for the observer.

The problem of what to observe

The problem of what to observe in artificial environments is somewhat more complex than it is in natural environments. The major reason for this complication is that what may be observed is not a "typical" behavior of that species, but rather a response made to the artificial situation. Therefore, it may have no generality beyond those circumstances.

It is often useful to study some types of behaviors in an artificial environment. The sexual behavior of the male rat, difficult to observe in the wild, has been extensively studied in artificial environments with great success and can serve as a fine example of deriving response categories within an artificial situation.

We can identify three major responses in the male rat with reference to the sexual behavior system. The first of these is called a *mount* and the entire mount sequence is shown in Fig. 8.2(a). The mount consists of three distinct phases, the approach to the female, clasping of the female with the forelegs which may or may not be accompanied by weak pelvic thrusting, followed by the dismount. The second major response is called *intromission*. Intromission is shown in Fig. 8.2(b). Intromission can be distinguished from a mount in that the penis is inserted into the female's vagina and is accompanied by a strong pelvic thrust. The third major response is ejaculation. The ejaculation response is shown in Fig. 8.2(c). This ejaculation response differs from intromission in as much as it lasts much longer and is accompanied by orgasm, which in itself is not observable, but is indicated by the "shivering" or "quivering" behavior that the male rat displays.

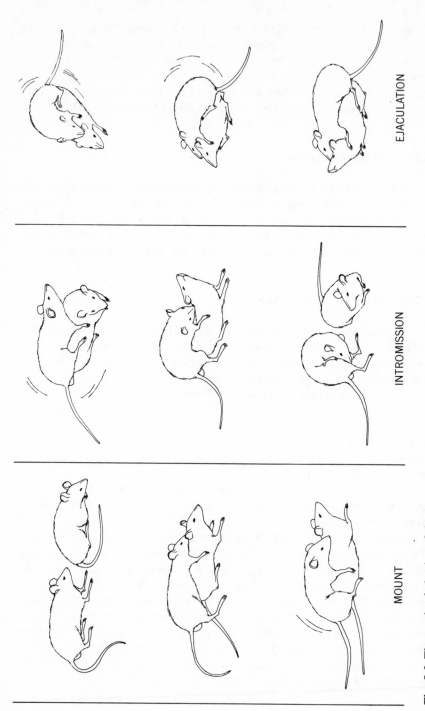

Fig. 8.2 The mating behavior of the rat.

Common Errors Made in Naturalistic Observation

There are basically two sets of errors that may be introduced into naturalistic observation. The first set is strictly mechanical: that is, identifying a piece of behavior as belonging in one category although it really belongs in another, failing to report the occurrence of a particular behavior, etc. These mechanical types of errors, although they should be avoided, can generally be minimized as the observer becomes more practiced in his endeavor. The second set involves errors of interpretation, is much more subtle, and can be made by even experienced naturalists. The basic rule to follow in preventing the occurrence of this error is that you must not read more into a set of observations than is there to begin with. You should report and be concerned only with the occurrence of particular behaviors and not try to explain why those behaviors occurred. To attribute particular types of motivation to the behaviors or to infer certain things about the internal state of the organism because you have made certain observations goes well beyond the data that is immediately available to you. If another observer were placed alongside you, would that observer agree that the types of motivations identified by you are actually operating? He may or may not.

The most common type of interpretation error is called the error of *anthropomorphizing*. To anthropomorphize simply means to *attribute to the animal certain human qualities* such as love, hate, thought, and so forth. Some examples of anthropomorphizing are listed below:

1. That race horse certainly loves competition.
2. My dog always gets jealous when I give attention to my child.
3. That deer, in moving when he did, must have been reading my mind.

Although many of us anthropomorphize in everday speech, we must take pains to avoid such a tendency in reporting naturalistic observations and in making certain interpretations of the naturalistic observation. In our attempt to be as accurate as is possible within such a procedure, it is not advisable to go very far beyond the initial data; i.e., beyond our observations. This error of going substantially beyond the data can be made on the basis of human observations as well. Some examples of this error in human observations are listed below.

1. John bit Fred on the arm because he dislikes him.
2. Frances teases all the boys because she is shy.
3. Gwen loves Fred and John, but hates Ed and Alex.

Here again, these statements imply more than can be contained in the data and are the examples of types of interpretations to be avoided in your observations.

chapter nine

scientific methods II:
introduction to the experiment

Definition of an Experiment

Much research in the behavorial sciences is done in the form
of an experiment. For an activity to be classified as an experiment, it must meet three general conditions:

1. The experimenter must manipulate (vary, systematically
change) some feature of the situation.
2. This manipulation must be made under controlled
conditions.
3. The experimenter must observe the effects of the
manipulation, i.e., he must collect data.

While we have already considered many aspects of data
collection in discussing Naturalistic Observation, the notion
of the experimenter actively varying some aspect of the environment under controlled conditions is unique to an experiment. The remainder of this chapter will be devoted to
explicating this notion.

The Concept of a Variable*

Included in the language of an experiment, as well as in other types of scientific research, is the term "variable." Most simply put, a variable is something that varies. More specifically, **a variable is some general property or characteristic of events, objects, people, etc. that may take different values at different times** depending on circumstances. Obviously, by virtue of the definition, a great many "things" can qualify as a variable. Here are some examples:

Length—an object may take on any of an infinite number of values.

Intelligence—a person may have an IQ of anywhere from zero to upwards of 200.

Sex—an individual may take on one of two values (male or female).

Hunger—an organism may take on any of a large number of degrees of hunger.

Notice that to qualify as a variable, two conditions need to be met:

1. There is a general property or characteristic involved.
2. The characteristic is measurable.

Further note that nothing is said of the scale of measurement involved. Thus, the variable of length is measured on a ratio scale, while the variable of sex is measured on a nominal (classificatory) scale.

Regardless of the scale of measurement, it is usually important to specify the manner in which the particular characteristic is measured. Sometimes the manner is clear, e.g., most of us agree how to classify male and female humans. Sometimes, however, ambiguity may arise. A classic example is the variable of anxiety. The ways in which anxiety has been measured (measurement operations) are as diverse as the imagination of psychologists. Some measure anxiety by the amount of harm with which an individual is threatened, others by the amount of "tension" a person is under, still others by a paper and pencil test in which a variety of questions are asked of a subject. All label the measured variable as anxiety, but we may legitimately ask if the *same* characteristic is measured under these different operations. The point that emerges is this: The nature of the variable is intimately related to the operations by which it is measured. A corollary of the point is: Always attend to the measurement operations of a variable as well as the verbal label of the variable—you may find, for example, that what you consider "anxiety" may not be what another scientist claims to be measuring.

---

*Our explication of the notion of "variable" is partly based on Kerlinger's (1964) treatment of the term.

There could, of course, never be a complete list of all the variables that might be studied in science, but you will find that within each field, it is generally possible to specify those which have received attention, i.e., those used in experiments. It is convenient, furthermore, in the context of an experiment, to classify variables into *dependent* and *independent variables*.

Independent variables

An independent variable in an experiment is the variable systematically varied by the experimenter. It will sometimes be called the *experimental treatment* when referring to the specific values of the variable in an experiment. Thus, if a researcher wishes to determine the effects of reinforcement on some aspect of the performance of rats, reinforcement would be the independent variable. We define reinforcement here as the number of food pellets given to a hungry rat after the rat gives a particular response. Further, suppose that the experimenter specifically examined the effects of no reinforcement, low reinforcement (one pellet), and high reinforcement (15 pellets). In the language of the scientist, we would say that there were *three levels of the independent variable* (the experimental treatment).

Dependent variables

A dependent variable is a particular variable on which the subject's performance is measured. To carry out the previous example, if the effects of reinforcement on learning were of interest, learning would be the dependent measure, or more correctly, those variables assumed to reflect learning would be the dependent measure. For example, the number of trials or errors taken to learn a task could be used as a dependent variable.

The combination of independent and dependent variables

The identification of the independent variable and the dependent variable within a study is usually very simple, since any time you can specify the purpose of a study, you must almost always specify the independent variable and the dependent variable. To illustrate, if an experimenter wished to determine the effects of caffeine intake upon cognitive functioning, the independent variable would be caffeine intake and the dependent variable would be performance on a test measuring some aspect of cognitive functioning (rate of solving arithmetic problems, digit span, etc.).

Note that the independent variable and the dependent variable are often intimately related to one another, in that the type of independent variable studied in an experiment will generally determine the nature of the dependent variable. This relationship between the independent variable and the dependent variable is often a theoretical question, and the precise relationship may differ from one theoretical exposition to another. If we were interested, for instance, in the effects of reinforcement (the independent variable), we would obviously choose a dependent variable related to learning (percentage of correct choices, speed, etc.). The specific dependent variable chosen, however, would often depend upon the theoretical framework within which the experiment has been conceived.

As has been implied, the purpose of an experiment is to measure the effects of the experimental treatment upon the behavior of a subject. Thus, scientists are looking to the experiment as a means of obtaining a *functional relationship* between an independent and dependent variable. The term functional relationship means a specification of the values on the dependent measure corresponding to those of the experimental treatment. For example, in the experiment on the effects of reinforcement on learning, assume that 10 rats were tested under no reward, 10 under low reinforcement, and 10 under high reinforcement. Using the number of errors made on a maze over a seven day period as the dependent variable, we might observe the following results:

Group	$\overline{X}$ # errors
No reinforcement	30.6
Low reinforcement	10.8
High reinforcement	5.2

These results are plotted in Fig. 9.1 and may be taken to represent a functional relationship between performance on a learning task and degree of reinforcement. The data can be interpreted to suggest that increases in reinforcement correspond with increased efficiency of performing in the maze.

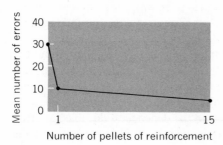

Fig. 9.1 Mean number of errors as a function of amount of reinforcement or rats learning a maze.

The Simplest Experiment

We may identify a prototype experiment as the simplest of all experiments. The simplest experiment that can be done is one involving two conditions:

1. **Experimental Condition**
2. **Control Condition**

Most generally, these conditions should be identical in all respects except one and this one difference relates to the independent variable. Typically, the Experimental Condition is one that is associated with some value of the independent variable. The Control Condition is one that is associated with some other value—usually, but not always, a zero value—of the independent variable. For example, a scientist may want to determine if Virus X can be destroyed by a particular chemical. Assuming a handy supply of the virus, he randomly and independently draws two samples of Virus X, and places each into comparable containers (i.e., comparable environments). Into one container (again chosen randomly) he places some neutral substance, such as water, while into the other is placed his chemical; he labels the former as the Control and the latter as the Experimental Condition. The conditions are identical (i.e., same initial environment, each had a new substance introduced) except that one has the chemical and the other does not. Since there is only one difference between the two conditions, any differences in the "health" of Virus X may be attributed to the presence or absence of the chemical.

Although we return to it later, it should be mentioned that what constitutes a control is often a theoretical question. That is, the theory dictates which variables should be controlled. In the preceding example, it was necessary to control for "introduction of a new substance" since it might be theoretically possible for the virus to react to a change in its environment, *per se*. But, to introduce water into the control environment because it is neutral is working on assumptions contained in the theorems and empirical laws of a theory. Thus, although the influence of theory on an experiment may occasionally be a subtle one, you may be assured that it is there.

The Concept of Control

Central to the definition of an experiment is the concept of control. The term "control" is used in everyday language with a variety of meanings, but when it is employed in connection with an experiment, **the control condition is used as a baseline, against which the effects of the experimental manipulation may be evaluated.**

Suppose, for example, you wish to determine the therapeutic value of a particular drug for combating one disease. In making this evaluation, would you simply take a group of patients, administer the drug, and then see whether or not they improved? Suppose that they did improve. Would they have improved if no treatment were administered? The only way to attribute the improvement to the drug is to have some kind of baseline or control to judge against.

How would you go about determining an appropriate baseline? Well, you might select two comparable groups of hospital patients suffering from the disease, administer a drug to one group that we will call the Experimental Group and not administer any drug to the second or the Control Group. Let us say that after observing both groups for some time, you notice that patients in the Experimental Group generally showed improvement, whereas patients in the Control Group showed no improvement. You might now be more justified in concluding that the drug does indeed work.

A control baseline is schematized below. In this schema we list a number of important variables that have potential importance in evaluation of the effect of the drug on the disease, e.g., age, sex, severity of disease, etc.

Variable	Experimental (Drug)	Control (No drugs)
A. Severity of disease	✓	✓
B. Age	✓	✓
C. Sex	✓	✓
D. Length of time in hospital	✓	✓
E. Drug	✓	—

The check marks in each column indicate that the conditions are roughly equal on these factors. Only the Experimental Group, however, received some amount of the drug. If any differences are observed between the two conditions, we could not attribute them to Variables A through D as they are equal in both groups. The only variable for the Experimental Condition not present (or present in zero amount) for the Control Condition is Factor E, the drug factor, which we then say controls for the effects of the drug.

Now, this control condition was a standard control procedure under these circumstances for some time, and can be used to illustrate a simple experiment. Sometimes, however, a simple experiment is too simple—

something that medical researchers learned gradually. A logical presentation of the above example is shown below:

Experimental	Control
A	A
B	B
C	C
D	D
E	

Since Factor E represents the only difference between the two conditions, it may be said that any observed group differences are probably the result of that factor. But is Factor E as simple as all that? Researchers began to realize that Factor E had at least two components, which we may label as E_1 and E_2. Patients who received the drug (Factor E_1) also received the following that was not encountered by the Control Condition: intake of a pill or injection, attention of nurses, notice of other patients for receiving "special treatment," etc. We will call this set Variable E_2. If this analysis is correct, we need to modify our schema to something like this:

Experimental	Control
A	A
B	B
C	C
D	D
E_1	
E_2	

It appears then that the improvement of patients in the Experimental Condition may have resulted from either E_1 or E_2. On the basis of this experiment, however, you could not specify which of these factors contributed to the observed improvement. We say, therefore, that independent variables E_1 and E_2 were *confounded* in the experiment, in that they were both present in the Experimental Condition and both absent (or present in zero degree) in the Control Condition. It is impossible, from this design, to determine which was associated with the observed improvement. Whenever the values of two or more variables are present in two or more experimental conditions, however unintentional this linkage may have been, we say these variables have been confounded with one another. Confounding should be avoided in an experiment at all costs. In fact, the whole concept of control is to eliminate the possible confounding that may take place within an experiment. Hence, what is called the Control Condition in the present example represents, in fact, a relatively poor control procedure in evaluating the drug effect.

What is the proper study to perform? One possibility might be the following study:

Experimental condition I (Drug)	Control condition I (Placebo)	Control condition II (No drug)
A	A	A
B	B	B
C	C	C
D	D	D
E_1	E_2	
E_2		

What we have now is the inclusion of a third group. This "placebo" group (placebo is simply a sugar pill) receives treatment identical to the Experimental Condition except that Placebo patients take a sugar pill instead of the drug. Patients in the Experimental and Placebo Groups receive a pill or injection, although they all assume that what is being administered to them is the drug. Even the nurses assume that the pill being given is really the drug for they do not know which patients are assigned to which group. This type of control procedure is called *double blind*, i.e., neither the subject nor those administering the treatment or recording the data know to which group a particular subject is assigned. Its purpose is to eliminate differential treatment of patients in each group. We shall return to this point in a later discussion of controlling for experimenter variables. At any rate, it is very often found when using a double blind procedure that placebo patients show marked improvement over control patients indicating that the various components of E_2—which are themselves admittedly confounded—contribute to improvement over and above the actual physiological effects of the drug.

In summary, a Control Condition serves as a baseline against which the effects of an Experimental Condition may be evaluated. For the example just given, the Placebo Group is the proper control for the Experimental

Condition, and the No Drug Condition is the proper control for the Placebo Condition. By "proper control" is meant one that differs in only one respect from the comparison (experimental) condition. Notice that the No Drug Condition is *not* a proper control for the Experimental Condition, in that E_1 and E_2 are confounded in this comparison. One of the greatest difficulties in experimental research is to design a control condition that is free from confounding.

Within any one experiment, a multitude of variables must be controlled in order to interpret the results easily. For convenience, we have dichotomized these variables into two sets, one relating to the participation of subjects in the study, and the other relating to the situation in which the subjects are observed. We will treat each set separately in the following two chapters.

chapter ten

scientific methods II: subject variables in the experiment

The Nature of Subject Variables

An inherent quality of subjects in a behavioral experiment is that they react differently with each subject introducing a different history and a different repertoire of responses into the experimental environment. These differences among subjects may be labelled as *individual differences,* and are found among most species studied in the laboratory. Thus, in the same way that no two humans are completely alike, neither are any two monkeys, rats, or lizards. One specific type of individual differences that is relevant in the conduct of an experiment is known as *subject bias.* Bias refers to subjects being predisposed to respond in a particular way in the experimental situation. This predisposition may result from either genetic reasons or from some past experience of the subject. Regardless of the reason, such predispositions are called subject biases.

The Importance of Subject Variables

One of the main concerns we have with subject variables is that they may confound an experiment. Suppose that you wanted to examine the effects of two amounts of food reinforcement on the acquisition of a bar-press response in rats. Two levels of the independent variable are chosen—one pellet and 20 pellets of reinforcement. The dependent variable is the number of bar-presses required to reach a stable performance level (asymptote). In addition, assume that there were 12 rats available for the study, 6 males and 6 females. What kind of considerations are made in placing the rats into the two groups? Well, one thing that should *not* be done is to assign all the male rats to one group and all the females to the other. This would *confound* amount of reinforcement (the independent variable) with sex and any observed group differences may result from either different levels of the independent variable or from the difference of sex.

There are still other precautions that must be taken. We are now interested in doing a memory study where a total of 20 people need to be tested individually. All subjects are to be run on one day, and will be assigned to one of two groups. How should the subjects be assigned to groups? Again, one thing that should not be done is to place the first 10 subjects to arrive at the laboratory into one group and the next 10 subjects that arrive into the second group. If this is done, you may have *confounded* levels of your independent variable with subject bias. This subject bias could take many forms, but might generally have to do with different types of subjects signing up at different times (morning or afternoon). These subject biases may or may not be relevant to a particular experiment. However, since we often do not know whether they are relevant, these biases are best dealt with by either eliminating or neutralizing them. There are basically three different procedures employed to control for subject biases. They are: using subject differences as an independent variable, matching subjects, and randomizing.

Control Procedures for Subject Variables I: Subject Variables as an Independent Variable

Perhaps the best way to control for subject variables is to include them in your experimental design. In this way you can *systematically vary* some subject variables and examine the manner in which they affect the dependent variable. There are two types of procedures available to include subject variables as independent variables. The first is to treat the subject variables as *levels variables*; the second is to use the *subject as his own control*.

The levels variable

An independent variable represents the manipulation performed by the experimenter, and there are two broad classes of manipulations open to the experimenter. One type of manipulation is to impose the *experimental variable* upon the subject. **An experimental variable is any variable manipulated or varied by the experimenter,** and examples of such experimental variables are amount of reinforcement, exposure time of stimuli, number of practice trials, etc. In each of these, the experimenter has virtually full control of the details of these variables (how much reinforcement he will give, what the actual exposure time will be, how much practice to allow, etc.).

A second type of manipulation is to "create" a *levels variable* from the subject population. **A levels variable represents a classification schema for traits already existent within the subject population.** Examples of such traits are sex, IQ, anxiety, amount of education, age, experience, etc. These variables, of course, are among those called subject variables.

Let us see how we can incorporate a levels variable into a previous example. Recall that we wished to examine the effects of 1 or 20 food pellets upon bar-press behavior, and of the 12 rats available, 6 were male and 6 were female. The best experimental design would then be as follows:

Amount of reinforcement

	1 pellet	20 pellets
Male	Group M1 3 Ss	Group M20 3 Ss
Female	Group F1 3 Ss	Group F20 3 Ss

Sex

The subjects in each cell within each level should be assigned to these cells by a random procedure. This design permits us to evaluate the effects of both amount of reinforcement, sex, and the combination of these factors upon the dependent variable.

If you examine this design, you might be tempted to say "Although we can now evaluate the effects of both amount of reinforcement and sex on bar-pressing behavior, we have done so at a sacrifice. Before, we had just two groups (1 pellet vs. 20 pellets) with 6 subjects in each. Now, we have four groups with 3 subjects in each. Not only must we now do more work (run four instead of two groups) but 3 subjects per group is a rather small number."

These points are both interesting and important. Notice that there are still 6 subjects being run under each reinforcement condition, and the data, as we will see later, will be analyzed by making use of all these subjects. And there are still 6 subjects per reinforcement condition so that no additional work has been made—you would have had to run all these rats anyway. Second, it *is* true that each group has only 3 subjects and this *is* a relatively small number. The only time that we must consider that there are 3 subjects per group, however, is when we deal with the combination of the two independent variables. The principle point of this example is that a levels variable may be incorporated into the design of an experiment to control for subject variables.

There are many occasions in which the incorporation of a levels variable into an experiment is desirable. For example, recent research has suggested that the anxiety level of subjects may be an important variable relating to behavior. The procedure in using anxiety as a levels variable can be examined as a specific case of more general procedures. The first step in this process would be to administer a test that presumably measures anxiety, such as the Taylor Manifest Anxiety Scale (Spence & Taylor, 1951; Taylor, 1951) to a large subject population, then select people in the top 20% and define them as High Anxiety subjects and select people in the bottom 20% and define them as Low Anxiety subjects. Your final step would be to incorporate these subjects into a levels variable (high and low anxiety) in combination with your main experimental treatment.

The subject as his own control

In the typical experiment, an investigator goes to great lengths to insure that his subjects are "naive." We mean by naive that the subjects have had no direct contact with the particular sets of independent variables to be used, and no contact with independent variables similar in some ways to the experimental treatments. Once a subject has participated in a behavioral experiment, he must be defined as being "non-naive" with respect to those particular variables. There are other types of experimental variables, however, that either can or must be experienced by "non-naive" subjects. In such cases, it is advisable to use the subject as his own control.

To use a subject as his own control you must run him in both the Experimental and Control Conditions. In this way, the subject's performance under the experimental treatment will be compared to his own performance under the control treatment.

Suppose you wish to determine the effects of LSD on cognitive functioning. One possible experimental design would be to select two comparable groups of subjects and administer the drug to one and a placebo to another.

Although this may be an adequate design, it is not the best one possible. First, unless you used large groups of subjects, it would be difficult initially to equate the groups on the dependent variable. Second, each person reacts in his own special way to most situations, and the idiosyncratic reactions to an hallucinogen would probably vary quite a bit from one subject to another. Even if LSD produces different behaviors in the experimental group from those in the control group, we would still be unable to determine the particular effects of the drug on any one subject.

Although it too has problems, a better experimental design to use in this case would be a *pre-post-test design*, in which a group of randomly chosen subjects is *initially tested before the treatment is given and then retested while the treatment is presumed to be active.* In this way, the pre-test is the control condition for the post-test, with the same subject providing data in both the control and experimental conditions. We have provided a set of hypothetical data here to illustrate some aspects of the pre-post design.

Subject #	Pre-test	Post-test
1	85	41
2	61	38
3	93	68
4	97	62
5	52	23
6	40	21
7	77	33
8	82	46

The higher the score, the higher the level of cognitive functioning as measured by the test. As can be seen, the subjects were highly variable without taking the drug, and were still highly variable afterwards as well. Careful inspection of the data, however, reveals that the drug, in this case, had systematic effects on each subject. Specifically, LSD appeared to reduce the degree of cognitive functioning between 40% and 60% in almost all cases. This information would not be available if two independent groups of subjects had been used. All we would know is that throughout the subjects' cognitive functioning was reduced about 50%. Some subjects might have improved, some remained the same, and others might have lost some degree of functioning. By employing the subject as his own control, we additionally learn that each subject showed similar effects to the drug.

Often, as we have already mentioned, the simplest experimental design is not always appropriate, in that more than just the experimental and control treatments must be utilized. If this is true, we would simply require an extension of the pre-post-test design to incorporate three or more levels of one independent variable. Perhaps we wanted to determine some long term effects of LSD. We might then want to retest the same subjects after given periods of time; this design is represented as follows:

Pre-test	Post-test	One day later	One week later	One month later

Procedures used to evaluate the results of the pre-post-test design and its extensions are given in Appendix A.

The advantages, then, of using designs in which the subject is his own control are:

1. Precision is gained in controlling for subject variables, since these variables are now constant from one treatment to another.

2. More information is gathered about the manner in which the treatment variable is affecting the dependent variable.

3. Fewer subjects are generally required for the completion of the study since each subject is run under two or more conditions, a consideration which at times may be extremely important to the scientist.

There are instances when designs employing the subject as his own control should not be used. The pre-post-test design specifically examines sequence or carry-over effects. When you do not want these effects, or are not sure of the nature of the sequence effects, such designs should not be used. For instance, you would not want to train rats on one pellet reinforcement and then train them on 20 pellet reinforcement to evaluate the separate effects of these amounts of reward. Having been trained on low reward will certainly influence performance under high reward. Additionally, you may at times have no choice in assigning subjects to groups. In educational research, for example, you will very often be forced to use classes that are already functioning. Control procedures for these will be discussed in a later section of this chapter.

Control Procedures for Subject Variables II: Matching

The use of subject variables as an independent variable is probably the best control procedure to employ. If the effects of some of these variables are already known, or if it is for one reason or another not feasible to include subject variables as an independent variable, you may employ a control procedure known as *matching*. **In the matching procedure, we attempt to equate subjects in each of the groups on one or more subject variables** to provide comparable groups. As an example, the matching procedure for a two-group experiment includes the following steps:

1. Measure each subject on the particular variable in question before the study is conducted.

2. Pair two subjects who have similar scores.

3. Randomly assign one subject to one of your conditions and the other subject to the other condition.

4. Repeat this process until all subjects have been assigned.

What the matching procedure accomplishes, then, is to equate two or more groups of subjects on an average value of some subject variable.

The main problems with utilizing matching procedures for equating subjects are that:

1. A matching procedure is only effective as a control for subject biases if the matched variables are related or correlated to the dependent variable; quite often the relationship of these variables to the dependent variable is unknown.

2. In order to match subjects we must pre-measure them, but this may not always be possible.

3. In pre-measuring our subjects we may inadvertantly bias their responding on the dependent variable, that is, they may now respond in a particular way as a result of the pre-measuring experience.

4. We must deal with what Marascuilo (1971) calls the *regression fallacy*. To understand the regression fallacy, we must consider the meaning of regression. Regression is a mathematical term which indicates, very roughly, that there is some kind of "retreat" to a less advanced position. This notion of regression can be illustrated by considering the phenomenon of *regression toward the mean*. Whereas one would expect the offspring of two extremely short individuals to be short as well, we would also expect the offspring to be taller than either of the parents (i.e., be closer to the mean height of the population). Likewise, the children of extremely tall parents, while expected to be tall as well, would also be expected to be *shorter* than either of the parents (i.e., be closer to the mean height of the population). In general, *measures of characteristics are generally expected to regress toward the mean under certain measurement conditions* (Marascuilo, 1971).

We may now see the application of the regression fallacy to the matched subjects procedure. In measuring the performance under the experimental condition, *the performance of each member of the matched pair may regress toward his own respective population mean independent of any effects of the experimental treatment.* This is the regression fallacy. If the regression influences the measure in the same direction as the experimental treatment, such treatment effects would then tend to be overestimated; if the regression influences the dependent measure in the opposite direction, such treatment effects would then tend to be underestimated. An example given by Marascuilo (1971, pp. 439-440) may make this clearer:

> This regression to the mean is unavoidable in any experiment in which bivariate data are correlated. In fact, this procedure works in some very strange ways in behavioral research. An example where it entails serious methodological problems is the following, taken from a doctoral dissertation proposal that fortunately was corrected before the collection of data.
>
> It was believed that the performance of Negro students in a literature program could be significantly improved by having them participate in the program. To show that the method was good, a controlled matched-pair study was anticipated. Both white and Negro students were to be given an achievement test and then the subjects were to be matched on the basis of the test scores. As was expected, the Negro students scored in the lower part of the distribution with the whites scoring in the upper part. Thus, when the matching was finally accomplished, only the top performing Negro students were included in the sample. Their matched partners were the poorest performing white students. If the treatment were to have no effect, one could predict the outcome of the study even before it was done. The white students on second testing will regress to the average of the white students and thereby experience a spurious increase in average performance. At the same time, the Negro students on second testing will also regress to the average of the Negro and thereby experience a spurious decrease in average performance. A test will show that the Negroes do poorly when in reality the treatment may have no effect. Fallacies such as this one are very common. Unfortunately, experienced researchers fall into the making of this error. Matching is a very useful procedure for increasing the efficiency of a study. However, there are appropriate and inappropriate methods for matching.

It may readily be seen, then, that the "fallacy" involves a potentially tenuous assumption that the matching procedure is a sensitive and powerful control procedure. Clearly, the more extremely the sample mean diverges from the population mean, the more likely it is that a matching procedure would be an inadvisable control method. Interestingly, many psychological investigations use a paper and pencil pretest to match groups on some particular characteristic (e.g., anxiety, authoritarianism, depression, etc.), and, in order to make clear predictions, the researcher may use *only those subjects scoring in either extreme for the post-test.* To compare the effects of amount of anxiety on some cognitive function, for instance, a paper and pencil test (e.g., Taylor Manifest Anxiety Test) is administered to a large group. Those individuals scoring the upper 20% and lower 20% would be classified as High and Low Anxious subjects, respectively, and only these subjects would be used later in the experiment. Under the above circumstances, we would expect a relatively large amount of regression toward the mean, and it is quite likely, therefore, that the strength of the variables being examined in such research would be relatively difficult to estimate.

Control Procedures for Subject Variables III: Randomization

Using subject variables as independent variables or using a matching procedure will still not take into account all possible subject variables. Besides this, many subject variables will elude measurement either because no adequate test of these factors is available or the subject population may be such that no pre-experimental measures can be taken. In cases where it is not convenient to use subject variables as an independent variable or when matching procedures are not feasible, we can then attempt to randomize subject variables.

A random selection of possible events means that every event has an equal opportunity or probability of being chosen. If we randomly and independently assign subjects to the groups in an experiment we assume that various subject biases will be parcelled into each group on the basis of chance; thus, a random process should more or less equalize subject biases. As you can imagine, the effectiveness of the randomization procedure is directly related to the size of your groups; that is, the larger your group size, the more likely it is that your randomization process "equals out" the subject biases. You can easily see why this should be. If the group size (n) is 1, the probability could be very high of picking a subject that responds in a biased manner. As you increase the n to 2, the probability increases of sampling two subjects that will "negate" each other in terms of subject biases. If n equals 3, the chances are better, and if n is 150, the chances are even better that you have negated any subject biases. This is one of the reasons that the n is often a critical factor in the conduct of an experiment. Since the larger the n, the greater the chances of equalizing subject bias, it is generally considered to be good research practice to include a sufficient number of subjects to allow subject variables to be "randomized-out." What is sufficient, of course, may vary substantially from one study to another.

After you have randomly and independently assigned your subjects to groups, you should take the precaution of designating which will be the Experimental and Control Conditions through some random process— such as flipping an unbiased coin—to further reduce the chances of subject biases confounding the interpretation of the data.

Even when we use subject variables as independent variables or match groups, there are only a finite number of such variables that may reasonably be considered. The remaining subject variables that cannot be accounted for by other procedures should be randomized among the groups in your experiment. Recall the example used earlier in which all subjects were scheduled to be run on one day for the memory experiment. The proper way to assign the subjects to groups would be as follows: Before the first subject enters the lab, flip a coin to choose the group in which he or she will be placed. The next subject is placed in the *other* group. Before the third subject enters the lab, flip the coin again, and so on, until all the subjects have been run. In this way, both the matching and randomization procedures are combined to properly assign subjects to conditions. That is, subjects are closely matched in terms of scheduled time slots and are then randomly placed in the two groups.

At this point we should specify some of the methods you can use to accomplish randomization. One of the easiest ways to randomize is to utilize a table of random digits such as that given in Appendix B, Table B. The main feature of such a collection of numbers is that they have no fixed relationship to one another. The use of the Table of Random Numbers to assign subjects to groups is as follows:

1. When you use the table, you should choose either one of the rows or one of the columns and go across or down, respectively, until that list of numbers is completed.

2. Assume we have four groups. Let us label Group A as 6, Group B as 7, Group C as 8, and Group D as 9.

3. Upon going down a column, we are concerned only with the digits 6, 7, 8, and 9; ignore all other numbers.

4. If we encounter a 6 first, Group A is placed on first place. If a 9 is found next, Group D is given second place. This is represented below:

Group A	Group B	Group C	Group D
1	4	3	2

5. Assume that we will want 8 subjects per group (a total of 32 subjects), so that we will now be concerned with the numbers 1 through 32.

6. Use the Table of Random Numbers looking for numbers between 1 and 32; here we look at two digit numbers, and ignore all other numbers. The first usable subjects number might be 05. Subject number 5 will be assigned to the group in first place (Group A). The second usable number might be 02. Subject number 2 will be assigned to the group in second place (Group D), etc.

7. After assigning the first four sampled subject numbers to groups, we now recycle by putting the fifth number in the group in first place, and so on, until all 32 numbers have been used. The final group structure is illustrated in Table 10.1. Thus, the first subject coming to the experiment will be run in Group A, the second in Group D, and so on.

Table 10.1 An Example of Random Assignment of Subjects in Four Experimental Groups

Group A (1) subject number	Group B (4) subject number	Group C (3) subject number	Group D (2) subject number
5	25	8	2
17	4	23	13
1	10	12	26
22	31	30	29
9	16	15	28
18	19	3	7
27	24	32	21
6	11	20	14

Another method that could be used in place of a random number table would be to place the numbers in a hat and have an unbiased observer draw them out. If there were two groups we could assign subjects to either group by flipping a coin, provided you first determined the order of assignment by using a random number table or drawing from a hat.

Nonrandom groups

In the event that you are forced to utilize already existent groups, such as often happens with many types of educational research, there are at least two control procedures that may be utilized. The first step is to pre-measure the groups on the variables suspected to be related to the dependent variable. If the groups do not differ from each other on the pre-measures, you may assume the groups are roughly equivalent; it is then permissible to begin the experiment. If, however, the two groups initially differ on your dependent measure, there are statistical methods available for "equating" your groups (see Winer, 1971). Essentially this procedure evaluates the relative change within each group rather than the absolute difference between the two groups. Utilization of nonrandom groups is certainly not a recommended experimental procedure and should be used only when no other alternative exists.

chapter eleven

scientific methods II: situational variables in the experiment

Just as no two experimental subjects are alike, no two testing conditions are alike either. Once a subject has been run, that increment in time, those precise conditions of temperature, humidity, state of the measuring instrument (amount of ink in a pen, creases in a piece of paper, etc.) can *never* occur again. In a word, each testing situation is unique, and this uniqueness lends a particular confounding to any and all experiments. The problem of reducing the confounding to render it ineffectual requires an additional set of control procedures that we will now examine for these four sets of situational variables: Environmental Variables, Task Variables, Experimenter Variables, and Yoked Controls.

Control Procedures for Situational Variables I: Environmental Variables

Holding environmental variables constant

Control of environmental variables is usually accomplished by holding the variable of interest constant. This can be done by conducting the research in places where the major features of the environment can be precisely regulated, for example, an experimental chamber that isolates the subject from all extra-experimental distractions such as noise, extraneous light, or irrelevant stimuli of any kind, while at the same time allowing the experimenter precisely to control temperature, humidity, and so forth. By holding these environmental variables constant we can usually assume that their influence is equated across all subjects and all groups. Note that a change in the value of one of the environmental variables (however inadvertently) for only one of the groups would result in a confounding of the variables. Variables such as an electrical failure, a sudden noise, or the experimenter getting sick are single instances unlikely to occur again. If such a change occurred, the two groups would no longer be equivalent on all variables except the independent variable. Consequently, if we find a difference on the dependent measure between two groups, we would be unable to establish the precise condition associated with the group differences, i.e., the "change" is confounded with the levels of the independent variable.

Environmental variables as independent variables

A second less feasible way to control for environmental variables is to incorporate them into the study as independent variables. Recall that this procedure was recommended as the best control for subject variables; we list this procedure in second place—and not in first—when dealing with environmental variables for the following reasons:

1. It is possible within the confines of a laboratory to hold many environmental variables constant. As was already mentioned, subjects are frequently run in experimental chambers that control temperature, lighting, and so forth. An experimenter can at least determine the effects of his independent variable under these "standard conditions."

2. Some environmental variables cannot be controlled at all. An example of this is time, since each instant of time can never be replicated. Weather, seasons, etc. can likewise not yet be manipulated by modern science.

3. There are huge numbers of environmental variables constantly operating, and it would probably take a series of generations to evaluate the separate effects of each.

4. Most environmental variables are simply not theoretically interesting. That is, behavioral theories generally do not specify the interaction of these environmental variables with subject variables. Since research is generated

from theory, until such time as environmental variables are integrated into a theoretical structure, it is unlikely that research will be so directed.

Randomization of environmental variables

A third, and even less desirable, method for controlling environmental variables is to randomize them across groups. We would want to utilize this control procedure when we cannot hold environmental variables constant or could not use them as independent variables. For instance, if we could not control the time of day a subject participated in the experiment, we could randomize this particular variable throughout our groups. This is not a recommended procedure, although in most cases it is the only procedure that can be easily utilized. That is, by randomizing environmental variables, we may magnify the individual differences already expected in an experiment.

Control Procedures for Situational Variables II: Task Variables

Task variables are situational variables directly concerned with the particular experimental procedure or measurement instrument utilized in collecting the data. These would include such variables as the duration and intensity of experimental stimuli, type of questions on a questionnaire, mode of stimulus presentation, the testing apparatus, nature of the required response, type of instructions (or pretraining) necessary, etc.

Holding task variables constant

Suppose that you wished to investigate the effect of type of reward on discrimination learning in children. You will reward one group with one M & M candy and the other with one marble for each correct response. Each child is tested individually and on each trial of the experiment is presented with two pictures. If the pictured objects are the same, the subject would press one lever; if they are different, the subject would press the other lever. On each correct trial, the child would receive a reward; one group an M & M and the other a marble. The independent variable in this study is the nature of the reward; the dependent variable is the number of correct choices per unit of time. The question now is: What task control procedures are required to insure that observed group differences would be caused by the independent variable? The following list outlines some of these considerations:

1. We would want to make sure that the difficulty of the material to be discriminated was equal for the two groups. This should be controlled by using the same pictorial material for both groups.

2. We would want to make sure that the responses required of the subjects were the same in both groups. Both, in this case, would be pressing a lever.

3. There are many other incidental variables related to the task we would want to control, such as the seating of the child before the apparatus, the timing of the trial presentations, duration of stimulus presentation, or any instructions given to the subject. We should control these variables by holding them constant across groups.

Randomizing task variables

In certain types of experiments, certain of the task variables should be randomized. For example, suppose you wished to determine the effects of prior experience with shock on the acquisition of an avoidance response by dogs. That is, in avoidance training, a signal is presented to the animal prior to the onset of an aversive stimulus (shock). If the dog emits the particular response designated by the experimenter as "correct" (running down an alley, jumping a hurdle, etc.) during the signal, it does not get shocked (i.e., it avoids the shock). If the target response is not emitted during signal onset, the dog receives shock. It is conceivable, however, that the learning rate of the avoidance task may be influenced by pre-experimental experience with the shock stimulus. You decide, therefore, that prior to acquisition training, some dogs should be placed in a chamber and be given 30 short but unavoidable shocks during a one hour period. How should the shocks be spaced over the time interval? To insure against any effects of the specific spacing of shocks to influence later performance, each subject should receive a different random spacing of the 30 shocks. That is, if the sequence of spacing of shocks was identical for each dog, you would have confounded "experience of 30 shocks" with "the sequence of 30 shocks." By giving each subject a different sequence, any differences between these and the control animals could not have resulted from the specific sequence of shocks but instead would be associated with only "experience with 30 shocks." The above experiment, by the way, is used as a demonstration of "learned helplessness" (Overmier & Seligman, 1967). The shocked dogs fail to learn the avoidance whereas the control dogs do learn, and this result is interpreted as indicating that the experimental dogs learn, during pre-training, that no action on their part can prevent the occurrence of shock. This learned helplessness is apparently carried over or transferred to the avoidance situation.

Counterbalancing task variables

Counterbalancing is a special control procedure for task variables having sequential properties. We mean by sequential effects that previous responses or stimuli will be transferred into an additional phase of the experiment. An example of this is seen in our discussion of subject variables. Specifically, we advised that a subject should not be used as his own control when unwanted carry-over effects may be present. The concept of counterbalancing represents an attempt to "balance out" the order or sequence in which stimuli are presented.

One counterbalancing procedure is to present stimuli (A and B, for example) in an ABBA order for half the subjects and an BAAB order for the other half the subjects where we must present several types of stimuli repeatedly to the same subject. The attempt is made to have B followed by A as often as A is followed by B. If an extended sequence like this is administered, the hope is that the carry-over effects will negate or counterbalance each other. You simply average all the measures under A and all those under B, and concern yourself primarily with this difference. And if you want to be especially clever you can compare B when it follows either A or B (you can do the same for A) to check for carry-over effects. Such procedures are often utilized when designing questionnaires that repeat similar questions several times.

A second method, somewhat better than straight counterbalancing, is to use a randomized counterbalancing procedure. This type of counterbalancing procedure structures the stimulus series so that there is no predictable order (such as there is in the ABBA sequence). One of the problems with a random series, through, is that it is possible to get some very long runs of one stimulus, thus providing a chance for response bias, e.i., subjects may expect that stimulus to occur later in the series in "bunches" or runs. To mitigate against this potential biasing factor, experimenters often put a constraint on the randomness (one can argue, of course, that once constraints are enforced, a series is no longer random) in the following form: Only "bunches" (runs) of limited length shall be allowed; that is, no event shall occur in succession more than four (or whatever) times. This "randomness with constraint" procedure is generally more frequently used than the ABBA procedure, apparently because the former series is less predictable (by the subject) than the latter.

Control Procedures for Situational Variables III: Experimenter Variables

One last type of situational variable that can influence your experimental results is the experimenter himself. Although you may be surprised to learn that the scientist himself needs to be controlled, you must remember that the experimenter is a person and elicits reactions from the subjects according to the image he projects.

We have already mentioned one method of controlling the influence of the experimenter in an earlier example. Recall the hospital drug study. One of our control strategies was to keep those who were interacting with the subjects, as well as the subjects themselves, ignorant of the group to which they were assigned. This *double blind* control procedure provides that those who are administering the experimental treatment are unaware of which subjects are in which group; in this way, they presumably cannot systematically treat the groups differently, e.g., give more attention to the experimental group.

One of the best ways to control for experimenter influence is to keep him ignorant of the particular group each subject is in. Most of the time, however, this is not feasible since it is often his duty to control the contingencies presented to the various groups. So what do we do? There is no simple solution to this problem. There are currently available a large number of programming devices that allow for the automatic collection of data as well as control of all experimental contingencies by machine. Such machines eliminate both the experimenter influencing subjects and any errors in recording data that the experimenter may inadvertantly make. The most sophisticated programming machine available is the laboratory computer and one of these machines can be programmed to run virtually any experiment except those requiring the experimenter and his associates to interact with the subject (social psychology experiments, or hand running subjects in some animal research).

If it is necessary for the experimenter to interact directly with the subject, there are a number of control procedures available. One of the best is to employ more than one experimenter and include the experimenter as an independent variable in the design. By doing this we can tell whether the various experimenters are producing different types of data on the dependent measure. But even here there may be problems. The influence of the experimenter has been extensively investigated by Robert Rosenthal at Harvard. In one study in 1966, Rosenthal used three relatively untrained experimenters to investigate a learning problem. The first experimenter was informed that he had a group of stupid rats, while a second experimenter was told that he had a group of bright rats. A third experimenter was not informed of the rats' "intelligence." Rosenthal found that the stupid rats learned at a slow rate, the bright rats learned at a fast rate, and the rats run by the uninformed experimenter learned at a moderate rate. In reality, all of the rats were from the same sample and for all intents and purposes did not differ in "intelligence." This experiment demonstrated that an experimenter's expectation of the outcome of the experiment could influence the data he collected.

In the event you cannot utilize two experimenters to collect data, there are at least two other alternatives providing some control for experimenter influence. One of these is a comparison of data collected by the experimenter to that collected by other experimenters who are doing similar types of experiments in other places. The assumption here is that if the experiments are highly similar, the data should likewise be similar or compatable. A second, less reassuring way to control for experimenter influence is to train the experimenter so that he will not behave differently toward the groups. This training procedure is utilized by a large number of laboratories throughout the country. The problem of using trained experimenters requires some consideration:

1. Untrained experimenters and trained experimenters will often collect dissimilar data. This alone indicates an experimenter influence on the dependent variable.

2. At times trained experimenters in one laboratory will collect different data from that collected by trained experimenters in another laboratory in researching the same problem.

3. Trained experimenters can at times be influenced by their pet hypothesis and may inadvertantly bias subjects.

Control Procedures for Situational Variables IV: Yoked Control

A yoked control is a special and very useful type of procedure that controls for many situational variables. The main feature of this control is that it matches the stimulus events presented to the control and experimental groups. The difference between the two groups is that there are no contingencies in effect for the control group, e.g., they are subjected to events without being able to do anything about them. In fact, it is the behavior of subjects in the experimental group that determines what happens to the yoked control group.

For example, Brady (1964) studied the effect of prolonged periods of stress in monkeys. The experimental monkey could press a lever to postpone shock for a given period of time. A control monkey was yoked to the experimental animal. The yoked animal also had a bar to press, but pressing the bar did not postpone the impending shock, it did absolutely nothing. Each time the experimental animal was shocked, the control animal was also shocked. If the experimental animal bar-pressed, and therefore postponed the shock, then the control animal was not shocked. Brady found two interesting results in this study.

1. The experimental animal learned to bar-press to postpone shock whereas the control monkey (whose bar-pressing behavior, if any, had no control over his receipt of shock) showed no evidence of increases in his bar-pressing. This indicates that the ability to postpone shock delivery was sufficient reinforcement to promote learning.

2. The monkey who could postpone the shock, called the "executive" monkey by Brady, eventually developed a serious case of ulcers, caused by his constant vigilance. The yoked control, experiencing the identical stimulus situation as a result of the yoking procedure, except for the need for maintaining vigilance, developed no physical ailments.

Overview

We have stressed the nature of control and procedures used to create a control condition. Generally, the central aspect of an experiment is the use of an appropriate control, for without this, it would be impossible to draw any information from an experiment. A proper control condition is one in which any confounding of variables is eliminated.

A proper control procedure is not only of general empirical concern, but is also of theoretical importance. The theory dictating the experimental manipulation will usually also dictate those variables to be controlled. A relatively simple example may help to make this last point clear. During the course of a particular research project, an interviewer is expected to ask a series of prescribed questions and record the responses. Some of the control procedures the interviewer could use are:

1. If possible, the interviewer should know nothing of the experiment and, of course, the groups to which subjects are assigned.

2. The interview should take place in the same room for all subjects.

3. The interviewer should ask the question with the same inflection, pace, and so on for all subjects.

4. Assuming that the interviewers would span more than one day, you may ask that he dress comparably on all working days, i.e., do not wear a suit and tie on one day and a sweatshirt and jeans on another.

One variable not usually controlled in such research would be the *color* of the interviewer's clothes. That is, in most practical, academic research, rarely is the interviewer told what colors to wear. To someone from the field of market research, where the color of a package may be an important variable in its sales figures, the failure to control the color of the interviewer's clothes would probably be unthinkable. That is, a variable may be judged as either trivial or vital depending on the theoretical framework brought to bear on a problem. Other substantially more technical, subtle, and complex examples abound in behavioral research enterprises. You should, therefore, always try to take a variety of theories into consideration —if possible—in the course of deciding those control procedures most appropriate for your particular experiment.

chapter twelve

experimental design

Definitions of Experimental Design

When the term "experimental design," or simply "design" is used in the context of research, it may mean one or more of the following:

1. **The term design may be used as a verb,** suggesting that a particular activity is taking place. Thus, the statement "I am designing an experiment to test this hypothesis" indicates that the person is considering what types of groups to run, which particular independent variables and dependent variables to include, etc.

2. The term **design** is also **used to describe a specific type of experiment.** Thus, in psychology a "transfer design," a "retroactive design," "short-term memory design," and so forth all refer to different **procedures** administered to the control and experimental groups **to test for that particular effect.** If these do not communicate an image to you, do not be concerned because they are idiosyncratic to certain areas of psychology and are only intended as examples.

3. A third meaning of **design**—more general than that mentioned in the second context—is a direct **reference to the arrangement, or choice, of the groups to be run in an experiment.** Thus, the running of Drug and Placebo conditions may constitute the design of a two-group study.

4. Another use of the term **design** is when it **refers to the statistical procedures to be used to anlyze the data to be collected.** Thus, "simple randomized design," "factorial design," "repeated measures design," all refer to arrangements of data analyzed by a statistical technique known as analysis of variance (ANOVA). Sometimes, but not necessarily always, it is appropriate to also specify the arrangement of the experimental groups (as in the third meaning given above). It is also in this fourth sense that the term **design** will be used throughout the remainder of the book.

The Emphasis on Experimental Design

The skills of a well-trained researcher are many, and among his most specialized skills is the ability to design a reasonable experiment. Interestingly, one of the few disciplines that attempts to train many of its members in experimental design is psychology. We can offer here only limited conjecture as to why psychology places such a strong emphasis upon expertise in design. Although there are clearly many more, we cite here some points which seem to bear on the answer.

First, much of the pioneering work in the behavioral sciences was concerned with individual differences, and the effects of this orientation are still being felt today. Two obvious lessons learned from this work were (a) people differed from one another, and (b) despite these differences, people seem to be overwhelmingly similar in many basic ways (the processes of learning, perception, and development, the effects of motivation upon behavior, and the operation of memory all appear to be comparable across *homo sapiens*). Accordingly, to determine these consistencies over and above the individual differences, many researchers have adopted the practice of running groups of subjects—as opposed to only one subject—in an experiment. It turned out, however, that in order to specify consistency against a background of individual variation, statistical procedures had to be utilized. And with an increasingly greater reliance upon statistics, research had to be designed (i.e., the groups had to be arranged) in such a way that the data as collected could, in fact, be amenable to statistical operations.

Second, behavioral science is still a new and rapidly growing science. Almost everywhere you turn, there are areas not yet explored. The researcher must therefore be *maximally flexible*, and not bound by specifics of other research areas (the technology or procedures used); yet, he must still know how to do research. The answer, apparently, has been to train in *design*, which may, in turn, be applied to *any* research area.

Experimental Design and Statistics

We trust that after finishing this book, you will be able to place the role of statistics in proper perspective. Some indication of that perspective has been given and will be given again, but it bears repeating. **Statistics is only a tool —one of many—available to the researcher. The primary use of statistics within the behavioral sciences has been to permit some estimate of the reliability of the differences obtained** in an experiment, although it has found other uses as well.

The design of experiments is intimately linked with statistics. All too often we have seen people ask how to analyze the data after completing an experiment. To the surprise of some of these individuals, they are told either that the data simply *cannot* be analyzed because their "design" does not permit analysis, or that analysis of the data will not be worthwhile, since the comparisons to be made are not justified (the experimental variables may be confounded with a host of other variables, etc.). Such problems may be substantially reduced by "fitting" the study to be run into an appropriate experimental design. This guarantees that the data may at least be analyzed by known statistical procedures. If you are looking for a general rule for designing experiments, it is: *never run an experiment without first fully knowing how you are going to analyze the collected data.*

Experimental design is also intimately related to control. No text written on design can tell you the proper control for your particular study. A control group, as discussed in Chapter 9, must *eliminate all the possible confoundings* in the experiment. Once you have decided on the nature of the control, you must then include it in your experimental design.

This chapter and the next one will be concerned with outlining some of the more frequently used experimental designs used in behavioral research. These designs will be broadly classed as either Independent Group Designs or Mixed Designs. Furthermore, these chapters will contain no statistics; rather, we wish only to introduce you to the various designs and point to their many aspects. All these designs are ANOVA (analysis of variance) designs, and the ANOVA procedures are presented separately in Appendix A. If further study of statistics is desirable, the student may also consult any good statistics book.

Independent Groups

To claim to have **independent groups**—or, more precisely, independent measures—**assumes that the measurements taken for each condition are independent of one another. Independence means that obtaining a score in one condition will in no way affect any scores obtained in any other condition.** The most common way of taking independent measures is to assign each subject randomly to one of the conditions of your study and to run each subject in such a manner that the only variables differently influencing his behavior are those related to the experimental manipulation.

You may recall that we discussed some of these considerations in running subjects in previous chapters, mentioning that confounding should be removed at all costs from your study. It should be emphasized here that the analysis of your experimental design and the interpretation of your results *depend upon* the absence of confounding.

Independent Group Designs

There are two types of independent group designs that we shall consider. One is the simple randomized design in which only one independent variable is being employed. The other is the factorial design which is appropriate when two or more independent variables are used in the same experiment.

Simple Randomized Groups Design

The simple randomized design is sometimes called a **one-way classification design** in that only one independent variable is used although an unlimited number of levels may be employed; that is, the independent variable is classified in only *one* way (e.g., number of practice trials, amount of alcohol ingested, etc.). It assumes that you have assigned your subject to the various groups according to a random process in that any subject in the whole population has an equal opportunity of being in any of the groups. In a simple randomized-groups design you must have at least two groups—although you may have more. The basic two-group randomized design is depicted in Table 12.1. No subject has been pre-tested in this particular example, although the possibility of pre-testing is not ruled out by the design. Only one independent variable (IV, labeled as A) is used with level a_1 representing the Experimental Condition and level a_2 representing the Control. Needless to say, all subjects are measured on the same dependent variable (DV)

Table 12.1 Simple Randomized Two Group Design

Group	Selection of subjects	IV	DV
Experimental	Random	a_1	y
Control	Random	a_2	y

As it stands, this is a simple experiment such as we discussed in Chapter 9. It is possible to add other levels of the independent variable to this basic design and this is illustrated in Table 12.2. These other groups depicted in Table 12.2 represent levels of the same independent variable. A simple randomized design may employ any number of independent groups, provided that (a) you maintain the assumption of independence, and (b) that the independent variable represents a one-way classification. Data collected from this type of procedure can be analyzed using a one-way analysis of variance as given in Section AI of Appendix A.

Table 12.2 Four Group Simple Randomized Design

Group	Selection of subjects	IV	DV
Experimental 1	Random	a_1	y
Experimental 2	Random	a_2	y
Experimental 3	Random	a_3	y
Control	Random	a_4	y

Factorial Designs

Terminology

A design equally if not more commonly used in psychological research is one in which two or more variables in the same experiment are used. A factorial design is one that has enough groups to account for all of the combinations of two or more independent variables.* The simplest factorial design is given in Fig. 12.1. The two levels of Variable A (a_1 and a_2) are **combined factorially** with the two levels of Variable B (b_1 and b_2) to form four

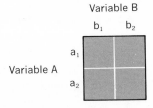

Fig. 12.1 A 2 × 2 factorial design.

independent groups. The above design may also be called a *two-way classification design*, in that the independent variables are classified along two dimensions represented by A and B. Since each independent variable has two levels, we may also call this a 2 × 2 (the "×" is read as "by") factorial design. The design given in Fig. 12.2 is still a two-way classification design, in that there are still only two independent variables, but it represents a 2 × 5 factorial design, since there are two levels of variable A and five levels of variable B.

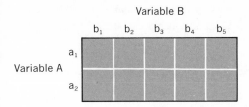

Fig. 12.2 A 2 × 5 factorial design.

You are not limited to only two variables for a factorial design experiment. If you wished to employ three independent variables, you would have a **three-way classification design,** the simplest of which is given in Fig. 12.3. This 2 × 2 × 2 factorial design involves the running of eight independent groups. Although it is rare to conduct an experiment using more independent variables than three, in principle it is possible to employ as many as you would like. Three seems to be a general limit, however, because once

*It is possible to have some cells in a factorial design that are not represented by a group of subjects (incomplete factorial designs). We will consider only those factorial designs in which all combinations of variables are represented by groups (complete factorial designs).

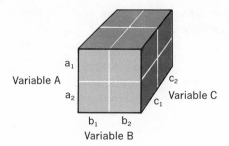

Fig. 12.3 A $2 \times 2 \times 2$ factorial design.

you exceed this number, it becomes extremely difficult to interpret the results of your ANOVA procedure.

The factorial design in practice

How do you come to choose a particular design for your study? Surprising as it may seem, once the experimental problem is formulated and the conditions decided upon, the design is virtually dictated by the preceding factors. All you need is to be familiar with what it is telling you. For example, when studying the effects of drugs on behavior, not only is the effect itself of interest, but often the effects of particular amounts of the drug are of interest as well. Thus, if you were interested in the effect of *Cannabis sativa* (marijuana) on memory, you might wish to design a study such as that described in Table 12.3. In this table the term "joint" refers

Table 12.3 Four Group Randomized Group Design with Two Control and Two Experimental Groups

Group	Designation	Selection of subjects	IV	DV
Experimental 1	E_1	Random	1 "joint"	memory task
Experimental 2	E_2	Random	2 "joints"	memory task
Control 1	C_1	Random	1 placebo	memory task
Control 2	C_2	Random	2 placebos	memory task

to an item containing *Cannabis sativa*. The utilization of the type design described allows us not only to assess the effects of the drug on the memory task, but also allows us to draw some conclusions as to the relationship between the amount of the drug ingested and performance on the memory task. Incidentally, as you may recall, it is a matter of standard practice in conducting this experiment, to have both the subjects and the experimenters unaware of group assignment (i.e., double blind procedure). Notice that there are four independent groups, and that all subjects are randomly assigned to conditions. We had to use two control groups in that the proper control for E_1 is C_1 and for E_2 is C_2. Although the conditions are listed in only one column, there are really two independent types of conditions (experimental vs. control, and one vs. two smokes). We may, therefore, rewrite this design as the *two-way classification design* presented in Fig. 12.4. As we shall presently see, it is important to recognize a factorial design if there is one within a listing of groups, since the ANOVA procedure will then allow you to obtain more information from the collected data than would be possible from a simple randomized design.

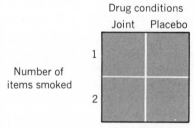

Fig. 12.4 Groups depicted in Table 12.3 arranged into a 2 × 2 factorial design.

A second, and perhaps more elegant, way to do the same study would be to pre-test subjects on a memory task similar to that used for the dependent variable and then use the difference in performance between the pre-test and post-test as your experimental data. This type of design is depicted in Table 12.4. The obvious advantage here in administering a pre-test to the subjects is that it controls for many subject variables. The reason for this is that we can subtract each subject's score made on the experimental task from his own score on the pre-test. This gives us a measure of change in performance, while subject bias remain constant. By using this change or difference score as our raw data, we greatly *reduce* the variability of our group scores. The reason this procedure reduces variability is that this difference score will greatly reduce the huge differences between subjects which may occur on the memory task. Another way of looking at this is to consider that the range of difference scores (a post-test minus a pre-test for the same subject) will be much smaller than the range of scores between the lowest scoring subject and the highest scoring subject.

Let us illustrate this with a concrete example. Weil, Zinberg, and Nelson (1968) were interested in the effects of *Cannabis sativa* on cognitive functioning. They wished to know whether the drug had different effects on chronic or habitual users than on naive users, and tested the subjects

Table 12.4 Four Group Design With Two Control Groups, Two Experimental Groups, and Incorporating a Pre-test

Group	Group selection	Pre-test	IV	DV
Experimental 1	Random	+	1 "joint"	memory task
Experimental 2	Random	+	2 "joints"	memory task
Control 1	Random	+	1 placebo	memory task
Control 2	Random	+	2 placebos	memory task

either 15 minutes after smoking or 90 minutes after smoking. Thus, a portion of their design had a 2 × 2 factorial type of subject (naive or chronic) as one independent variable, and the length of time after smoking the marijuana (15 or 90 minutes) as the second independent variable. The dosage in this particular test was held constant at a high level. These investigators gave all subjects a pre-test and then administered the experimental treatment. Reproduced in Fig. 12.5. are the difference scores obtained by these investigators for their groups. The difference score was obtained by subtracting the post-test score from the pre-test score, with a minus difference score indicating more errors made under the drug than not, and a plus score indicating fewer errors made under the drug. The data in Fig. 12.5 suggest that marijuana impairs cognitive functioning in the naive subject and either slightly increases or leaves cognitive functioning unchanged in the chronic user.

	Fifteen minutes	Ninety minutes
Naive subject	+ 5 −17 − 7 − 3 − 7 − 9 − 6 + 1 − 3 $\overline{X} = -\ 5.1$	+ 8 − 5 − 1 − 8 −18 − 4 − 3 −10 $\overline{X} = -\ 3.9$
Chronic user	− 4 + 1 +11 + 3 − 2 − 6 − 4 + 3 $\overline{X} = +\ \ .25$	−16 + 6 +18 + 4 − 3 + 8 $\overline{X} = +\ 2.8$

Fig. 12.5 A part of the data collected by Weil and others (1968) on the effects of marijuana on memory.

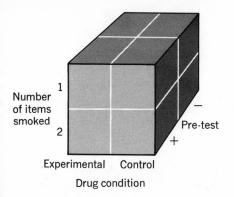

Fig. 12.6 The groups depicted in Table 12.5 arranged into a 2 × 2 × 2 factorial design which allow assessment of all these IVs.

It is possible, however, that during pre-testing the experimenters in some way may have influenced the responses of subjects on the dependent variable. To determine the effects of the pre-test on the dependent variable, we could run the experiment presented in Table 12.5. This eight group experiment is outlined in Table 12.5. All that we have done is include the pre-test as an independent variable. In matrix form this design is presented in Fig. 12.6.* It may be seen that the design of the eight group study was not very difficult to generate. Once you are familiar with the concept of the factorial design, the arrangement of the groups falls nicely into place.

Table 12.5 An Example of a Set of Groups Which will Allow Assessment of the Effects of a Pre-test on the *DV*

Group	Group selection	Pre-test	IV	DV
Experimental 1	Random	+	1 "joint"	memory task
Experimental 1	Random	−	1 "joint"	memory task
Control 1	Random	+	1 placebo	memory task
Control 1	Random	−	1 placebo	memory task
Experimental 2	Random	+	2 "joints"	memory task
Experimental 2	Random	−	2 "joints"	memory task
Control 2	Random	+	2 placebos	memory task
Control 2	Random	−	2 placebos	memory task

Main effects

The independent variables in a factorial design are arranged so that for most purposes we are assessing the effects of each independent variable on

---

*This design is really a complex mixed factorial design. Such designs will be discussed in the following chapter.

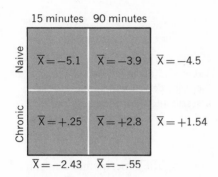

Fig. 12.7 The Weil and others (1968) data summarized to show the differences between the various levels of each IV on the DV.

the dependent variable separately from every other independent variable. Each independent variable is called a *main* variable. The term "main effect" refers to a significant difference between the mean of one or more levels of a main variable and the grand mean for that variable.

Reproduced in Fig. 12.7 is the factorial design shown in Fig. 12.5, with row and column means included. First consider the means given for the rows. These means represent the average performance of the Naive and Chronic user during the experimental test period. The means incidate that—on the whole—Naive subjects ($\overline{X} = -4.50$) made more errors on the memory task than chronic users ($\overline{X} = +1.54$). This would indicate that the *main effect* of Type of Subject (Naive or chronic user) had a significant* effect on the dependent variable. Now look at the column means. The means represent the average performance after 15 minutes and 90 minutes (regardless of the Type of Subject). These means indicate that both types of subjects made more errors on the task after 15 minutes than they did after 90 minutes. Such a result would indicate that the length of time since intake of the drug also had a significant effect on the dependent variable (performance) regardless of the subject.

The factorial design, then, allows us to assess the effects of two levels of two different independent variables on the same dependent variable within one experimental situation. We could also assess the effects of more than two independent variables on the dependent variable or more than two levels of an independent variable on the dependent variable by simply including more groups in our design.

---

*We will use the term "significant" in this chapter and the next without providing any of the relevant statistics. The reader should assume in all cases that the appropriate statistical operations were performed.

Let us emphasize the following two points with regard to main effects:

1. **One speaks of a main effect of a particular variable upon some dependent measure** as opposed to a specific reference to the levels of the independent variable. Thus, in referring to the previous example:

Incorrect—There was a main effect of 15 minutes vs. 90 minutes.

Correct—There was a main effect of time since drug intake, with the drug having a greater detrimental effect upon cognitive functioning after 15 minutes than after 90 minutes.

Notice that we not only need to report the occurrence of a main effect, but should also describe the group differences obtained.

2. **Main effects refer only to differences from one column mean to another or one row mean to another.** To state that a main effect of time since drug intake is significant directly implies that one level of this independent variable is significantly different from another level. With only two levels, as in the previous example, it is easy to describe the main effect. With three or more levels, the description may have to wait upon further consideration. To illustrate, consider the experimental results given in Fig. 12.8. Given that the results in Fig. 12.8 indicate a main effect of time since intake of drug, what may now be said? We can probably say that the largest difference here was significant but in order to be certain we need to do further analyses which are outlined in Section AI of Appendix A.

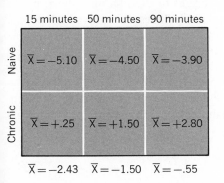

	15 minutes	50 minutes	90 minutes
Naive	$\bar{X} = -5.10$	$\bar{X} = -4.50$	$\bar{X} = -3.90$
Chronic	$\bar{X} = +.25$	$\bar{X} = +1.50$	$\bar{X} = +2.80$
	$\bar{X} = -2.43$	$\bar{X} = -1.50$	$\bar{X} = -.55$

Fig. 12.8 A set of hypothetical data arranged according to a 2 × 3 factorial design.

The interaction

Thus far we have concerned ourselves with the effects of main independent variables. We have indicated that it is possible for one or more independent variable to affect the dependent variable in a factorial experiment. It is also possible, using a factorial design, to assess the *joint effect* of two or more independent variables on the dependent variable. **The unique** joint effect of two or more independent variables on a dependent variable is called an interaction.

What do we mean by the concept of **unique joint effect?** Essentially this means that our subjects are doing "one thing" at one level of an independent variable and "another thing" at a different level of the independent variable. This may sound somewhat complicated, but let us illustrate this concept by a simple example. Assume that we are interested in educational research and wish to study the effect of two different teaching methods (t_1 and t_2) on two different groups of students—high IQ (bright) and low IQ (dull). If you think about this experiment you may decide that it is possible that one teaching method may work well with bright kids, but not with dull kids, whereas the other teaching method may work well with dull kids but not with bright ones. A set of hypothetical results of the above experiment is given in Fig. 12.9. The numbers represent the average improvement of each of the groups on a standard test following exposure to the experimental treatment. You should study Fig. 12.9 carefully and note the mean values of the various groups on the dependent variable. First evaluate the results of the main independent variable of Teaching Methods. The performance of the groups under this variable is represented by the row means. Thus, students on the whole averaged an increase of 24 points under Teaching Method one (t_1), and an increase of 24 points under Teaching Method two (t_2). Did the independent variable of Type of Teaching Method exert a main effect? No, it did not. Now look at the main independent variable of Type of Student—bright or dull. On the whole, bright students improved 24 points, whereas dull students improved 24 points. Did the independent variable, Type of Student, have a main effect on the dependent variable? No, it did not. Hence there are no main effects in this experiment. Does this mean that neither of our independent variables influenced the dependent variable? Inspect Fig. 12.9 again and look at the cell means. Doesn't it look like our main independent variables are doing something to these means even though neither variable has a major effect?

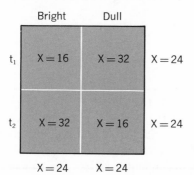

	Bright	Dull	
t_1	X = 16	X = 32	X = 24
t_2	X = 32	X = 16	X = 24
	X = 24	X = 24	

Fig. 12.9 Data arranged according to a 2 × 2 factorial design which depict a significant interaction.

If there were no effect at all shouldn't our data look like that depicted in Fig. 12.10? This indicates, then, that there should be an effect of our experimental treatment on the dependent variable as depicted in Fig. 12.9. It is just that this effect is not caused by the influence of either of our main independent variables alone, but rather, both of them are acting *jointly to determine performance* on the dependent variable. Look at Fig. 12.9 again and notice that for a bright subject, t_2 is more effective than t_1, but for a dull subject, t_1 is more effective than t_2. Here we have an example of an interaction in which neither main effect was significant. We have plotted the data given in Fig. 12.9 in Fig. 12.11 to show this effect more clearly. Notice that in graphing the means the resulting curves—one represented by bright students and the other by dull students—are not parallel. This indicates that the subjects are doing "one thing" under one level of the independent variable and "another thing" at a different level of the independent variable. That is, for bright students, t_2 is more effective—this is one relationship—whereas for dull students, t_1 is more effective—this is yet another relationship.

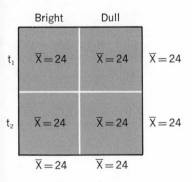

Fig. 12.10 A 2 × 2 factorial design in which no main effect or the interaction is significant.

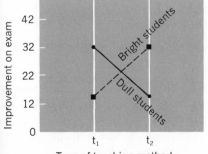

Fig. 12.11 A graph of the data given in Fig. 12.9 which shows the interaction (non-parallel lines) more clearly.

Let us examine the interaction depicted in Fig. 12.11 in a slightly different way. Can we say anything about what will happen in our experiment if we know only whether the students are bright or dull? Our answer to this should be no, that is, that there is no main effect of IQ. Can we say anything about what will happen in our experiment if you know only the teaching method to which the student will be exposed? Your answer again should be no because there is no main effect of Teaching Method. What you need to know in order to say anything about the results of the experiment is whether the student is bright or dull *and* the Type of Teaching Method employed. The reason we need information on both of these variables is that, in this example, neither alone tells us anything about the students' performance on the dependent variable; rather *both* of these variables act jointly to determine performance. This is what is meant by the concept of interaction. For convention's sake we would say the Teaching Method X (read as "by") Type of Student interaction was significant if we obtained the results depicted in Fig. 12.11.

We hope this last example communicated what is generally meant by the term interaction. We should now point out in a more precise way what is meant by the term. Interaction is a term borrowed from the field of statistics, and, as you might expect, it is given a precise definition by statisticians. Main effects are based upon a consideration of the row and column means, the interaction is based, as you saw from the previous example, upon a consideration of the individual cell means.

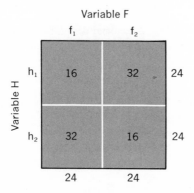

Fig. 12.12 A 2 × 2 factorial design with a significant interaction.

Let us transfer the data from Fig. 12.9 to Fig. 12.12. We determined that although neither main effect was significant, the variables acted jointly to produce *differential* effects, that is, the results depended upon the particular combination considered. More specifically, it was said that for an interaction to be observed one type of relationship held at one level of a variable and another type of relationship held at another level of that variable. From Fig. 12.12, we may say that for h_1 (one level of H) scores increase from f_1 to f_2 whereas for h_2 (another level of H) scores decrease from f_1 to f_2. This is represented in Fig. 12.13. We may schematize this, as shown in Fig. 12.14. Pictorially, when the schema in h_1 differs from the schema in h_2, that is, when these relationships are not parallel, we say that we have an interaction. Thus, none of the following schematic results in Fig. 12.15 depicts an interaction, since a parallel or similar relation exists between h_1 and h_2 in all the examples.

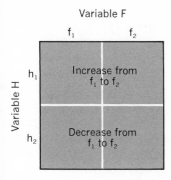

Fig. 12.13 Schematic of an interaction.

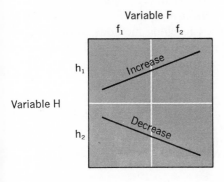

Fig. 12.14 Schematic indicating the nonparallelism of the lines which represent a typical interaction.

The statistician's definition of an interaction rests upon whether or not the relationships or curves are indeed parallel. We all presumably know what it means to have two parallel lines. In Fig. 12.16, Line a is parallel to Line b when $d_1 = d_2$. The psychologist, being less rigorous, will say Line a is parallel to Line b when d_1 **does not differ significantly from** d_2. Thus, **for an interaction to be significant, the lines must significantly depart from a parallel relation.**

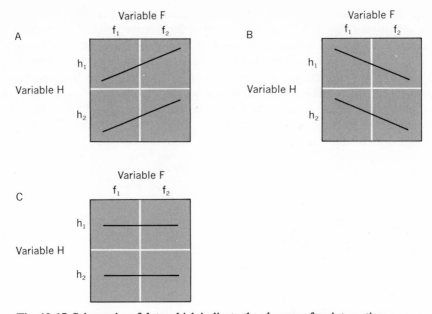

Fig. 12.15 Schematics of data which indicate the absence of an interaction.

Let us take some other examples from hypothetical data collected on the same educational research problem used earlier. Consider the data depicted in Fig. 12.17. First consider the effects of Type of Teaching Method. Students improved 24 points under both teaching methods, thus Type of Teaching Method did not influence subjects' performance. Now look at Type of Student. Dull students improved more than Bright students, thus Type of Student as an independent variable was probably significant. Now look at the cell means. Are the two main variables acting *jointly* to determine performance? The answer is no. That is, the same relationship holds for t_1 as for t_2. Schematically, we represent this in Fig. 12.18. Not only do the Dull students do better than the Bright students, but they are *equally* superior (i.e., a parallel relation exists) under each testing method.

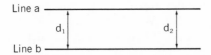

Fig. 12.16 Pictorial definition of parallelism.

Now let us examine the data given in Fig. 12.19 and ask the same questions about it. First we can see that t_2 improves performance more than t_1,

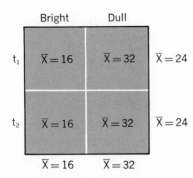

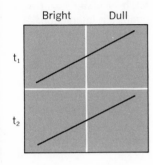

$\overline{X} = 16$ $\overline{X} = 32$

Fig. 12.17 Data indicating one main effect and no interaction.

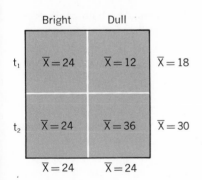

Fig. 12.18 An example of a significant main effect and no interaction.

Fig. 12.19 An example of a significant main effect and a significant interaction.

thus Type of Teaching Method is probably significant. Second, since both Bright and Dull students improve their scores on the average of 24 points, the main effect of Type of Student is not significant. Now look at the cell means. Is there an interaction? Your answer should be yes. As you can see, t_2 is more effective than t_1 when the students are dull, while both methods work equally well on bright students. In this case we have an example of one main effect being significant and, in addition, the interaction is significant. Consider the data in Fig. 12.19 replotted in Fig. 12.20. Here you

should be able to see the interaction more clearly. (Remember an interaction is indicated when the lines depart from parallelism.)

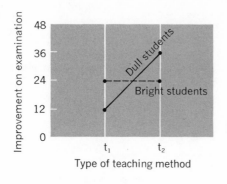

Fig. 12.20 Graph of a significant main
effect and a significant interaction.

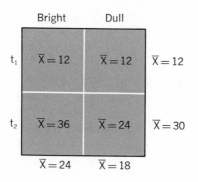

Fig. 12.21 Example of both main effects
significant as well as the interaction.

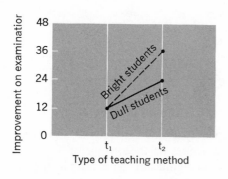

Fig. 12.22 Graph of the data given in
Fig. 12.21.

Now consider the data given in Fig. 12.21 and replotted in Fig. 12.22.
First we should note from the row means in Fig. 12.21 that t_2 led to more
improvement (on the whole) than t_1, while the column means in the same
figure indicate that (on the whole) bright students improved more than dull

students. Thus, both main effects of Type of Teaching Method and Type of Student were significant. Now consider the possibility of an interaction. Are the types of students doing something different under the particular types of teaching methods? Yes, they are. While t_2 is a more effective teaching method than t_1 it improves bright students *more than* dull students; hence Type of Teaching Method interacts with Type of Student. Thus, it is possible to have both main effects and the interaction significant.

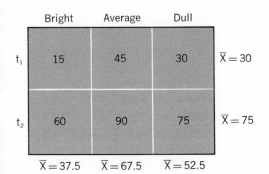

Fig. **12.23** Hypothetical data presented in a 2 × 3 matrix.

Consider a more complex example which is given in Fig. 12.23. We now have bright, average, and dull students exposed to one of the two teaching methods, and have obtained the given results. Both main effects are significant. This means that t_2 was more effective than t_1 and that at least bright students differed from average ones (we cannot yet compare the dull students to bright and average without the appropriate statistical techniques). Is there an interaction? With data as complex as these, it is a good idea to plot them. This is done in Fig. 12.24. As can be seen from Fig. 12.24, although they go "up and down," they do so *together*, that is, they are parallel. Therefore, there is no significant interaction.

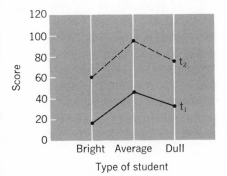

Fig. **12.24** Effectiveness of two teaching methods as a function of type of student.

Whenever you use a factorial design you must consider whether or not the interaction is significant and, if it is, exactly how to interpret the interaction in terms of your experimental variables. As you have already seen, the major advantage of the factorial design over a simple randomized design is that **it allows us to assess the joint effects of two or more main variables on the dependent variable.**

chapter thirteen

mixed designs

Repeated Measures

We have already encountered a simple repeated measures design in discussing a subject as his own control. This was the pre-post-test design. Essentially, a subject is measured under both the experimental and control conditions. Generally, a **repeated measures design is one in which a subject is measured under more than one treatment condition.** Using a repeated measures design accomplishes at least two major goals.

1. **It tends to reduce the total amount of variability in an experiment,** in comparison to a nonrepeated design. This is because a subject is used as his own control, that is, many of the Subject variables are controlled (i.e., held constant) from one treatment condition to another. (See Chapter 10 for a a more complete discussion.)

2. **A repeated measures design permits the investigator to record measurements of the subject's behavior over a period of time.** Recall that in a nonrepeated design, only one score may be used per subject in the data analysis. Frequently, though,

we wish to measure a subject repeatedly in an experiment and include this as a variable. When this is done, a repeated measures design must be employed.

Mixed Designs

A mixed design is one which has variables classed in more than one way. Typically, in behavioral research these classes are *independent groups* and *repeated measures* where the independent groups constitute an experimenter defined levels variable. An experimenter defined levels variable is called a fixed factor. One or more factors in these designs can be represented by independent groups. The other factor or factors are a repeated measure. Usually this repeated factor represents measures on the dependent variable taken across time. Such a design allows us to assess the effect of "time" on our dependent measure.

The T × S Design

The simplest repeated measures design is the Treatment × Subjects (T × S) design. In this design, there are two classifications of variables—they are classified either as a Treatment variable (fixed factor) or as a Subject variable (repeated factor). A relatively simple T × S design is given in Fig. 13.1. The Treatment effect is the independent variable with, in this example, four levels; the Subject variable simply refers to the number of subjects in the study—in this case, six. Each subject in this example experiences each Treatment level, with t_1 experienced first, t_2 next, and so on.

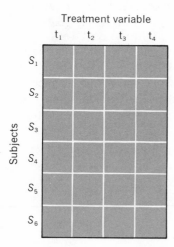

Fig. 13.1 Simple treatments × subjects design.

In the T $\times$ S design, the main effect of Treatments is the primary concern. The issue is whether or not one level of the Treatments variable differs from any other level. The main effect of Subjects would reflect the fact that individual differences among subjects were obtained, but since it is often difficult to interpret (Winer, 1971), this main effect is very often not even calculated. The T $\times$ S interaction would indicate that the subjects were behaving differently across Treatment conditions. This interaction, as we will see in Appendix A, is used as an estimate of the error variance in the experiment.

Applications of the T $\times$ S design

The simplest application of the T $\times$ S design is the pre-post-test type of experiment discussed in earlier chapters. This design is presented in Table 13.1. Subjects are first pre-measured on some dimension before the experimental treatment is administered, and then measured during such time as the treatment is supposed to have its effect. Essentially, the scores of each subject on the post-test are compared to his own pre-test scores in evaluating the effect of the independent variable.

Table 13.1 Hypothetical Results from a Pre-test, Post-test Design

Subject	Pre-test	Post-test
S_1	50	70
S_2	60	83
S_3	58	64
.	.	.
.	.	.
.	.	.

Most generally, the T $\times$ S design is appropriate whenever subjects are to be observed over some period of time. Thus, in an especially simple learning experiment, the data might be arranged as indicated in Table 13.2. One might count the number of the subjects' correct responses for blocks of five trials. We would expect that the number of such responses would increase as training is continued. The reliability of the increases would be reflected in the main effect of Trials (our Treatment variable). In this example, we would expect the main effect of Trials to be significant. The interpretation of these results would run something like this: We have measured the number of correct responses given over training, and this dependent variable is taken as reflecting the amount of learning taking place. We may thus conclude that the subjects in this experiment have accomplished some learning over 15 trials of practice.

Table 13.2 Number of Correct Responses for Subjects in a Learning Experiment Over 15 Training Trials

Subject	Trials 1-5	Trials 6-10	Trials 11-15
1	5	12	19
2	7	10	15
3	4	9	13
4	3	14	20
5	8	18	25
6	7	11	21
7	6	12	18
8	5	8	14
9	2	6	10
10	3	7	12
	$\overline{X} = 5.0$	$\overline{X} = 10.7$	$\overline{X} = 16.7$

One major limitation of the T $\times$ S design is that the treatment conditions must be administered in the same fixed order for all subjects. In certain cases, such as the ones previously mentioned, there is only one order in which the treatments could be given. In others, however, you might be somewhat reluctant to create a standard order for fear of influencing the results. This influence may take many forms and produce a variety of possible results. As an illustration, you might be interested in discovering whether boys get more sexually aroused in viewing pornographic movies or reading pornographic books. Owing to the expected large between-subjects variability you decide to use a repeated measures design in which the subjects will be exposed to both visual and printed materials. Which type of material do you present first? Presenting the visual material first may influence responses to the printed matter, and vice versa. In addition, simply being in such a situation may influence responses, i.e., responses may vary as a function of the amount of time spent in the context of pornographic material. You may decide, therefore, despite the large between-subjects variance that is expected, to run a two-group simple randomized design. We would recommend, however, that you choose a Latin Square Design.

The Latin Square Design

The Latin Square Design is used when you want to *counterbalance* two or more conditions. Counterbalancing, you will recall from our discussion in

Chapter 11, attempts either to neutralize or examine any sequential or carry-over effects which may be present in an experiment. In a Latin Square Design, each treatment appears once in each temporal position. With regard to the pornography example, the Latin Square Design depicted in Table 13.3 provides an elegant method for anlysis of the order effects discussed above. That is, you can (a) determine any differences between the first presentation of visual and printed material; (b) compare each type of material after the other has been presented; (c) examine the effects of time by seeing if any systematic behavior changes occur for both groups from the first to the second stimulus series.

Table 13.3 Pornography Study Using a Simple Latin Square Design

	First exposure	Second exposure
Group I	Visual	Printed
Group II	Printed	Visual

Latin Square designs are especially useful when you need to evaluate any sequential effects. You are not only limited to the 2 $\times$ 2 matrix design. We have outlined a 3 $\times$ 3 matrix in Table 13.4, in which A, B, and C are three levels of a particular independent variable. Each of three possible orders of the three levels is represented by independent groups. Those subjects in Group I, for instance, experience the order A, B, and C; subjects in Group II experience the order B, C, A; and subjects in Group III experience the order C, A, B. There are many complexities that may be incorporated into Latin Square designs, and if you are interested, we suggest that you consult more technical references (e.g., Myers, 1966; Winer, 1971).

Table 13.4 3 $\times$ 3 Latin Square Design

Group I	A	B	C
Group II	B	C	A
Group III	C	A	B

Another Simple Mixed Design

Another simple mixed design is presented in the 2 $\times$ 2 matrix in Fig. 13.2. Typically Variable A would represent measures taken under different conditions on the same subjects. Both the repeated and nonrepeated factors in this example each have two levels although you need not necessarily be limited to two levels of each factor.

Repeated measure (A)

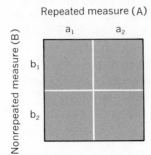

Fig. 13.2 A simple mixed design in which variable A is a repeated variable and variable B is a nonrepeated variable.

Application of the simple mixed design

The major application of the simple mixed design is that it enables a comparison of at least two independent groups as they perform across different conditions or over time. Take the learning example used in the section on the T × S design. This design may now be expanded to that presented in Table 13.4, along with some hypothetical data. We have recorded the mean number of correct responses for each trial block for those subjects in Group I (Learning Task I) and those in Group II (Learning Task II), and have plotted these data in Fig. 13.3. Both main effects and the interaction are probably significant. We may say, then, that Group I *learned at a faster rate* than Group II. Such a comparison of groups over some time-related variable is extremely valuable to the experimenter, and finds many applications in behavioral research.

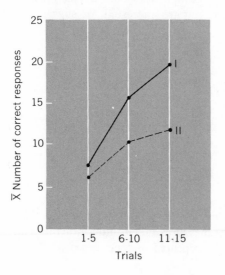

Fig. 13.3 Mean number of correct responses as a function of trials for two learning tasks.

	Trials 1-5	Trials 6-10	Trials 11-15
Learning task I	7.3	15.4	19.7
Learning task II	6.8	10.3	11.2

Fig. 13.4 Mean number of correct responses over trials for two learning tasks.

Complex Mixed Designs

Whenever more than two variables are used in a design, and some are repeated and others are nonrepeated, we call such designs complex mixed designs. Although there is virtually an unlimited number of potential designs, it is rare that an experiment will go beyond three variables. The reason for this general self-imposed limit is understandable—the more complex the design, the more difficult may be a description and/or interpretation of the obtained results. A simple mixed design (one repeated and one nonrepeated factor) considers only two variables, and therefore, the interaction will be in the general form of A × B. Because there are only two factors, this is called a *double interaction*. It is always possible to describe and usually possible to interpret a double interaction. In a design using three variables, the highest order interaction or the one involving the most factors is a *triple interaction*. Although triple interactions often are difficult to interpret, they may at other times be quite understandable. The highest order interaction in a four-variable study is a quadruple interaction, and the chances of being able to interpret an A × B × C × D interaction are not encouraging. An interaction of five variables (A × B × C × D × E) is very likely to be completely meaningless to most researchers. The frequency of employment of mixed designs varies, naturally enough, with the probability of being able to interpret the highest order interaction. Simple mixed designs are most common, followed closely by three-variable mixed designs; those using four variables may be found if you search the literature carefully enough, and the use of five variables in one study is rare indeed.

As we mentioned, the complex mixed designs employing three variables are the most commonly employed. There are only two popular versions of this design, and these are presented in Fig. 13.4. Of course, each of the variables may have any number of levels associated with it. The ANOVA procedures appropriate to each of these designs is detailed in Appendix A.

Complex mixed design: I	Complex mixed design: II
2 nonrepeated variables	1 nonrepeated variable
1 repeated variable	2 repeated variables

Fig. 13.4 Two complex mixed designs employing three variables. The nonrepeated are variables assumed to be fixed.

How to Choose the Appropriate Design

We have presented a large number of designs in the last two chapters, and by this time you may be asking how to choose the appropriate one for an experiment. This choosing process is relatively straight-forward, but the facility with which you complete the task depends upon your familiarity with the designs outlined. We will therefore take you through a series of decision steps to facilitate your choice. Once you are familiar with these steps, you will no doubt find a suitable short-cut to our procedure.

STEP 1—FORMULATE THE PROBLEM Obviously, the first step in any research is to formulate some idea of the subject matter that you wish to investigate. The idea must be only somewhat specific. For example, you probably know that if a response is consistently followed by reinforcement, that response appears to be strengthened. You also know that if you now withhold the reinforcement (an extinction procedure), the reponse will appear to be weakened, that is, it will occur less frequently, will be made with less effort, etc., until it is finally extinguished. You may formulate a problem, then, concerned with those variables which affect the extinction of a consistently reinforced response.

STEP 2—REVIEW THE LITERATURE After formulating the general problem, you should attempt to secure information pertaining to it. That is, you should familiarize yourself with the available information on the problem by using whatever sources the library can supply. Suggestions as to how to do this are given in Chapter 16.

STEP 3—INTEGRATE THE LITERATURE After taking complete notes on the various investigations reported in the literature, you should attempt to integrate these studies. In other words, attempt to draw some general conclusions from the information, indicating those variables which influence extinction, and the way in which they do so. Following through with our example, you might find that the amount of reinforcement used, the amount of training (i.e., acquisition) administered, and the spacing of trials—that is whether the trials follow each other by 30 seconds or 24 hours—are all important in affecting extinction performance.

STEP 4—SPECIFY YOUR INDEPENDENT VARIABLES Let us say that you choose to study the effects of only one of those variables—reinforcement magnitude—planning to consider in a future experiment the joint effects of this variable and others. It will be necessary, therefore, to *control* the effects of the other variables while *varying* reward magnitude. As recommended in Chapter 9, you plan to hold all factors except the independent variable *constant* across your experimental groups.

A further specification is also necessary in that the levels of the independent variable must now be considered. On the basis of your literature review, it might seem that the results of those studies using a small reinforcement reported one type of result, whereas those studies using a large reinforcement reported a different pattern of results. You therefore decide that one group should be given a large reward, another a small reward, and, for the sake of thoroughness, to run a third group to medium sized reward.

STEP 5—SPECIFY YOUR DEPENDENT VARIABLES   What do you wish to measure? Your literature review indicated that most of the relevant studies employed a locomoter response, in which the subject transversed a straight alleyway to obtain the reward. Furthermore, investigators typically measured the time the subject took to complete his run. For consistency (so that you may compare your results to those in the literature), you too should adopt this procedure.

STEP 6—THE INCLUSION OF A REPEATED MEASURE   Do you wish to repeatedly measure subjects over the period of the experiment or will you take only one measure. You know that the response will gradually weaken as the subjects are run trial after trial to nonreward. It might be interesting to trace the course of this weakening. Therefore, you decide to include a repeated measure; that is, you will observe the subjects' times during each trial of extinction (as well as acquisition).

STEP 7—DIAGRAM THE DESIGN YOU HAVE GENERATED   Since you have decided to have one nonrepeated variable (reward magnitude) and one repeated measure (trials), you have constructed a simple mixed design. This design is drawn in Fig. 13.5. We have, for convenience, blocked extinction by five trials. For most purposes, then, once you have formulated a problem and decided on the independent variable(s) and the dependent variable you wish to study, the design of the experiment will virtually "construct itself."

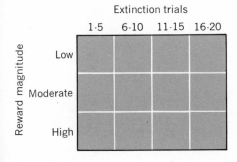

Fig. 13.5 Design operative during extinction.

chapter fourteen

scientific methods III: field research

Consider the continuum presented below. We have scaled the degree to which the experimenter interferes with, manipulates, or controls the environmental conditions under which the subject is observed. The two types of methodologies thus far discussed, naturalistic observation and laboratory experimentation, represent the two extremes on this scale. In a naturalistic observational setting, the observer interferes with the environmental conditions as little as possible. In the laboratory, the environmental conditions are literally built to the specifications of the scientist, and are virtually under his total control. Much research, however, may be conceived as occupying the middle ground between these two extremes, and we label such procedures as *field research*.

Continuum of environmental control

Naturalistic observation	Field research	Laboratory experimentation
No control	Partial control	Nearly complete control

Field research or field studies are usually conducted in a natural or quasi-natural environment with respect to the particular subject. This type of environment takes on the name **field** to differentiate it from the laboratory situation. Such research also demands that the scientist play some active role—in the sense that he must somehow intervene—in the data collection. The fact that the scientist is active precludes such investigations from being classed as naturalistic observation; also, the fact that the scientist cannot fully control the environment of his subjects because he is not in a laboratory precludes the use of the laboratory experiment classification. For these reasons, the field study comprises the middle ground as depicted in the schema just described.

The methodology used in the fields study is basically a combination of the principles already outlined with respect to naturalistic observation and laboratory experimentation. This "combination" notion is represented by the overlapping circles drawn below:

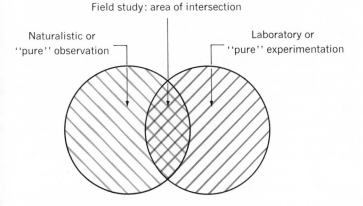

For although the scientist is playing a somewhat active role, he may on occasion need to employ the observational techniques used in naturalistic observation. By the same token, his observations may take place after some feature of the environment has been manipulated, and so may more closely resemble a true experiment in this instance. It is therefore necessary for the scientist to have a working knowledge of the various control procedures known to the laboratory researcher, as well as the observational techniques used in naturalistic research.

An additional point may be mentioned here. The terms "field research" and "field studies" actually encompass a variety of separate methodologies which, although sharing a common base, differ substantially among themselves. After discussing some of the commonalities of these procedures, we will treat each separately.

The Nature of the Field Study

Since a field study is a product of two basic methodologies, it follows that an understanding of the latter should provide an understanding of the former. While this may be true, the field study still retains some degree of uniqueness; some of the issues concerning this uniqueness are outlined in the following subsections.

The issue of control

Experimentation implies the use of a control condition against which the effects of the experimental treatment may be compared. In naturalistic observation, the concept of control is unnecessary since the task is simply to record a series of observations. Being a hybrid, some of the field study methodologies do incorporate control procedures whereas others do not.

The issue of independent variables

Experimentation implies the use of one or more independent variables each of which may have two or more levels. Naturalistic observation implies that it is not possible to manipulate an independent variable, since the whole idea is to interfere as little as possible with the environment. Some of the field study methodologies involve the manipulation of independent variables, whereas others do not.

The issue of the dependent variable

In laboratory experimentation, the dependent variable is highly specialized and constitutes only a very small portion of the possible things that may be going on. Very often the situation is constructed so that some measurement must take place—the only thing not under control is the value of that measure. For example, the rat in a runway *will* give a time score because the clock is always moving while he is in the apparatus, the human at the memory drum *will* give a response which will be either an omission, an incorrect answer, or a correct answer. In the open field, we find the exact reverse. The observer of natural behavior must record *everything* relevant to his task. He may be lucky and record a great deal, or he may be unlucky and record very little—that is the gamble he takes. In the field study, you typically "split the middle." That is, although the setting is structured there is usually no way to *insure* that the relevant behavior will take place.

There is also a problem about the nature of the behavior occuring in a field study. In the laboratory, the researcher may impose upon his subjects the most extreme or bizarre task requirements. For example, rats have been trained to make exactly some number of press reponses on some protrusion on an inside wall of a commercially produced metal and glass box to obtain some carefully pre-weighed amount of manufactured dry food; furthermore, humans have sat in front of a drum revolving at some fixed rate attempting to recall the exact order of small groups of letters having little meaning and which cannot be found in even the most complete of dictionaries. These extremely artificial conditions are defensible on the grounds that they permit the researcher in the rat example to examine basic learning and in the human example to examine memory processes.

On the other hand, and by definition, only "natural" behavior can occur in the naturalistic observation situation. In the field study, some sort of compromise between these two extremes is usually realized. The behavior cannot be radically different from that which ordinarily occurs, but the scientist is often able to construct the situation in such a way that some behavior—which he believes indexes the process he is studying—is among the responses his subjects are likely to give.

The issue of field study locations

As we have already noted, laboratory experimentation is conducted in laboratories and naturalistic observation is conducted in the natural environment of the organism. A field study is typically conducted in an environment someplace between these two extremes, but depending upon the nature of the research the exact place may be closer to either the natural or laboratory setting. On the one hand, recall the Etho-Box described in Chapter 8. Here, the environment of the organism is almost equivalent to the natural setting. We can, however, introduce into the Etho-Box an external event (under the control of the scientist) and observe the organism's reactions to this event. We may introduce a predator, a new type of food, lower or raise the temperature, change the illumination, etc. This type of field study would closely resemble laboratory research since this may be conceived as an example of the pre-post-test design. Pre-test represents the setting before the change, and post-test represents it after the introduction of the change. Differences in behavior would presumably arise because of the stimulus change.

On the other hand, we may bring the subjects into some arranged setting and observe particular aspects of their behavior under these predetermined conditions. For instance, we may instruct a small group of undergraduate students to engage in a discussion on a given topic. The students may be observed from a separate room, with the interest of the scientist focused upon the social interactions of members of this group and particularly upon the emergence of a group leader. This piece of research seems more closely aligned with naturalistic observation since the investigator intervenes only slightly by confining behavior to discussion of a topic, and then simply records those reactions given by members of the group that appear to be related to his particular interests.

What is a Field Study?

A field study involves the observation of organisms under circumstances where:

1. **The relevant environment is "roughly" natural.** Notice the term "relevant environment," and recall the examples mentioned above. For the animal in the Etho-Box, the "relevant environment" was his total environment, meant to closely simulate the natural setting. For our student discussion group, the relevant environment was *only the social circumstances*— the fact that they were physically in a social psychology research room was irrelevant from the standpoint of the scientist and presumably from the standpoint of the students as well. Also, exactly how "roughly" the field environment approximates the natural environment will differ considerably from one situation to another.

2. **The observations of the scientist are focused on some specific aspect of the behavior of the subject.** That is, the scientist will generally record *less* diverse data than he would doing naturalistic observation, but will generally record *more* diverse data than he would in doing laboratory experimentation.

The Range of the Field Study

On the basis of what has been said so far, it is apparent that in a field study we find a wide range of diverse procedures and techniques falling into this general classification. Four of the most common procedures classified as field research are the **survey technique, correlational research, longitudinal research,** and the **field experiment.** Each of these will be discussed in turn.

The Survey Technique

We define the survey technique as any procedure involving the investigator entering a subject population and measuring some specific set of responses.

In this technique you will find neither the manipulation of an independent variable nor the setting-up of a control condition. The survey is more like a probe to describe the state of affairs existent in the population at any one time. The most widely used survey techniques are probably the *interview* in which a small number of people are extensively questioned face-to-face and the *questionnaire* in which a large number of people are asked to complete a relatively brief form usually via a mailing procedure.

Advantages of the survey technique

Each methodology is designed to answer particular types of questions, and in so doing, defines the advantages enjoyed by the methodology. We have outlined below some of the advantages of the survey technique:

1. At the very least, it can supply information regarding the opinions, attitudes, etc. of a population on a given issue.

2. It can be used to answer questions (i.e., test hypotheses) the scientist has generated before starting the research. For example, the way certain sub-groups in the population vote may be the subject of a variety of hypotheses.

3. It may provide a basis for deciding how to deal with certain issues. That is, you may wish to collect a great deal of interview and questionnaire data regarding attitudes towards contraception before launching into a birth control campaign in a community. On the basis of the collected data, you may wish to plan your campaign one way rather than another.

4. The survey technique may provide a source for new hypotheses. Trends in the data may catch your attention and suggest new lines of investigation. Thus, you may plan additional research on the basis of the results of your current research.

Limitations of the survey technique

Thus far, we have been discussing the survey technique on the assumption that it has been both efficiently and correctly carried out, and that the obtained data have been both properly analyzed and reasonably interpreted. Good survey research, however, is very difficult to accomplish because there are a great many limiting factors. We will postpone a discussion of the proper analysis and interpretation of the data to Appendix A (see Sections AIII and AIV) and deal here with some of the limiting factors involved in conducting survey research.

1. If a questionnaire is being employed, you must always consider the

validity of the actual questions. That is, you must ask if the questions are really tapping the information in which you are interested. To collect information on cigarette smokers' attitudes toward quitting which of the following two questions would you ask:

Question A:	Question B:
Check the most appropriate answer	Check the most appropriate answer
____I would like to stop smoking cigarettes ____I would not like to stop smoking cigarettes	I plan to stop smoking cigarettes ____tomorrow ____next week ____next month ____next year ____don't know ____never

Each of these questions taps somewhat different aspects of smoking termination behavior, and should not be used interchangeably. It is often a difficult task to construct questions appropriate to your original interest, and the matter should be given a great deal of thought.

2. If a questionnaire is being used, you should avoid creating what is called a *halo* effect. **A halo effect introduces a source of error into the research in that it tends to bias the responses of subjects.** Let us give an example of a halo effect. Subjects are given a painting and are asked to rate the degree to which they like it on a Lickert scale provided by the experimenter. Which of the two following scales would you use? If you chose Scale A, you

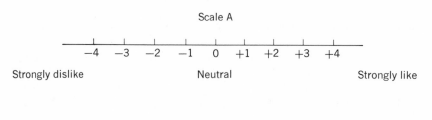

Scale A

-4 -3 -2 -1 0 +1 +2 +3 +4

Strongly dislike   Neutral   Strongly like

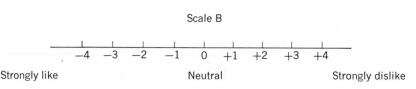

Scale B

-4 -3 -2 -1 0 +1 +2 +3 +4

Strongly like   Neutral   Strongly dislike

will most probably introduce a halo effect into the research. "Dislike" has a negative connotation, and the "negativity" of the scale values being associated with the "Dislike" rating would only serve to magnify or *halo* the actual rating behavior. Likewise, by having positive numbers associated with "Like" ratings, these judgments may also be magnified (or *haloed*.) Scale B acts as a balance somewhat by reversing the valences associated with the ratings. Unfortunately, this may result in a "negative halo effect" since subjects may be reluctant to rate that which they strongly like as a large minus value. What do you do? If you must use numbers, use Scale B since scientists, being conservative creatures with respect to their work, prefer to eliminate (or reverse) the halo effect. In practice, we would recommend using a scale without any numbers at all. Such an alternative scale is presented as Scale C, in which subjects simply check the appropriate blank space.

Scale C

— — — — — — — — —

Strongly dislike   Neutral   Strongly like

3. In either questionnaire or interview research, it is often necessary to assume that subjects are responding in an honest and straightforward manner. In the large bulk of instances, this assumption is a reasonable one to make.

4. Interview research is plagued with its own limitations over and above those already mentioned. The biases of the interviewer himself, the environment in which the interview takes place, the sex of the interviewer, etc. are all factors that need to be considered. Any one of these factors can be such as to make interpretation of the results difficult at best.

5. Even if all of these above problems are dealt with, you may need to entertain the possibility that you have tapped a *cyclical* or *transitory effect*, i.e., an effect that vacillates over time. Most researchers, for example, know better than to distribute a questionnaire to a class on the day of an important exam since the students' responses in such a case are entirely unpredictable. Other factors, such as the state of the economy, may strongly influence the outcome of a political poll.

6. Since questionnaires are typically distributed to a large sample of subjects via a mailing procedure, and since these people are asked to mail the completed questionnaire back to the researcher, one never finishes the study with as many questionnaires as were originally mailed out (typically, about one-third of the mailed questionnaires are returned). The magic question then becomes: Do the obtained results also reflect the attitudes, etc.,

of those people who did not return the survey? There is a distinct possibility that the answer to that question is NO. If the answer is NO, we have what is known as a **biased sample,** in that the sample results may then no longer be justifiably extrapolated to the **whole population.** That is, the sample is no longer representative of the population of original interest.

The partial returning of questionnaires is only one of many ways that can produce biased samples. A superb example of biased sampling can be shown from this real occurrence. *Literary Digest* conducted a public opinion poll in order to forecast the outcome of the 1936 presidential election. Several million postcard ballots were circulated to people whose names were randomly and independently drawn from telephone directories and automobile registration lists. On the basis of the sample, *Literary Digest* predicted a landslide victory for the Republican candidate, Alfred M. Landon. What went wrong? A post mortem analysis of the research told the simple story. At the time of a severe economic depression, only those people who were fairly well off would own phones and cars, and they would indeed, most likely vote Republican. But the overwhelming majority of voters were far too poor for such luxuries, and these untapped masses voted for Franklin Roosevelt. The *Literary Digest* sample was super-biased—it sampled a small and *nonrepresentative* portion of the entire voting population. The conclusions drawn from the sample could be generalized *only to those people who owned phones and cars and not to "all potential voters"*—which, of course, was the target population.

An example of the survey technique

Surveys have been taken on a variety of topics, and we present to you the results of one particular study concerned with reasons for entering the field of psychology. A total of 174 psychologists checked the various factors that influenced their decision to enter the field. Table 14.1 summarizes these results.

Correlational Research

With the survey technique we have seen the use of a method that involves entering the population with a particular measurement device, usually with the intent of describing the status of the population at a given time period.

Table 14.1 Factors Considered as Most Important in Leading to the Decision to Enter the Field of Psychology (After Clark, 1957[a])

Factor	Percentage checking this factor
Wanting to know more about human beings and their behavior	56
Being influenced by a particular teacher of psychology	54
Interest in the scientific investigation of human behavior	47
Becoming interested in the field through the content of courses in psychology	46
Becoming interested in the field through reading books in psychology	44
Interest in applying psychological techniques in such areas as clinical, educational, or industrial psychology	43
Desire to work with individuals or groups	32
Courses were easy for me	29
Doing research in this field	25
Need to understand myself	19
Desire to solve society's problems	16
The prestige of psychology	5
Having been helped in personal problems by a psychologist	4
Desire to enter a field offering fairly lucrative rewards	1

[a]The group on which these data are based consists of 174 members of The American Psychological Association who received their doctorates during the years 1940–44. Clark, K. E. (1957), *America's psychologists: A survey of a growing profession.* Washington: American Psychological Association.

Correlational research is similar to the survey technique in this way, but takes the survey procedure one step further in that the investigator **enters the population with two or more measurement devices with the intention of determining the extent to which variables measured by these devices are related to one another.** That is, instead of simply determining how people react to the question of birth control, a correlational study might also measure people on one or more other variables (e.g., degree of religious commitment, amount of formal education, etc.). The question would be to what extent are attitudes on birth control related to degree of religious commitment or amount of formal education.

Correlational research is a very important methodology to most social sciences—so important, in fact, that we have chosen to devote all of Chapter 15 to the subject.

Longitudinal Research

Longitudinal research generally attempts **by examining a population over a prolonged period of time,** to describe the development of some process. Notice that we said "prolonged." All research takes place over time— something that is accepted as fact—but sometimes this "time element" is itself of prime interest. When this occurs, the research may be called a longitudinal study. Longitudinal research focuses on a given sample, usually relatively small in size, and follows the members of this sample for some designated period of time. The purpose of such research is to examine the subjects intensively along some particular dimensions in order to see the development of their behavior patterns.

Longitudinal vs. cross-sectional research

One of the fields within behavioral science making extensive use of longitudinal and cross-sectional research is developmental child psychology, and it will be useful to indicate the difference between longitudinal and cross-sectional research within this field. Suppose that you wished to determine how cognitive functioning develops with age—a problem that can be investigated both by a cross-sectional study and by a longitudinal study. Although these methodologies are not mutually exclusive (indeed, you would probably want to use both in any thorough research project), each can supply certain kinds of information not easily available from the other.

The cross-sectional study can focus on a narrow area of cognitive function-ing and identify certain variables whereas the longitudinal study tends to examine broader questions. Hence, you are more likely to do a cross-sectional study as a laboratory experiment and a longitudinal study as a field study.

To conduct a cross-sectional study, you could choose a specific task that you believed reflected cognitive functioning, such as oddity learning. The first stage of oddity learning typically is identified by the presentation of three stimuli, two of which are identical. One set of oddity stimuli is given below, along with the three possible arrays of these stimuli.

Array 1   △   ○   ○

Array 2   ○   △   ○

Array 3   ○   ○   △

The child is trained by randomly presenting these arrays one at a time until he consistently chooses the triangle, the "odd" stimulus, at which point he is shifted to a second set of oddity stimuli, such as that illustrated below:

Array 1   ☐   +   +

Array 2   +   ☐   +

Array 3   +   +   ☐

Again, each array is presented randomly until the child learns to choose the odd stimulus. This procedure is continued until the child will con-sistently pick the odd shape the first time he sees a new set of stimuli. Since the choosing of oddity is eventually independent of the specific forms, but is dependent on some abstract appreciation of the notion of "difference" per se, we say that the child has a functioning concept.

The ability to solve an oddity problem changes with age, among other things. To demonstrate this, you may design the hypothetical cross-sectional experiment outlined below:

Group 1 3 yrs-4 yrs	Group 2 4 yrs-5 yrs	Group 3 5 yrs-6 yrs	Group 4 6 yrs-7 yrs
S_1	S_{21}	S_{41}	S_{61}
S_2	S_{22}	S_{42}	S_{62}
.	.	.	.
.	.	.	.
S_{20}	S_{40}	S_{60}	S_{80}

If you count the percentage of each group solving the problem, you might find the following: Group 1—15%, Group 2—35%, Group 3—60%, Group 4—85%.

This experiment is a cross-sectional study because we in some sense took a "cross-section" through time; that is, we sliced through a constant interval of time and sampled children who were either 3, 4, 5, or 6 years during the same interval of time. To state this another way, the experiment was conducted using 20 different children in each of the age categories.

It would be possible to take this study one step farther. Assuming that only 15% of the 3–4 year olds were successful, you might then wish to expose such children to certain procedures that might facilitate their ability to solve an oddity problem. Such as experimental design is given below, in which a different sample of 3–4 year old children is given either Procedure A, B, C, or nothing prior to oddity training.

Group designation	Experimental treatment
Control	No pretraining
A	Procedure A
B	Procedure B
C	Procedure C

If you found that only Procedure B increased the ability to solve oddity, you have gone a long way toward identifying the appropriate factors needed to develop this particular cognitive ability.

The longitudinal study provides a somewhat different perspective. First, you might start with children between the ages of 3 and 4 years and test them on a variety of tasks (oddity might be only one of 20 or 30). At various intervals of time (perhaps at one year intervals) you would *retest these same children* on comparable tasks. Along with case histories that might be obtained, it would be possible to describe the *development of each child* over the observation period, as well as noting the commonalities and differences found among the sample of children.

Notice the difference between the cross-sectional and longitudinal orientations. Longitudinal research is substantially broader in scope and tends to treat a general issue; cross-sectional research is narrower in scope and tends (if successful) to focus rapidly on a particular problem. The results of the longitudinal investigations will almost always produce some success, although the results are not nearly so dramatic as with cross-sectional investigations which can lead to clear success or failure. Longitudinal research may provide enough of a picture of what may be happening to conduct cross-sectional research. Each is necessary to answer certain kinds of questions; both are necessary to supply a fuller understanding of the complex issues with which the scientist may be concerned.

Uses of longitudinal research

Although most behavioral scientists can make good use of longitudinal research, many sub-disciplines, because of the nature of the problems investigated within their scope, have made extensive use of this methodology. We cite only three additional applications to provide you with an idea of the types of questions that may be answered by longitudinal research.

1. Educators have relied upon longitudinal research for some time. Each time a major change is made in the educational curriculum, its effects need to be carefully evaluated. Educators typically work on a seven or twelve year cycle, under the assumption that any long range effects of the change may take that long to manifest itself. They will focus on a group of students at the time of the change, and follow these students through a number of years of school. If these students appear to have benefitted from the new program, the program may either be retained or made more widespread in the school district.

2. Social psychologists may also use longitudinal research, particularly in the study of small groups. By observing the functioning of a group from the time it first forms, through its development, and perhaps to its termination, it may be possible to analyze in detail many aspects of group

dynamics (e.g., the development of functions and structures of organization of the group members) displayed.

3. It is also possible to use longitudinal research in a therapy situation to describe the changes, if any, occurring over the course of the therapy.

Advantages of longitudinal research

There are basically two major advantages of this methodology. The first is that it allows an opportunity to observe some phenomenon over a prolonged period of time. Through such extensive and intensive study the scientist is likely to learn a great deal about the phenomenon under investigation. The second advantage is that, by observing the same subjects over time, and therefore repeatedly measuring them, a considerable amount of control is exercised over subject variables. As was seen in Chapter 10, holding these variables constant across conditions is a highly effective way to control for individual differences.

Limitations of longitudinal research

Perhaps the most obvious limitation of longitudinal research is in maintaining the validity of the sample. Since longitudinal research may take years to complete, many persons in the sample may "drop out" for one or another reason. In some research the students may move out of the school district; in other settings, some members may quit the group, or perhaps terminate their therapy. The resulting sample may then turn out to be somewhat biased along certain dimensions and thus cause some concern to the investigator.

There are two other more subtle, yet equally important limitations. First, by definition, subjects are being repeatedly measured, and the question of unwanted sequential effects must be considered. That is, will the fact that subjects were previously measured influence (in any way) the results on later measurement? In an experiment, this question can be answered by incorporating a counterbalancing procedure. In longitudinal research no counterbalancing is possible since the earlier measurement must *always* precede the later measurement. Although there may be ways to indirectly answer the question (e.g., occasionally skip a measurement of some subjects and make between-subjects comparisons to those who were measured), these procedures are very cumbersome and take more effort than they are worth. The best the scientist can do is to make the assumption that such sequential effects are minimal and that they would not negate the eventual conclusions.

The other limitation to longitudinal research is that it is almost impossible in many instances to evaluate the effect of the observer. Unless sophisticated technological devices are employed permitting observation at a distance, the observer himself is a part of the total environment in which the observed behavior is taking place. Whether the observed events would also have taken place in the observer's absence is all too often a question lacking a satisfactory answer.

The Field Experiment

As we discussed the survey technique, correlational research, and longitudinal research, we noted that there was generally an increasing amount of intervention on the part of the scientist. With the field experiment comes maximal intervention, in that a field experiment is truly an experiment in the same sense as the term was used in Chapter 9. The simplest field experiment is one that employs two conditions, namely, Experimental and Control; independent variables are manipulated, dependent variables established, and control procedures enacted in the same way as was discussed for the laboratory experiment. The difference, and it is a crucial one, is that here the experiment takes place in the field—the subject's natural environment.

Advantages of the field study

One of the most pervasive arguments against the use of laboratory experiments is that such research is conducted in highly artificial surroundings and may not be generalizable to the "real world." The field study is felt by many to be a more satisfactory procedure in this regard, since this type of research takes place in the actual setting in which the scientist is interested. And the experimental subjects, operating as they do in their normal lives, should give a truer picture of their natural behavior. This *validity* issue constitutes the major advantage of this methodology.

Limitations of the field study

Although the advantage of conducting field experimentation is generally acknowledged by most scientists, very few researchers actually charge into nature to conduct experiments. To the majority who stand on the sidelines, their own reluctance to engage in that particular form of research is clear—to do "good" field experiments is extremely difficult. Let us outline a few of the limitations of field experimentation that run parallel to many points made in reference to naturalistic observation in Chapter 8.

1. **The study that seems,** logically at least, **to be the crucial study to run may be ethically impossible.** For example, social isolation studies have been done with both rats and monkeys, but it would be highly inadvisable to isolate human infants from all social contacts for the first 10 years of life and then proceed to perform a series of tests to determine the effects of the isolation.

2. Along with the ethical problems, **the researcher may also run into vested interests.** Although you may be fully prepared to run a study in a particular school, the principal, or some parent group, may decide that, while the experiment does seem interesting, they would rather not have their children used as "guinea pigs."

3. The major limitation with regard to field experimentation is that certain methodological difficulties always arise, some of which cannot be overcome in a particular study. The scientist must then make the choice of whether or not to continue with the project and accept the difficulties that are clearly involved. Here are some of the frequently experienced difficulties:

a. Any apparatus or materials needed for the research should be a part of or at least "blend in" with the natural setting. Therefore, the best suited materials may frequently not be used; the scientist may have to settle for second or third best and thus be unable to completely achieve the desired conditions under which the behavior is to be measured.

b. The entire experimental situation, particularly the task required of the subject, may also represent a poor compromise.

c. The dependent measure, because it needs to be adapted to the field setting, may not measure precisely the effects in which the scientist is interested. In a field setting it is impossible to guarantee that the subjects will emit the desired behavior in the first place, although it may be possible to maximize the chances of such behavior.

d. Perhaps the greatest of all the limitations is that, in a field setting, the investigator typically varies more than just the independent variable, since the independent variable cannot, in the field, be totally isolated from other variables. Most field studies, then, are to a greater or lesser degree, confounded.

For the above reasons, many scientists prefer not to engage in field experimentation, with the largest deterrent the necessary confounding present in most field studies. There is a point, however, when these limitations must be endured in order to get on with some meaningful research. Let us trace the development of a seasoned researcher by considering three phases of his development. The first phase is the learning phase, in which the research principles outlined in this book are stamped into his memory and often put into practice in his own research.

This hypothetical person then moves into the second phase in which he works on a number of research projects and becomes vitally concerned with removing any and all confounding from his own research and is quick to spot inadequacies in the research of others. If this researcher, during Phase II, sits on research committees or is present at an oral defense of a master's or doctoral thesis, he is usually the most feared committee member, for he is likely to spot any transgression of standard research practice.

Many researchers, however, gradually move into a third phase as a result of growing tolerance and sophistication. Our hypothetical researcher realizes now that a careful analysis of nearly every experiment raises some difficulty. He comes to appreciate the fact that all experiments have embedded within them some degree of confounding. Even two rats who simply receive different amounts of reward also differ on a number of other factors (e.g., amount of time eating in the experimental situation, the amount of digestive juices activated, perhaps the amount of hunger reduction, amount of noneating behavior emitted in the experimental situation, and so on). What happens is that he eventually stops counting. He learns to accept a certain absence of clarity with respect to "unimportant variables" in his research in order to formulate at least general impressions.

This, then, takes us back to field studies. It is true that field studies are, for the most part, inevitably confounded, usually to a greater extent than laboratory experiments, but you should try to avoid throwing the baby out with the bathwater. Field studies can be extremely insightful and should, in many cases, be conducted despite the obvious methodological difficulties. The experimenter should always be aware of such problems, but at the same time should intelligently weigh the pros and cons of his research before deciding whether or not to run his study.

Examples of field experiments

We have chosen two fairly divergent examples to show you the potential range of field experiments, but the variety is, like the other methods, virtually unlimited.

STUDY 1—ON THE STREETS OF NEW YORK* Milgram, Bickman, and Berkowitz (1969) were interested in some of the factors drawing people into already existing crowds. In order to delineate the testing environment

---

*Milgram, S., Bickman, L., & Berkowitz, L. Note on the drawing power of crowds of different size. *Journal of Personality and Social Psychology*, 1969, *13*, 79–82.

and experimental procedure objectively, they first defined a few basic concepts:

(a) *stimulus crowd*—the original crowd size, varying from 1 to 15, was comprised of the investigators' associates;

(b) the *available population*—those pedestrians who passed within a certain distance (50 feet) of the stimulus crowd;

(c) *observable action*—the available population must emit some behavior so that it can be decided whether or not a given subject "joined" the stimulus crowd.

The subjects were 1,424 pedestrians on a busy New York City street who passed along a designated 50 feet of sidewalk during 30 one-minute trials. This sample can probably be best classified as an incidental sample. The investigators implicitly assumed that these pedestrians were representative of some larger population. The exact specification of the population was, however, not provided (some possibilities are: all pedestrians on that street at that time, all New York City pedestrians, all New York City residents, all Big City residents, all Americans, all Humans).

The procedure of Milgram et al. followed this general pattern: at a signal, the stimulus crowd entered the designated area, stopped, looked up at a sixth-floor window for 60 seconds, and then disbanded. Stimulus crowds were either of size 1, 2, 3, 5, 10, or 15 individuals, and six trials were conducted for each stimulus crowd size. The order of the 30 trials was randomized. Film records were taken for each trial, and the investigators read off the dependent variables from the film record. Two dependent variables were used: (a) the number of people who looked up at the sixth-floor without breaking stride, and (b) the number of people who actually stopped and joined the crowd in looking up. The pedestrians, of course, were never aware that they were serving in a social-psychological experiment.

Notice that this study qualifies as an experiment since an independent variable (size of stimulus crowd) was manipulated and dependent variables were employed in such a way as to *always* get a measurement. In such a design, each group essentially serves as a control for every other group. Some of the results, by the way, were (a) more people looked up without breaking stride than stopped, and (b) the amount of looking up increased as the size of the stimulus crowd increased.

STUDY 2—SUMMER CAMP STUDIES* This next piece of research combines the field experiment with a longitudinal methodology, and we summarize, in a very simplistic way, the fine research conducted by Muzafer and

---

*Sherif, M. Experiments in group conflict. *Scientific American*, November 1956. Offprint No. 454. Reprinted in *Frontiers of Psychological Research*. Selected and introduced by Stanley Coopersmith. San Francisco: W. H. Freeman and Company, 1966. Pp. 112–116.

Carolyn Sherif (pronounced Shĕreef) and their associates. The problem is group conflict, and in order to deal with natural groups, Sherif chose to work within a summer camp situation. Boys between the ages of 11 and 12 with homogeneous backgrounds were intensively screened. All boys were socially well-adjusted, had somewhat above average IQs, were from stable white, Protestant, middle class homes, did not know one another, and had no idea that they were part of a study.

All kinds of data were collected throughout the study. Tape recorders and cameras were used when possible, sociograms (questionnaires designed to tap the quantity and quality of social interaction among subjects, e.g., who is your best friend, who would you prefer to spend the afternoon with, who is the best baseball player, etc.) were administered, and informal observation of the boys accounted for much of the data.

The actual procedures differed from one summer to another, but all the studies shared a common base, in that we can identify, roughly, about three different phases. In Phase I, the groups are officially formed and allowed to develop, but in isolation from one another. This development is indicated by the boys fitting themselves into different roles, including both status (e.g., leader) and function (e.g., cook) roles, and friendships being established.

Once the first phase had run its course, Phase II, the study of intergroup relations, was initiated. The hypothesis was that when two groups have conflicting aims, the members of one group will become hostile toward members of the other group. Accordingly, competitive activities were initiated. Although the competition started out "in a spirit of good sportsmanship" the situation soon developed into open hostility between groups. Sherif observed that as intergroup hostility increased, intragroup cohesion increase.

Phase III was instituted to try to stop the war. The additional hypothesis was made that just as competition leads to friction, working for a common goal should produce harmony. At first, the groups were simply brought together socially, but rather than ease the tension, it provided additional opportunities for hostile interchanges. Finally, Sherif resorted to a series of urgent (and seemingly natural) camp-wide emergencies which, in order to be solved, required the groups to work together (e.g., water line breakdown, truck breakdown, etc.). Gradually, the groups began to tolerate and even like each other, and intergroup friendships began to form. The war was over.

The summer camp research stands as a set of classic studies, and clearly exemplifies excellent field experimentation. Conditions are experimentally manipulated, and dependent measures were recorded. The longitudinal component was smoothly incorporated as observations were made not only between phases, but within phases as well, and the resulting data can be interpreted.

chapter fifteen

scientific methods III: correlational procedures

The Concept of Correlation

The term correlation is probably familiar to most of you and is used in psychology in a way similar to everyday usage. When we say that two variables are correlated, we mean that two variables are related, or "go together." It is possible to compute a number, called a **correlation coefficient,** telling us the **degree to which** two variables have been observed to "go together." More specifically, **a correlation coefficient is a number computed from a set of data and summarizes the extent to which variations in one measure "go together" with variations in another measure.** There is a variety of correlation coefficients available, their usage depending upon the type of data collected. Each of the coefficients has a different name.

Correlational procedures may be applied to data collected by certain methodologies.* We term these methodologies **correlational research.** As was mentioned in Chapter 14, correlational research is one of the field study methods. Further recall that in correlational research, the investigator enters the

---

*This does not imply that correlations cannot be performed on data collected using experimental procedures.

to-be-sampled population with two or more dependent measures. His intent is to determine the degree to which these various measures are related to one another. In this present chapter we will deal with some of the intricacies of correlational research.

Correlational Research

Correlation vs. experimental research

Experimental research refers to those techniques, procedures, designs, etc. pertaining to the conduct of an experiment. For an endeavor to be considered an experiment, at least one independent variable must be manipulated and its effects upon a dependent variable recorded. In addition, an experiment must consist of at least two conditions, i.e., an Experimental condition and a Control condition.

Correlational research differs from experimental research in that in the former **there is no manipulation of an independent variable;** *therefore, no distinction is drawn between an Experimental and a Control condition.*

Purposes of correlational research

Because correlational research differs from experimental research, it should be clear that each is used for different purposes. Experimental research, as mentioned in earlier chapters, attempts to establish the necessary and sufficient conditions for the occurrence of a particular phenomenon. This is a positive step toward the postulation of a causal relationship. In this sense, correlational research is even more basic, in that its purpose is to determine the extent to which two events are even related. That is, it would be foolish to create an elaborate experiment to determine if X is both necessary and sufficient for the occurence of Y without first demonstrating that X is indeed related to Y.

How is correlational research done?

Most generally, correlational research attempts to determine if (and the extent to which) X is related to Y in a given population. Logically, the scientist proceeds, then, to record any and all instances of X and any and all instances of Y. The procedure is typically more elaborate than this, however, since in most behavioral research X and Y are always present; that is, they can always be measured. The issue, then, is **whether variations in X correspond or correlate** with variations in Y.

A clear example may help to illustrate these points. Assume that we wish to learn the extent to which a student's high school Grade Point Average (GPA) is related to his college GPA. Consider the former to be X and the latter to be Y. Our population might consist of those students having graduated from a nearby state university. One way of conducting this study is to randomly sample a given percentage of students from the population, check each of their transcripts to determine their high school and college GPAs, record these data, and then perform the appropriate statistical operations to yield a correlation coefficient. The data would be recorded in the form presented below:

Student	High school GPA (X)	College GPA (Y)
1	X_1	Y_1
2	X_2	Y_2
3	X_3	Y_3
.	.	.
.	.	.
.	.	.
N	X_N	Y_N

You should pay careful attention to two points contained in the schema:

1. The data are recorded in such a way that we know the particular X score and the particular Y score associated with each student. It should be clear that in order to determine the degree of the relationship, the X and Y scores *must* be appropriately paired. In other words, since you are interested in how much X and Y "go together," you must collect your data in exactly that way.

2. As you can see, there are two different measurements recorded, X and Y. To be consistent in our language, we would say that there were two dependent variables used in this study. Of course, there is no independent variable.

It may be seen, then, that correlational research involves applying at least two dependent variables to the population or to a random sample thereof. What we hope will be learned is the extent to which these dependent variables are related to one another in that population.

Uses of correlational research

There are three major uses to which correlational research may be put. They are (a) simply to describe the degree of relation between X and Y, (b) to serve as a basis for designing experimental research, and (c) to predict. The first has been mentioned already and will be given no further comment here. The second was touched on earlier when we pointed out that X and Y should be known to be related before you would attempt to determine if X was necessary and sufficient for the occurrence of Y. We will therefore limit our discussion to the third mentioned use, prediction.

Recall the example used earlier in which we collected high school and college GPAs on a random sample of students. Assume that an analysis of those data indicated a high correlation, that is, the two dependent variables were highly related. As you would suspect, the way in which these dependent variables are related may be stated as follows: The higher a student's high school GPA, the higher is his college GPA. The first thing you should realize is that this is an overall statement relating to the students in general. There would be some instances where a student with a relatively low high school GPA finished college with a very high GPA, and vice versa. Other kinds of individual fluctuations may also occur in the data as well, so that the overall correlation provides only a rough guide to some general trends rather than an accurate description of each and every student.

Given this general relationship between the two dependent variables, you might wish to draw an inference from the data. Specifically, you might say that if a student finished high school with a high GPA, the chances are fairly good that he would probably finish college with a high GPA. This inference, made on the basis of an observed high correlation, is reasonable and—if you were sitting on a college admissions board—useful as well in that it would provide at least a partial foundation for determining admission policies. To use other words, you are *predicting* that a student with a high score on the X dependent variable will **probably** have a high score on the Y dependent variable. Thus, correlation and prediction are closely related to one another.

How accurate will your prediction be? That is, given a particular X value (high school GPA) how accurately can you predict the corresponding Y value (college GPA)? Clearly, under most circumstances, you will most likely **never** be able to predict **exactly.** The reason is that although the correlation may be high, it is not, so to speak, perfect. A **perfect** correlation would indicate no student-to-student fluctuations, and we may assume that in an actual investigation of GPAs, we would scarcely find such a perfect correlation. On the other hand, suppose that the data analysis indicated no correlation, that is, zero correlation. If high school GPA were totally **unrelated** to college GPA, we should be completely unable to make anything but **chance predictions;** in other words, a zero correlation affords no linear predictive information.

Most correlations fall someplace between perfection and zero, and so, they may be of some predictive value. Obviously, the higher the correlation, the more accurate the prediction will be. We should reemphasize here that **exact** predictions are neither possible nor to be expected in these circumstances, rather, our prediction becomes an **estimate** of what we would **expect on the average.** The higher the correlation, the better the estimate should be.

Limitations of correlational research

Correlational, as experimental, research has its own limitations. Observations need to be made and theoretical frameworks need to be already in existence, and these will limit any scientific endeavor as discussed in Chapter 1. Many of the problems to be overcome in constructing experimental research must likewise be overcome in correlational research (see Chapter 9). There are some things, however, that deserve special mention in this chapter that relate to the interpretation of a correlation coefficient and will be discussed later.

The Correlational Coefficient

As already mentioned, the end result of the statistical procedures used here is called a **coefficient of correlation,** or more briefly a **correlation coefficient.** The most widely used of these procedures results in the **Pearson Product-Moment Correlation Coefficient,** and is designated by the letter r. Our discussion will limit itself, at this time, to the Pearson r.

The value of r

The lowest value the Pearson r can take is $r = 0.00$. This represents zero correlation and would indicate that X and Y are unrelated to one another in the sample. The highest value the Pearson r can take is $r = 1.00$. This indicates a perfect correlation, and would indicate that X and Y are completely related to one another in the sample. Values of r closer to one reflect more relatedness; values of r closer to zero reflect less relatedness.

The valence of *r*

A complete statement of a Pearson correlation coefficient includes not only a number but also a valence; that is, *r* may be either positive or negative. The **number** summarizes **how much** of a relationship was observed, whereas the **valence** summarizes **what kind** of a relationship was observed. A positive valence indicates that increases in the X measure correspond to increases in the Y measure, or, if you prefer, decreases in the X measure correspond to decreases in the Y measure. We say that height and weight are **positively correlated** in that, generally speaking, taller people also tend to weigh more, or shorter people tend to weigh less. Clearly, a positive correlation may be high or low depending upon how close the **value** is to 1.00 or 0.00 respectively. A negative valence indicates that **increases** in one variable (e.g., X) are associated with **decreases** in the other variable (e.g., Y). We say that the number of "accidental" pregnancies is negatively correlated with acquaintance with birth control procedures in that **fewer** such pregnancies result when **more** information about birth control procedures is made available to the participants.

Remember that the valence of *r* simply refers to the *direction* of the relationship and the number or value summarizes the *degree* of relationship. Thus, a correlation of $r = +.82$ represents the same degree of relatedness as $r = -.82$; in the first case, however, increases in X are associated with increases in Y, whereas in the second case increases in X are associated with decreases in Y.

How to Picture a Correlation

It is possible to "draw a picture" of a correlation by constructing what is called a **scatter diagram.** To construct a scatter diagram, all you need is a set of axes (an X and Y axis) and some data to plot. We have supplied a set of axes below:

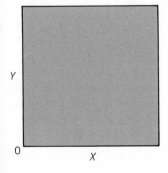

Recall that data in correlational research is collected in pairs; that is, each subject contributes an X score and a Y score. To plot your data, all you have to do is find the appropriate coordinates and put a dot there. This is illustrated in the following scatter diagram:

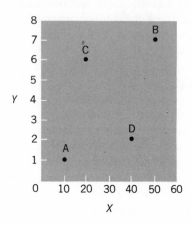

Subject	X score	Y score
A	10	1
B	50	7
C	20	6
D	40	2

Subject A gave a score of 10 on the X measure and a score of 1 on the Y measure. The dot in the lower left corner of the scatter diagram represents this juncture. Subject B gave a score of 50 on the X measure and a score of 7 on the Y measure; his dot is in the upper right corner. The other two data points were placed by the same procedures. Thus, each data point represents two measures (an X and Y measure) on each subject.

We have illustrated examples of various types of correlations in Fig. 15.1. Figures 15.1(a) and (b) reflect perfect correlations in that the data show no deviation from a general (universal) relation (i.e., a straight line). As you can see, perfect prediction is possible under these circumstances. In Fig. 15.1(a), r is positive in that increases in X are associated with increases in Y; in Fig. 15.1(b), r is negative in that increases in X are associated with decreases in Y.

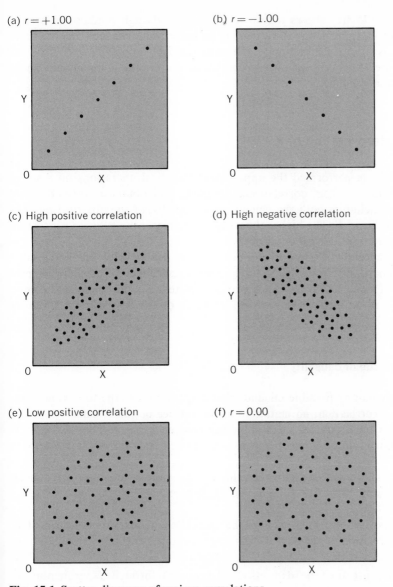

Fig. 15.1 Scatter diagrams of various correlations.

Figures 15.1(c) and (d) illustrate high correlations. Since the data show some *variability*, perfect prediction cannot be made; however, an estimate of a *Y* value given a particular *X* value should be fairly good in that there is *not that much* variability.

Figure 15.1(c) shows a low correlation. Although predictions of a Y value given a particular X value may be better than chance (because there is *some* relation), such estimates would be relatively imprecise.

Figure 15.1(f) shows a zero correlation. Here, predictions would be no better than chance.

The Interpretation of r

After having performed the appropriate statistical operations on a set of data produced from correlational research, you obtain a correlation co-efficient including both the valence and the value of the observed relation between X and Y. The higher the value or the closer the Pearson r is to 1.00 the greater the correspondence between variations of X and Y, and the more accurate will be your estimate of a particular value of one variable given a particular value of the other. This is actually as far as your interpretation of r can be taken. But a broader context should be discussed here, and it will be instructive to consider some of the issues in this broader context.

The issue of causality

To avoid any possible misunderstandings, we make the following statement: **A correlation, no matter what the valence or value, cannot be interpreted as demonstrating a causal linkage between X and Y.** This statement is true from a logical point of view as well as one that is the result of common sense.

Logically, we must go through three stages more or less in order to speak of cause and effect (see Chapter 1). These are:

1. The occurrence of Y must be correlated with the occurrence of X. This correlation might start us thinking that something of a causal relationship may exist between X and Y.

2. It must then be demonstrated (perhaps through experimental research) that X is both necessary and sufficient in a given context for the occurrence of Y.

3. Finally, on the basis of the first two steps, X may be theoretically tied to Y by the postulation of a cause-effect relation.

Correlational research, since it does not incorporate Experimental and Control conditions, cannot be brought through stage 2 of the above formulation, much less stage 3. In other words, it represents that described in stage

1, that is, the identification of some sort of reliable association between two dependent variables.

From a common sense point of view, it would also be incorrect to interpret correlation as causality. Consider these cases of a high correlation:

1. Height is positively correlated with weight.
2. The setting of the sun is highly correlated with the rising of the moon.
3. The amount of money spent to purchase a new car is positively correlated with the weight of the car.

Does increased height **cause** increased weight? Does the setting of the sun **cause** the moon to rise? Does your monetary output **cause** a car to gain weight? The answer in each case is obviously no. The correlation presumably occurs because of a set of intervening factors. Taller people weigh more because there is more body substance—the amount of which is probably genetically based and therefore determines both height and weight. The "movement" of the sun and moon results from the rotation of our planet. A more expensive car may cost more because more steel, engineering, and craftmanship went into the development of that car.

We may summarize as follows. Correlation is but one of many aspects of causality and cannot itself be interpreted as such. It therefore follows that by virtue of a linkage being causal, a correlation must exist; but it also follows that not all correlations should be accepted as indicating a causal linkage. Consequently, if you discover a correlation in your own research, you will need to engage in much additional work before you can hope to speak in causal terms.

The issue of the value of *r*

The issue of the calculated value of *r* is a critical aspect of the context within which any interpretation is made. Here is a hypothetical example to initially make the point. Researcher A finds that GPA is positively correlated with ability to solve a particular set of puzzles. He reports a correlation of $+.27$, and refers to this as a "low positive correlation." Researcher B reads the report of the first researcher and decides that A's research could be improved if all subjects sampled had comparable IQ scores. Researcher B runs the study with the addition of holding IQ constant, and observes a correlation of $+.45$, a "moderate positive correlation." Researcher C reads both reports and decides that, although B improved upon A's work, B may also be improved upon. After all, C reasons, IQ is a composite of both verbal and analytic ability. Since C conceives of puzzle solving as primarily an analytical skill, why not eliminate IQ and use instead a test of analytic ability. Upon incorporating this change into his study, C observes a correlation of $+.92$, a "high positive correlation."

If we grant that such a sequence of events could conceivably occur, what lesson may be learned? We may state this lesson as follows: **The value of the correlation is relative to the particular circumstances under which it was observed.** To speak of *the* correlation, implying some law-like stability, is clearly a misunderstanding of the statistic. That is, Researcher A, in measuring GPA, was "masking" the operation of analytical ability by introducing a host of other (and, as it turned out, extraneous) variables into the situation. Researcher B improved this state of affairs to some extent by focusing upon IQ, but could still not eliminate all the extraneous factors. Even Researcher C was not entirely successful since he, too, fell short of a perfect correlation.

It seems to us that we are led to a particular conclusion with respect to the preceding example. In principle, if not in practice, it should be possible, through a series of further refinements, to eventually reach a correlation of 1.00. If this is admitted, then the following implication may be drawn: **If a correlation exists, then it should be a perfect one. Correlations less than unity reflect the operation of unspecified factors.** Thus, to the extent that a correlation is less than 1.00, unspecified factors are introducing variance into a nonvariant relationship. In other words, correlations in nature should be either 0.00 or 1.00, and the extent to which intermediate correlations are found reflects our ignorance of the relevant factors.

A variance interpretation of r

Using the Pearson r as a base, we may give a fairly precise description of our ignorance, i.e., an estimate of those extraneous factors. For very good reasons*, the simple operation of squaring r permits us to make variance statements. For example, if r equals .50, then r^2 equals .25. We may then be justified in saying that 25% of the variance of one of the dependent variables is predictable from the variance of the other dependent variable. In other words, we know 25% of that information necessary to make a perfect prediction. Stated another way, we are 75% "ignorant" of the relevant factors comprising this relationship. Table 15.1 gives you some idea of our relative "knowledge" and "ignorance" for the range of possible r values.

An examination of Table 15.1 reveals some interesting points. First, we do not make marked gains in "knowledge" with correlations much below

---

*We do not wish to discuss the statistical justification for many statements made in this sub-section. For a brief but well presented review of the variance interpretation of r, we suggest seeing Ferguson (1971, pp. 115–117). Much of this sub-section draws upon Ferguson's discussion.

.60. In fact, our equality between "knowledge" and "ignorance" (50%–50%) corresponds to a correlation of about .70. From .70 to 1.00, we literally double the amount of predictability we have. As you can see, then, it is probably more meaningful to speak of r^2 rather than r.

Table 15.1 Amount of Variance Predictable for a Range of Values of r

r	r^2	% ''knowledge''	% ''ignorance''
.00	.00	0	100
.10	.01	1	99
.20	.04	4	96
.30	.09	9	91
.40	.16	16	84
.50	.25	25	75
.60	.36	36	64
.70	.49	49	51
.80	.64	64	36
.90	.81	81	19
1.00	1.00	100	0

This brings us to a second point. Recall our discussion of scales of measurement in Chapter 2. Applying the various sets of rules, we can easily see that percentage is a ratio scale of measurement. We may therefore say that 40% is twice as large as 20%; 50% half as large as 100%, 4% four times as large as 1%; and so forth. If 4% is four times as large as 1%, then a correlation of .20 essentially gives us four times the predictive power than a correlation of .10. We have supplied the relative "distances" between various correlation coefficients in Fig. 15.2. As can be seen from Fig. 15.2, the intervals between r values are not equal. It appears, therefore, that **the scale of measurement appropriate to r itself is only an ordinal scale.** Thus, it

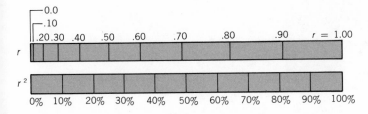

Per cent of ''knowledge''

Fig. 15.2 Intervals between various r values at various percentages of "knowledge."

is permissible to say that an r of .50 represents more of an observed relationship than an r of .20. The following two statements, however, are quite inappropriate to make:

1. *Improper*: An $r = .80$ represents an equal increase in degree of relationship over $r = .70$ as $r = .70$ represents over $r = .60$. This is improper because such a statement can be made only on interval data or better.

2. *Improper*: An $r = .50$ represents twice as great a relationship as an $r = .25$. This statement can be made only on ratio data.

Assumptions Underlying the Pearson r

A correlation coefficient may be calcuated on any set of data, since the statistical operations are simply manipulations of numbers. For the researcher to "make sense" out of the coefficient (use r to describe the relation of X and Y in the sample), however, he must make a total of five assumptions. These assumptions must be met in the data; if they are not, any statements he may put forward may be, in the strong meaning of the term, non-sense.

Assumption #1—Linearity

Linearity means that a given distribution can be best represented by a straight line function as opposed to a curved line (or curvilinear) function. Consider the scatter diagram presented below:

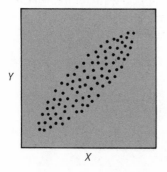

Although the data are somewhat variable, the best fitting (i.e., the most representative) function relating X and Y is a straight line. The best way to determine the curve of best fit is to engage in various curve-fitting (mathematical) procedures (i.e., method of least squares). By far, the most usual way, however, is simply to plot your data and visually determine whether or not you can meet the linearity assumption. For comparison, we have presented a curvilinear relation below:

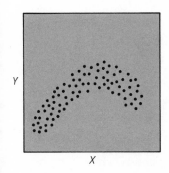

Although most data collected by behavioral scientists conform to linearity, you might occasionally come across curvilinearity. It is then necessary to use an alternative to the Pearson *r*.*

Assumption #2—Symmetrical distributions

Both the *X* variable and the *Y* variable must be distributed in a symmetrical manner. Each of the distributions in Fig. 15.3 is symmetrical and represents a sample of some of the appropriate ones.

Assumption #3—Unimodal distributions

In order to conform to this assumption, the frequency distributions of *X* and *Y* can have no more than one major mode. Even the rectangular distribution pictured in Fig. 15.3(a) is unimodal. Other unimodal distributions are given in Figs. 15.3(b) and (c). Contrast these to Fig. 15.3(d) in which a multimodal distribution is presented.

Assumption #4—Comparable distributions

Not only must the distributions of *X* and *Y* be symmetrical and unimodal, they must be comparable as well. That is, both may be rectangular

---

*You could use a *correlation ratio* in such cases. The appropriate procedures are to be found in Guilford (1965, pp. 308–317).

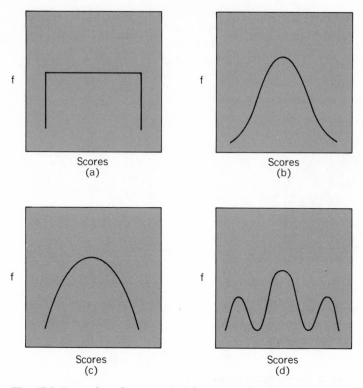

Fig. 15.3 Examples of symmetrical frequency distributions.

or normal, etc., but, for example, one may not be rectangular while the other is normal.

Assumption #5—Continuous measurement

In interpreting the Pearson r, it is necessary to assume that both the X and Y variables represent a continuous scale of measurement. Provided that these variables reflect a continuous scale of measurement, we should mention that you may, for one reason or another, wish to impose discrete categories upon the data. It would still then be possible to calculate a Pearson r on these classified data. If, however, either X or Y or both are *truly categorical* designations (e.g., male or female, Democrat or Republican, etc.), then you must use the appropriate alternative coefficient. These alternatives are mentioned later in the chapter.

Modifying your assumptions

In testing the significance of the Pearson *r*—something we will discuss shortly—we need to "tighten-up" these above mentioned assumptions. The assumption of linearity holds as given above, however, you cannot simply assume that the population is a symmetrical, unimodal distribution—you must assume that X and Y have been randomly sampled from *normally distributed* populations, and that these populations have *similar variances*.

Failing to meet the assumptions for Pearson *r*

If the data cannot meet one or more of the assumptions underlying *r* or you are not terribly sure that the data can meet them, then it may be more appropriate to use another correlation coefficient known as the Spearman Rho. We have included a consideration of the Spearman Rho later in this chapter.

Calculating the Pearson *r*

The calculation of *r* is rather simple and straightforward. We present two alternative methods that are mathematically identical. If a desk calculator is available, you will find the first method presented easier; if no such machine is available, then the second one might prove more efficient.

Method #1—Raw score formula

The raw score formula for calculating the Pearson *r* is as follows:

$$r = \frac{N\Sigma XY - (\Sigma X)(\Sigma Y)}{\sqrt{\{N\Sigma X^2 - (\Sigma X)^2\}\,\{N\Sigma Y^2 - (\Sigma Y)^2\}}}$$

In this formula, X and Y are original scores in variables X and Y, N is the number of pairs of scores considered, and Σ (read as sigma) represents the operation of summation. We have presented a set of data in Table 15.2 together with the calculation.

Table 15.2 Raw Score Method of Calculating Pearson's r

Subject	X	Y	X^2	Y^2	XY
1	17	4	289	16	68
2	13	4	169	16	52
3	12	9	144	81	108
4	11	13	121	169	143
5	9	6	81	36	54
6	9	13	81	169	117
7	7	11	49	121	77
8	3	10	9	100	30
9	6	6	36	36	36
10	2	18	4	324	36
$N = 10$	$\Sigma X = 89$	$\Sigma Y = 94$	$\Sigma X^2 = 983$	$\Sigma Y^2 = 1068$	$\Sigma XY = 721$

$$r = \frac{N\Sigma XY - (\Sigma X)(\Sigma Y)}{\sqrt{\{N\Sigma X^2 - (\Sigma X)^2\}\{N\Sigma Y^2 - (\Sigma Y)^2\}}}$$

$$r = \frac{10(721) - (89)(94)}{\sqrt{\{(10)(983) - (89)^2\}\{(10)(1068) - (94)^2\}}}$$

$$r = \frac{7210 - 8366}{\sqrt{(9830 - 7921)(10{,}680 - 8836)}}$$

$$r = \frac{-1156}{\sqrt{(1909)(1844)}}$$

$$r = \frac{-1156}{\sqrt{3{,}520{,}196}}$$

$$r = \frac{-1156}{1876.219}$$

$$r = -.616 \qquad p > .05, df = 8$$

$$r^2 = .38$$

Method #2—Deviation formula

The deviation formula for calculating the Pearson r is as follows:

$$r = \frac{\Sigma xy}{\sqrt{(\Sigma x^2)(\Sigma y^2)}}$$

In this formula, deviation scores (the lower case xs and ys) are generated by subtracting the group mean from each score. Thus, if a given X is 10 and the group mean is 13, then:

$x = X$–Mean
$x = 10$–13
$x = -3$

We use the same data from Table 15.2 to calculate the Pearson r with the deviation procedure. This is outlined in Table 15.3. Notice in Table 15.3 that both Σx and Σy are equal to zero. Stated verbally, this reads the sum of all deviations around the mean is equal to zero, and indicates in a graphic way, that the mean represents the center of the distribution. Hence, it is fitting that the mean be one of the measures of central tendency.

The Question of Significance

Having calculated a Pearson r, you next need to answer the question of reliability considered in Chapter 7. This question may be stated in one of the following three forms:

1. Is the correlation coefficient significant?
2. Did the correlation arise on the basis of random variation of scores?
3. What is the probability of the observed correlation being reliably greater than zero?

The determination of the significance of r is accomplished in an analogous way to the determination of the significance of F in Chapter 7. The computer now, however, provides a sampling distribution of the r statistic. For $df = 30$ or greater, the sampling distribution of r closely resembles the normal curve, with the mode, median, and mean all at $r = 0.00$.

Table D in Appendix B summarizes the probability of obtaining a given r value at the appropriate df from the sampling distribution of r.

To determine the significance of r we enter this table in the first column at the appropriate df (equal to N-2) and determine where your correlation falls with respect to the tabled values. For example, say you calculated an r of $-.603$ with an N of 14. The df for this example, then, is $N - 2$ equals 14 $-$ 2 equals 12. Consulting Table D, you find that you need an r of .458 or better to have significance (actually, this is borderline significance) at α equals .10. Your r can therefore be represented by $p < .10$.

Table 15.3 Deviation Method of Calculating Pearson's r

Subject	X	Y	$(X - \bar{X})$ x	x^2	$(Y - \bar{Y})$ y	y^2	xy
1	17	4	8.1	65.61	−5.40	29.16	−43.74
2	13	4	4.1	16.81	−5.40	29.16	−22.14
3	12	9	3.1	9.61	−.40	.16	−1.24
4	11	13	2.1	4.41	3.60	12.96	7.56
5	9	6	.1	.01	−3.40	11.56	−.34
6	9	13	.1	.01	3.60	12.96	.36
7	7	11	−1.9	3.61	1.60	2.56	−3.04
8	3	10	−5.9	34.81	.60	.36	−3.54
9	6	6	−2.9	8.41	−3.40	11.56	9.86
10	2	18	−6.9	47.61	8.60	73.96	−59.34
$N = 10$	$\Sigma X = 89$ $\bar{X} = 8.9$	$\Sigma Y = 94$ $\bar{Y} = 9.4$	$\Sigma x = 0$	$\Sigma x^2 = 190.90$	$\Sigma y = 0$	$\Sigma y^2 = 184.40$	$\Sigma xy = -115.60$

$$r = \frac{\Sigma xy}{\sqrt{(\Sigma x^2)(\Sigma y^2)}}$$

$$r = \frac{-115.60}{\sqrt{(190.90)(184.40)}}$$

$$r = \frac{-115.60}{\sqrt{35,201.96}}$$

$$r = \frac{-115.60}{187.622}$$

$$r = -.616$$

$$r^2 = .38$$

You also find that an r of .532 is required for significance for α equals .05. You meet this level as well. When α equals .02, however, you need an r value of .612 or higher for significance, and you fall somewhat short of this level. Assuming that you set α at .05, the proper way to record your result, including the coefficient, the df, and the probability level, is as follows:

$$r\,(12) = -.603, p < .05.$$

Spearman's Rank-Difference Correlation

Uses of Rank-Difference Correlation

Spearman's Rank-Difference Correlation coefficient, designated as ρ (rho), is generally used as a "quick" substitute for r when the sample size is small (less than $N = 30$), and must be performed on *ranked* data. For calculations on the same set of data, r is usually slightly larger than ρ, but no more than .02 units at maximum difference. Furthermore, ρ appears to be only slightly less reliable than r. Since much behavioral data is already in ranked order form, and since all quantitative data is easily transformed to ranks, it is not surprising that Spearman's ρ has proved very popular.

Because the coefficient ρ is based on ranked data, many of the assumptions demanded in properly interpreting r may be considerably lessened when computing ρ. Since ordinal measurement (ranking) is based upon a quantitative measurement scale, we must, by definition retain the assumption that X and Y may be continuously measured. On the other hand, X and Y need not be symmetrically distributed or unimodal, since the ranking procedure eliminates interval equality between scores. Furthermore, the assumption of linearity can be loosened to include even certain curvilinear relationships. That is, as long as the relationship is monotonic (i.e., consistent, shows no reversals) in that X and Y both increase or one always increases as the other always decreases, ρ may be meaningfully interpreted.

There are other similarities between the Pearson r and the Spearman ρ. One of these is that both statistics themselves are represented by an ordinal scale of measurement. A second similarity is that both can be converted to a different statistic allowing us to speak of predictable variance; r is converted to r^2 and ρ may be converted to ρ^2. As with the Pearson r, it may be more meaningful to speak of ρ^2 rather than to speak of ρ.

Calculation of ρ

The computation formula for ρ is as follows:

$$\rho = 1 - \frac{6\Sigma D^2}{N(N^2 - 1)}$$

Table 15.4 Calculation of Spearman's ρ

X	Y	X rank	Y rank	(X rank - Y rank) D	D^2
359	95	1	1	0	0
347	85	2	3	−1	1
328	80	3	4	−1	1
312	90	4	2	2	4
298	30	5	14	−9	81
287	70	6	6.5	−0.5	0.25
271	75	7	5	2	4
248	60	8	9	−1	1
239	55	9	10	−1	1
212	65	10	8	2	4
195	35	11	13	−2	4
189	70	12	6.5	5.5	30.25
170	40	13	12	1	1
166	50	14	11	3	9
				$\Sigma D = 0$	$\Sigma D^2 = 141.50$

$$\rho = 1 - \frac{6\Sigma D^2}{N(N^2 - 1)}$$

$$\rho = 1 - \frac{6(141.5)}{14(14^2 - 1)}$$

$$\rho = 1 - \frac{849}{14(196 - 1)}$$

$$\rho = 1 - \frac{849}{14(195)}$$

$$\rho = 1 - \frac{849}{2730}$$

$$\rho = 1 - .31$$

$$\rho = +.69$$

$$\rho^2 = .48$$

in which D is the difference between subject's X rank and Y rank, and N is the number of pairs of scores observed. Table 15.4 demonstrates the calculation of ρ. Notice from Table 15.4 that ties are resolved by taking the average rank of those tied scores. Remember that the highest rank must equal N.

Significance of ρ

To test the significance of ρ, enter Table E, Appendix B at the appropriate N to determine which level of significance, if any, you may have achieved. In the example in Table 15.4, we may write the following summary:

$$\rho\,(14) = +.69, p < .05.$$

Other Correlation Coefficients

Both the Pearson r and Spearman ρ are based on the assumption that both X and Y are continuous variables. In the examples already used, this continuity was reflected in the actual scores used in the analyses. We should now like to make the following two points:

1. Even though both variables are continuous, you may, for a variety of reasons, wish to impose a dichotomy upon this continuity for either one or both of the dependent variables. For example, you may dichotomize all students taking some exam into either a "Pass" or "Fail" category, or label people as either "High" or "Low" scores on some personality paper and pencil test, even though all subjects received some numerical grade (i.e., a continuous scale of measurement was used). Although you would be correct in performing a Pearson r on such data, there are available "easier" or "faster" calculational devices.

2. It may be that one or both dependent variables are really dichotomous (e.g., male or female, students or nonstudents, etc.). In these cases, you *must* use statistical procedures other than the Pearson r.

We have therefore outlined some of the coefficients of correlation used in these particular cases in Table 15.5, and recommend that you consult an appropriate source (e.g., Guilford, 1965, pp. 317–339) in times of need.

Table 15.5 Some Correlation Coefficients and the Situations in Which They May Be Used

Name	Symbol	Status of X Variable	Status of Y Variable
Biserial Coefficient	r_b	Continuous but arbitrarily dichotomized	Continuous—not dichotomized
Tetrachoric Coefficient	r_t	Continuous but arbitrarily dichotomized	Continuous but arbitrarily dichotomized
Point-Biserial Coefficient	r_{pbi}	Truly dichotomous	Continuous—not dichotomized
Phi Coefficient	ϕ	Truly dichotomous	Truly dichotomous

section four

the communication of
research

After the research project has been designed, conducted, and analyzed, the results must be put together into a logical form that should serve the purpose of communicating your research to others. The purpose of the chapter that follows is to show you the ways in which the American Psychological Association recommends that research be reported. This form, or a slightly modified version of it, is generally acceptable in most of the behavioral sciences. Where there are ambiguities, we have chosen to adopt the form used in the Journal of Experimental Psychology.

communication of research findings

Where is Research Reported?

There are many different types of sources reporting or summarizing research results of which three are valuable *general* sources of information. The first of these is textbooks. Usually a text will report summaries of research in a variety of areas, and as a consequence they can provide general background information about particular areas. One disadvantage with textbooks is that they are usually at least two years out of date when they are published. The reason for this is that most journals where the primary research is reported—and thus the textbook writer's source—have a publication lag of about a year. In addition the text itself has a publication lag of about a year.

Another thing to consider with regard to textbooks is the theoretical orientation of the author. The author's theoretical orientation will dictate the particular research he summarizes and its context. Hence, we need to use care in taking an author's interpretation of particular research results literally. If a set of results is particularly important or relevant, it is better to consult the original source rather than rely on a textbook author to report them.

A second source is called "integrating articles." These integrating articles are found in the professional journals of the field and provide an attempt either to make an integrative review of the research in the area, or propose a theoretical model that may explain a subset of the area research. Such reviews are written for the scientist, in that some prior knowledge is assumed. They are also extremely useful to the student who has some background in the research area. The integrative article differs from a text in that a great number of *specific* studies are covered, and the detail and level of analysis are typically more sophisticated than the corresponding textbook.

The third type of source available for background in an area is the published set of research reports. Ultimately, all researchers must consult this literature in order to achieve any expertise in an area. A research report communicates in detail the findings of a specific set of experiments by an investigator. The task of this chapter will be to discuss the nature, content, and style of this type of research report.

How to Use the Library

The library is an indispensable tool of the scientific researcher. Exploration of a specific area—and increasing familiarity with previous work done—will naturally raise questions yet to be answered. It is not our purpose to tell you how to use the library—your own experience or a short conversation with a cooperative librarian can provide you with an understanding of the library you are using. Rather, we would like briefly to outline some of the facilities available to you for locating appropriate reference material. Since much of your time in this type of course will be spent in searching for and reading research reports—that is, the journal literature—we will be concerned mainly with this type of source.

The card catalogue

One thing that the card catalogue does not do is list the journal literature. The best you can do is find texts that deal at least partly with your research area. You will probably be able to glean a few primary journal references from their bibliographies or reference sections. Beyond this, the card catalogue will do you little good for the kind of research being discussed here.

Psychological abstracts

The American Psychological Association (APA) publishes about fourteen different journals. One of them, *Psychological Abstracts,* is published monthly and is the only APA journal to contain no original articles.

The *Psychological Abstracts* index is organized according to the topic covered in a research report. Hence, by looking up the relevant topics in the index you will typically find listed references to several abstracts of research reports that dealt with that topic. Through careful use of the *Abstracts* it is possible to gain references to most if not all research reports on a given subject. In addition the abstract of a given report will generally give you enough information to decide whether you should read the original research report. Consequently, proper use of this particular source can be a time saver for the researcher and student alike.

Other research reports

Each research report contains a list of references, and although these lists are not necessarily complete, there is nothing wrong with supplementing your reading with them. Often, if you are lucky enough to find some fairly recent pertinent articles, most of the literature will be available through these reference sections, and your efforts with the *Psychological Abstracts* will be considerably reduced.

Annual reviews

Each year a series of volumes is published that reviews a variety of topics in a number of different fields. These reviews are usually technical and written for a sophisticated audience. Nevertheless, if the topic in which you are interested has been reviewed in recent years, the reference list as well as portions of the textual material may prove useful.

The Purpose of a Research Report

The purpose of the research report is to communicate your results and their implications to the scientific community. In the behavioral sciences a standardized form of doing this has been adapted to minimize confusion and to provide a concise form and some uniformity in style. Consequently you should be aware of the format of the research report as well as the style of writing that is most acceptable for research report purposes.

One thing to keep in mind when writing a research report is that you are communicating your experimental results to other members of the scientific community. This means that not only must you accurately represent the results that you have found, but you must convince them that your data are valid, reliable, reasonable in view of the particular experiment conducted, and that the conclusions that you have drawn from your experimental data are logical and justified. In addition, because of the prevailing tradition, it is necessary to describe your particular research effort as being a logical extension of previous research.

Some Stylistic Considerations

Tense

Since the research has been conducted prior to the writing of the report, **it is almost always appropriate to use the past tense.** Thus:

Incorrect: This experiment is designed to demonstrate . . .
Correct: This experiment was designed to demonstrate . . .

The only time that a statement would be written in the present tense is when it refers to something general, i.e., a statement held to be true both in the past and future. Thus: The partial reinforcement effect indicates [not indicated] that partial reinforcement results in greater resistance to extinction than continuous reinforcement. This reflects a general relationship and thus is time independent. Time independent statements are written in the present tense.

Person

In writing research reports, the use of the first person is vehemently discouraged. Thus:

Incorrect: I performed an analysis of variance and demonstrated that . . .
Correct: An analysis of variance indicated that . . .
Incorrect: We felt that this experiment clarified previous research . . .
Correct: It is felt that this experiment clarified previous research . . .

Standard abbreviations

Since certain words or terms are used very often in writing reports, it is to everyone's advantage to abbreviate some of them. For example, units of measurement are abbreviated. Here are some standard abbreviations:

cm = centimeters
sec = seconds
ft   = feet
V   = volts
mA = milliamps

Other abbreviations

Each research area within the major discipline has its own jargon, and in writing a research report, you may use some terms over and over in the paper. It makes everyone's task easier if such terms are also abbreviated. Since these terms may be general only to the research area, however, not all readers will be familiar with them. Thus, the first time you use a term which will be used repeatedly in the paper, you designate your abbreviation, and from then on, you use only your abbreviation; thus:

The partial reinforcement effect (PRE) indicates that partial reinforcement (PR) results in greater resistance to extinction (RE) than continuous reinforcement (CRF). The PRE is observed regardless of the measure of RE used, and is observed regardless of whether the CRF group is matched to the total number of trials or to the number of reinforced trials received by the PR group.

You must at the same time, however, exercise some discretion in the use of abbreviations. The intent is to make the paper more readable rather than making it like a coded message. Only if the term is cumbersome and will be used relatively frequently should it be abbreviated.

Source citation

Previous research that has been done, ideas previously introduced into the literature, conclusions previously drawn on the basis of particular data, etc., all need to be accurately and properly referenced in your research report. Unlike the form most familiar to you, however, footnotes are not used for this purpose. Rather, the name of the author(s) and the date of publication are given in the text. There are two formats which may be used, depending on whether the author's name is or is not going to be a part of the sentence:

Format 1: The phi-phenomenon was introduced by Wertheimer (1912). Wertheimer (1912) introduced the phi-phenomenon.

Format 2: The phi-phenomenon was introduced shortly after the turn of the century (Wertheimer, 1912).

The full reference is then given in the Reference section at the end of the report. When an article is written by two authors, the formats are as follows:

Format 1: Mowrer and Jones (1945) suggested a discrimination hypothesis.

Format 2: The discrimination hypothesis (Mowrer & Jones, 1945) is still in use today.

Notice that in Format 1 the word "and" is written out, the date is enclosed by parentheses, and no commas are used. In Format 2 the term "and" is replaced by an ampersand and a comma separates the authors from the date of publication.

When you wish to cite more than one refernce, it is best to place them in parentheses after stating your point. The citations should be placed alphabetically, separated by semi-colons. For example:

Recent evidence has suggested that exposure to pornographic material increases with educational level of the population (e.g., Brown, 1971; Drake, 1962; Jones, 1968a; b; Jones & Smith, 1964; Rogers, Smith, & Brown, 1970).

The following points should be noted:

1. Notice that "e.g.," was placed before the list of references. **E.g. is read as "for example" and should be used when the list following it is not exhaustive but rather representative.** You should take care in holding down to a minimum the total number of references used and present as best a representational sample of previously published work as you can.

2. The list is alphabetical, not chronological.

3. Jones published two articles in 1968 that you wish to cite. They are designated (a) and (b) by alphabetical order of the title of the works.

4. Within a reference, commas between authors are used only if there are three or more authors.

5. The sentence ends *after, not before,* the parentheses.

An Overview of the Report

In general the research report contains:

1. A **title** that conveys the essential purpose of the experiment.

2. An **introduction section** that describes published data and theoretical background that leads up to your experiment.

3. A **Section on methods** that presents your experimental design, your subject population, the apparatus, and the procedures you used in the acquisition of the data.

4. A **results section** in which you give the essential details of the data which you have acquired.

5. A **discussion section** in which you interpret the data that you have collected, point out the ways they relate to other data that have been published, and the implications of your data.

6. A **list of references** cited in the text of your paper.

7. The **tables and figures** to which you have referred in your paper.

8. A short **abstract** that simply summarizes your overall experiment.

The order in which we take up discussion of particular sections of the research report is not in the sequence they appear but rather in the way it may be expedient to write them. Thus, our discussion of the Method section comes first, since it is the easiest section to write and will often facilitate the writing of the other sections. When you finally come to the point of putting it all together, however, it should be arranged in the order we will indicate later.

Method Section

The section of the paper that many people write first is called the Method section. There can be several sub-sections in the Method section.

The first sub-section under Method is usually the *Subjects* section. In the subjects section you should describe in detail the subject population used. Also included is all the pertinent information that defines any special conditions to which subjects were exposed, such as special housing, lighting, or other considerations such as deprivation. For instance, if the subject population that you utilized in your experiment was college sophomores, an adequate description should contain the statement that the subjects were college sophomores and the number of males and females in the study. It is also important to describe how the subjects were selected for the experiment, especially if the process was not random.

The second sub-section under Method is the *Apparatus* or *Materials* section. The difference here is that the apparatus section entails the use of equipment rather than, as may often be used, simply a paper and pencil test. Examples of pieces of apparatus would be a T-maze, a memory drum, a display panel upon which subjects would be guessing, etc. Examples of materials would be surveys, questionnaires, or any other item which could not be conceived of as a piece of equipment, i.e., something that is not built. Within the apparatus or materials section you should describe in detail all the apparatus which was used in the acquisition of data. Enough detail should be included so that someone could, if desired (and this is not infrequently the case), duplicate your apparatus from the reported description. For example, if you are attempting a study of how humans remember certain types of verbal material the apparatus upon which the material is presented (memory drum, slide projector, etc.), the amount of time the item is exposed to the subject, the size of the material, etc. are important considerations, and changes in these factors may likewise result in a difference in obtained results. Thus, you must be very careful to present, as accurately and in as detailed a manner as possible, precisely what the apparatus consisted of as well as the other details of the experiment. If you used a specialized piece of apparatus which you have built yourself, all its essential details (e.g., measurements, color, etc.) should be presented. If the apparatus that you used is a commercially available piece of equipment then it is sufficient to call it by its common name.

A third sub-section in the method section is the *Procedure* section. In this section you should describe the manipulations made in the acquisition of your data. It would be appropriate to include the experimental design under procedure, description of the groups, description of all the stimulus conditions you controlled while collecting the data, such as the inter-trial interval, particular sequences of stimuli that may have been used, or any other parameter that defines what you did to particular groups. The amount of detail included within a Procedure section is somewhat variable, but as a general rule there should be enough of the details of the procedure used so that someone reading your Procedure section could tell exactly what you did to all the subjects, how you collected your data, and could, if the occasion merited it, replicate your procedure. The general rule to remember is to include what happened to the subjects from the beginning to the end of the experiment. If there are several groups, you should outline the general procedure experienced by all subjects in all groups, and then give additional specifics for each particular group.

A fourth sub-section that is sometimes included in the Method section is a *Design* section. The Design section usually describes the particular groups that were run and sometimes descriptions of stimulus presentations and other pertinent information. Such a section, if utilized, usually follows the Procedure or Subjects section. Unless your design is particularly complicated there is no reason to have a section by itself entitled design; rather it is better to include the design within the procedure section. A general rule to use in deciding whether or not to include a design section is whether the procedure becomes unnecessarily complicated when describing the groups.

If it does, then it may be better to separate the group descriptions into a separate section rather than presenting them within the procedure section.

Results Section

The Results section is one of the most difficult sections for the student to write correctly. The reason for this is that many students do not have any intuitive feel for what sorts of data to present here. It is difficult to decide what data best describe the results of your experiment, and it is just such data that needs to be presented in the Results section. One way to make a decision as to what data to present is to think about the purpose behind the study. If your hypothesis suggests that the various groups should differ in some particular way, i.e., you might have supposed that the groups would have acquired the material to be learned at different rates, then the bulk of your Results section should be addressed to the data that bear upon that question. Additionally, an examination of the Results sections of other published works might establish tentative guidelines for your own report.

Care should be used in describing your results in concise language before introducing any statistical test. If you found that one group did not perform as well as another group, the first sentence of your Results section should state something such as Group A performed better on that particular task than Group B. In the sentence following this you should give the statistic and probability value to substantiate your first statement. Presentation of results in this manner simplifies things for the reader. For example:

> The results indicated that meaningful material was learned more rapidly under high than low anxiety conditions, the means being 5.72 and 9.45 trials to learn respectively, and that nonmeaningful material was learned more rapidly under low than high anxiety conditions, the means being 10.30 and 21.47 trials respectively. This trend was confirmed by the finding of a significant interaction, $F (1, 86) = 14.86, p < .01$.

If you present some results in either figures or tables, the following form is to be employed:

> ... the Meaningfulness $\times$ Anxiety interaction is presented in Fig. 1. From Fig. 1 it may be seen that learning rate increased as anxiety increased for the meaningful material but decreased as anxiety increased for the nonmeaningful material.

Tables and figures are placed at the end of the report. This is merely convention. It is important that when you refer to tables and figures within the Results section that you refer to them in such a way that it does not interrupt your discussion of the data. Rather, the reader should be able to continue reading the text and at the end of the paragraph to be able to go back to the table or figure. The purpose of a table or figure, then, is to present data in much greater detail than could be conveniently done in the text.

Usually within the Results section there is very little, if any, interpretation of the data. You merely summarize your data without giving any theoretical interpretation of it. Such summaries should be as short and as concise as possible, and, additionally, no more data should be presented than serves to clarify the results of your experiment. This means that in many cases your report of results will be in terms of group scores rather than individual scores.

Discussion Section

In the Discussion section you interpret your results. The purpose of this section is to impart the implications of your particular set of results. Thus, you should point out the parallels between your results and any other results that have been reported within the scientific community, the differences between your results and other results, and any inconsistencies or extensions of present theory suggested by your data. In the case where your results can serve as steps or arguments for revising a particular theoretical position or extending it, such extensions or revisions should be presented in the Discussion section. However, you should be careful that your interpretation does not go logically beyond the limits of your data.

Introduction Section

In this section you should attempt to present the theoretical framework within which your study was conceived and also some of the relevant empirical work. In this way, your particular experiment is presented as a logical extension of past thinking and research.

This section should be viewed as an inverted pyramid in that statements at the beginning of the introduction section are general statements, broadly defining the problem and are followed by a set of logical deductions from that base. The last paragraph of the introduction (or the last few sentences) should contain rather specific statements of your experimental manipulation. This could be viewed as the apex of the pyramid. Information included in the introduction section should be fairly specific and logically arranged. Generally, you would not want to have fewer than three paragraphs nor more than seven paragraphs in the introduction section. It is for this reason we suggest that the introduction be written last and why it is the single most difficult part of the paper to write. You may find it difficult to organize the vast amount of data that is available on a given topic into a cogent, three to seven paragraph statement of the nature, scope, and design of the particular study.

Abstract

The abstract is a brief summary of your research report. Usually a sentence or two is included introducing the rationale for conducting the experiment, followed by a couple of sentences describing the subject population, and the experimental design employed. The main results should be given along with probability values, if a significant difference among conditions was found. Finally, you should include a statement that adequately summarizes the way in which you interpreted your results. A method for determining exactly what goes into an abstract is to conceive of the abstract as representing all the major sections of your paper. A good strategy in writing your abstract is to construct a couple of sentences adequately summarizing each of the major sections of your paper and placing them together in such a way that the product reads easily.

The abstract needs to be very tightly worded, since you must say all that is required in a maximum of 120 words.

Title

The title is one of the most important parts of the paper, since a person often decides whether or not to read a paper on the basis of the title alone. Therefore, it is essential that the title convey the main aspects of your experiment within the limits of 15 words or less. For instance, if your experiment is on some general phenomenon such as transfer of learning, the title of your article should contain the words "transfer of learning." If you were doing a study on marijuana smoking in college students you would want to include the term "marijuana smoking" in the title along with college students and perhaps the particular performance measure which you have utilized with the experiment. A possible title could be something like "The effects of marijuana smoking on the driving ability of college students."

References

In the Reference section you simply list in alphabetical order all of the articles which you have cited within your research report. Spell out the names of Journals rather than abbreviate them. Underline Journal names and book titles. List the references alphabetically by the last name of the first author. In the case of references for the same author(s), these should be presented in chronological order from oldest to newest. Here is a sample of a hypothetical Reference section:

Amsel, A. The role of frustrative nonreward in noncontinuous reward situations. *Psychological Bulletin*, 1958, 55, 102–119.

Capaldi, E. J. Partial reinforcement: A hypothesis of sequential effects. *Psychological Review*, 1966, 73, 459–477. (a)

Capaldi, E. J. Stimulus specificity of nonreward. *Journal of Experimental Psychology*, 1966, 72, 410–414. (b)

Capaldi, E. J. A sequential hypothesis of instrumental learning. In K. W. Spence & J. T. Spence (Eds.), *The psychology of learning and motivation*. New York: Academic Press, 1967.

Capaldi, E. J., & Kassover, K. Sequence, number of nonrewards, anticipation and inter-trial interval in extinction. *Journal of Experimental Psychology*, 1970, 84, 470–476.

Capaldi, E. J., & Spivey, J. E. Inter-trial reinforcement and after-effects at 24-hour intervals. *Psychonomic Science*, 1964, 1, 181–182. (a)

Capaldi, E. J., & Spivey, J. E. Stimulus consequences of reinforcement and nonreinforcement: Stimulus traces of memory. *Psychonomic Science*, 1964, 1, 403–404. (b)

Capaldi, E. J., & Spivey, J. E. Schedule of partial delay of reinforcement and resistance to extinction. *Journal of Comparative and Physiological Psychology*, 1965, 60, 274–276.

Hull, C. L. *Principles of behavior*. New York: Appleton-Century, 1943.

Sheffield, F. D., Roby, T. B., & Campbell, B. A. Drive reduction versus consummatory behavior as determinants of reinforcement. *Journal of Comparative and Physiological Psychology*, 1954, 47, 349–354.

Tables and Figures

Tables appear on a separate page, labeled at the top; immediately underneath is a brief description of what it represents. The table should be clearly labeled and should also be symmetric and neat.

Figures should be drawn legibly and neatly with both the ordinant and the abcissa clearly labeled. Lines drawn on the figures should clearly indicate those groups, variables, or other things being presented. The figure caption is not placed on the actual figure itself but rather is typed on a separate page, labeled Figure Captions. Each curve should be drawn in the figure and should have its data points connected with straight lines. To differentiate between two or more curves, *do not use different colors* (reproductions are only black and white)—use different types of lines (unbroken, dashed, dotted, etc.).

Footnotes

For most purposes, you need not be concerned with footnotes. Footnotes should be infrequently used, unless for some reason or other they simply *must* be present. In the event that footnotes are needed, they are referenced in the standard way and are presented near the end of the paper, typewritten, double spaced, on a page labeled Footnotes, and typed consecutively: Footnote 1, Footnote 2, and so forth.

Construction of the Research Report

The research report is constructed as follows. Care should be taken to make sure the correct format is followed.

1. Abstract. This is the first page and contains the heading Abstract as a centered heading and the 120 word summary of your results.

2. Title page with beginning of introduction. This is the second page of the report. On this page the title is centered with the author(s) names and professional affiliation presented as centered headings below the title. Following this is the introduction. There is no label as such on the introduction section.

3. Method. This is a centered heading placed below the introduction. Each sub-section in this section is indented five spaces, underlined, followed by two dashes, and the text of that subject. For example:

Method

Subjects—The subjects were 180 female college freshmen enrolled in a Psychology 1A class. The range of their ages was 18 to 36 years with a mean age of 20 years.

4. Results. This is a centered heading following the end of the Method section.

5. Discussion. This is a centered heading following the end of the Results section.

6. References. This is a centered heading on a *new* page, following your last page of discussion. This section contains a list of all works cited in your report.

7. Footnotes, if any.

8. Figure captions.

9. Tables

10. Figures.

Note that the paper should be typed *continuously* from the first page of the introduction until the end of the discussion section; all subsequent sections, such as references, footnotes, figure captions, start on separate pages even though a particular one may not fill up a complete page. The numbering of pages is accomplished in the following way: The page containing the abstract is neither numbered nor counted; the first page of the introduction is not numbered but is counted. The page immediately following page 1 of the introduction is numbered page 2, the next page 3, etc. All pages are numbered and counted through (including) the page containing the figure captions. Page numbers should appear in the upper right corner of each sheet; author name(s) should appear in the upper left corner of each type-written sheet. If you wish to submit a paper for publication it is usually necessary to submit copies in duplicate or triplicate. You should consult particular journals for style and submission requirements before final preparation of your research report.

appendix A
the analysis of research

In this book so far we have seen that the basis of the scientific enterprise resides within a theoretical framework, that there are various methodologies available to the scientist in developing or expanding upon a theory, and we have seen that there are a number of very useful research designs which may be used to answer specific kinds of questions. The conduct of research, however, does not end after the scientist has completed collecting data. These data, in and of themselves, do not supply the full amount of required information. The scientist must, as we have seen in Chapter 7, deal with the question of the reliability of the data; that is, given that an experimental condition produces a different mean than the control condition, would this same type of result continue to hold if the experiment were repeated several times? The scientist must test the data with the appropriate statistical procedures to answer this reliability question, but before using such a procedure, the data should be checked to be sure they meet the procedure requirements. The purpose of this section is to present a sample of the most frequently applied statistical procedures.

Statistical procedures are never applied at random to the data that the scientist collects in the course of his research. As we have already seen, the scientist has designed his research with the statistical procedure already in mind. Once the data are collected and the procedure is selected, he simply should run the data through the procedure to answer the reliability question. We must, however, keep in mind that the choice of a research design is dependent upon the scientist's knowledge of the available statistical methods.

The Notion of Parametric and Nonparametric

Traditionally, statistical procedures or designs are divided into two gross categories—**parametric** and **nonparametric.**

An examination of the word "parametric" quickly reveals that there are two components, *para* and *metric*. Very generally, **the term "metric" refers to a measurement operation** and, of course, in science in order to collect any kind of data, you must measure something. The term "para" modifies, in a sense, the term metric. "Para," as a prefix, refers to the notion of "beside, alongside, beyond," suggesting, then, that the term parametric refers to "something beyond measurement." What is this "something" which must take place beyond the measurement? The proper use of parametric statistics includes not only measurement but a variety of **assumptions** regarding certain characteristics of both the collected data and the population from which the same has presumably been drawn. Nonparametric statistics, on the other hand, essentially deny the "para" component of the term parametric, meaning that the assumptions underlying the use of parametric statistics are not necessarily met. Let us present the assumptions of parametric and nonparametric statistical tests.

Assumptions of parametric statistical tests

Parametric statistical tests make three general assumptions about the collected data or reference population.

First, **the selection of subjects from the population was random and independent,** that is every subject in the sample had an equal chance of being chosen from the population and the selection of one subject in no way influenced the sampling of any other.

Second, **the observations were drawn from normally distributed populations.** This assumption is usually very difficult, if not impossible, to verify, in that it would require measuring every individual in the population. The whole point of drawing a sample is to avoid the tremendous task of measuring each and every member of the population. In order to estimate whether or not the normality assumption may be reasonably made, we statistically examine the sample. If the scores themselves have a shape of a normally distributed frequently polygon, then we should feel fairly confident that the scores would be normally distributed within the population. To the extent that the sampling distribution departs from a normal shape, we should feel less confident that scores in the population were normally distributed.

Third, **the variance of each set of scores or group of scores must be comparable,** that is, the variance from subject to subject in each group must be nearly the same. This comparability of variance among the sets of scores is called **homogeneity of variance.**

Assumptions of nonparametric statistical tests

For the proper use of qualitative or nominal nonparametric statistics, the scientist needs to make only one major assumption with regard to his data: **The selection of subjects from the population was random and independent,** i.e., every subject in the sample had an equal chance of being chosen from the population and the selection of one subject in no way influenced the sampling of any other.

You will note that this assumption is the very first assumption made with regard to parametric statistical tests. **If the scale of measurement is quantitative (ordinal or higher) then we must also assume homogeneity of variance.**

It follows, therefore, that we may readily apply nonparametric statistical tests to nominal and ordinal data as well as to interval and ratio data.

The choice between parametric and nonparametric statistics

If your data meet all the necessary conditions for using parametric designs, you still have a choice as to which of the two types of statistical designs to use. What considerations enter into your decision to use either parametric or nonparametric statistics? We suggest that you follow this general rule: **When the data meet all the assumptions underlying the interpretation of parametric statistical tests, you should use parametric in preference to nonparametric designs.** (However, ANOVA procedures are robust enough to tolerate some violation of parametric assumptions.) The reasoning behind the rule can be only alluded to here, but it regards the concept of "power." Generally, the "power" of a statistical design refers to the "ability" of that design to yield a significant group difference (provided that one really exists in the population). When all the assumptions are met, many of the more commonly used parametric designs are more powerful than nonparametric ones; the parametric designs should therefore be chosen over the analogous nonparametric statistical designs.

A list of some of the available nonparametric tests and the conditions under which they are appropriate is given in Table A.1. The calculations of these statistics are given in Appendices A-III and A-IV.

Table A.1 Nonparametric Statistical Tests

	Type of Data	
Experimental design	Qualitative (Appendix A.III)	Quantitative (Appendix A.IV)
Two matched groups	McNemar test	Wilcoxon matched-pair signed ranks test
Two independent groups	χ^2 (chi square)	Mann-Whitney U test
Two or more matched groups (T $\times$ S)	Cochran Q test	Friedman two-way analysis of variance
Two or more independent groups	χ^2	Kruskal-Wallis one-way analysis of variance

A list of some of the available parametric tests listed according to the experimental design is given in Table A.2. Calculations of these tests are given in Appendices A-I and A-II.

Table A.2 Parametric Tests Classed According to Experimental Design

Experimental design	Test
Two or more independent groups	ANOVA MODEL I
T × S design (two or more matched groups)	ANOVA MODEL R-I
Two-way classification (independent groups)	ANOVA MODEL II
Two-way classification (one repeated measure)	ANOVA MODEL R-II
Three-way classification (two independent—one repeated)	ANOVA MODEL R-III
Three-way classification (one independent—two repeated)	ANOVA MODEL R-IV

The Frequency of Use of Statistical Procedures

Most of the articles published today in behavioral science journals include some form of statistical treatment of the collected data. It might be of some interest to you to learn about the "popularity" of the statistical tests and whether this popularity has changed over recent years. Edgington (1964) sampled six journals published by the American Psychological Association from 1948 to 1960—a portion of which is reproduced in Table A.3. The data in Table A.3 indicate that the statistical procedures that are available are used with comparable frequency by scientists, with a very slight emphasis upon ANOVA techniques.

Table A.3 Relative Usages of Various Statistical Designs—1948–1960 (after Edgington, 1964)

No. articles sampled	ANOVA[a]	t	Correlation[b]	χ^2	Other non-parametric
4,145	37%	30%	30%	14%	15%
				←——— 29% ———→	

[a]Includes analysis of covariance.
[b]Includes both r and ρ.

Table A.4 Relative Use of Various Statistical Designs for 1970*

No. articles sampled	ANOVA[a]			t	r	ρ	χ^2	Other non-parametric	Total no. of statistical tests
	I	R-I, II	Other						
578	4%	6%	37%	22%	11%	2%	7%	11%	1,239
	←—— 48% ——→				←— 13% —→		←—— 18% ——→		

*The authors are grateful to Dr. George L. Parrott for making these data available to us.
[a]Does not include analysis of covariance.

A recent unpublished study by George L. Parrott and Phyllis Baker of California State University, Sacramento, paralleled and updated Edgington's (1964) report. Parrott and Baker used a similar cross section of psychological journals, and employed comparable categories. A portion of their results is outlined in Table A.4. On the basis of the data given in Table A.4, and comparing these to the data in Table A.3, the clear indication is that the ANOVA designs are becoming increasingly popular and dominant in experimental work within psychology. This dominance appears to be growing at the expense of all of the other procedures, but particularly at the expense of correlational procedures.

One-Tail vs. Two-Tail Tests

We mentioned earlier that the reliability of mean differences is tested on a probability basis, that is, if the probability of obtaining the calculated value of your statistic from the sampling distribution is equal to or less than .05, that difference would be considered a reliable one. Many of the statistics which will be outlined in this section may be "tested" (determining its probability of occurrence) by either a one- or two-tailed procedure. All we wish to say on this point is:

1. If the direction of the mean difference is predicted before conducting the research, then ordinarily a **one-tailed** test should be used.

2. If no direction is predicted, then ordinarily a **two-tailed** test should be used.

Generally speaking, the use of a two-tailed test is more conservative than a one-tailed test (will lead to fewer Type II errors, in that fewer significant differences will be obtained). Some of our tables list values of the statistic needed for a judgment of significance at several alpha levels for both one- and two-tailed tests, and it may help you to know that the alpha level for a one-tailed test is exactly one half the alpha level of a two-tailed test. All probability figures for the results of the statistical tests presented in the following chapters are for **two-tailed** tests unless stated otherwise.

A Note on Perspective

The sections in Appendix A focus on statistical procedures for the analysis of data, and once again we suggest that you separate the trees from the forest. The use of statistics is simply one of many tools available to the scientist and—like any tool—they are only a means to an end. The end point for the scientist in our discussion here is a short but cogent statement of the outcome of his research. The use of statistical tools helps permit the scientist to construct his statement.

Obviously, then, this text is not meant to be a statistics book. Such a book would attempt to have you understand the intricacies of the statistical procedures themselves. All too often, the scientist himself does not understand the underlying statistical reasoning behind these procedures; this may or may not be acceptable, depending on a number of considerations. The point is that statistics usually occupies only a small percentage of the time spent on research, and although it is still a vital part of the research enterprise, we are asking you to keep statistics in proper perspective.

The following information should be treated as reference material. We therefore suggest that each procedure be studied as your needs require.

analysis of independent group designs

Independent group designs are those in which **each subject contributes exactly one score to the data analysis** and in which each subject was randomly assigned to a group. Consequently, each value of the independent variable in the design is represented by a **different** group of subjects.

There are only three general types of independent group designs which are widely utilized in behavioral research. these are the one-way, two-way, and three-way classification designs. These classifications are assumed to be fixed in that a variable is assigned different values by the experimenter. Our purpose here will be to present the **statistical procedures** for the analysis of data collected according to these fixed model independent group designs.

ANOVA MODEL I

Overview

A one-way classification design consists of several values of one independent variable and is analyzed by a **one-way**

analysis of variance (one-way ANOVA). The calculations made utilizing the ANOVA procedures result in an *F*-ratio. A short description of the *F*-ratio is given in Chapter 7 and should be reviewed before proceeding.

Recall that the *F*-ratio is the ratio of the variance between groups to the variance within groups. To compute an *F*-ratio we must estimate these two variances. In the process of obtaining an estimate of these two variances, we first calculate a statistic called the sum of squares (SS) for each **source of variance**. From the SS we calculate the mean square (MS) by dividing the sum of squares by the appropriate (**df**) degrees of freedom. The mean square is an **estimate** of the variance.

Computation procedures and numerical example

The computation of an *F*-ratio for data collected according to a one-way classification design is fairly simple. First arrange your data by groups as shown in Table I.1. Next you should compute some simple statistics on these data. These are given at the bottom of Table I.1. The data in Table I.1 are latency measures collected under several different dosage levels of d-amphetamine or speed. The basic question we wish to answer is: Does this drug affect latency of response, and, if so, is the affect differentially related to dosage level.

Table I.1 Response Latencies in Seconds for a Drug Experiment

Placebo (Fake drug)		Dose 1 (Low)		Dose 2 (Medium)		Dose 3 (High)		
S_1	3.5	S_{10}	3.5	S_{20}	3.3	S_{29}	4.7	
S_2	3.6	S_{11}	3.1	S_{21}	2.4	S_{30}	3.4	
S_3	4.0	S_{12}	2.7	S_{22}	2.9	S_{31}	3.3	
S_4	3.1	S_{13}	3.0	S_{23}	3.5	S_{32}	4.6	
S_5	3.0	S_{14}	3.6	S_{24}	2.8	S_{33}	4.2	
S_6	3.7	S_{15}	3.3	S_{25}	2.6	S_{34}	4.0	
S_7	3.5	S_{16}	3.6	S_{26}	3.0	S_{35}	3.6	
S_8	3.4	S_{17}	3.4	S_{27}	3.2	S_{36}	3.9	
S_9	3.0	S_{18}	3.0	S_{28}	3.1			
		S_{19}	2.9					
$\Sigma X_1 =$	30.80	$\Sigma X_2 =$	32.10	$\Sigma X_3 =$	26.80	$\Sigma X_4 =$	31.70	$\Sigma\Sigma X_1 =$
$\Sigma X_1^2 =$	106.32	$\Sigma X_2^2 =$	103.93	$\Sigma X_3^2 =$	80.76	$\Sigma X_4^2 =$	127.51	121.40
$X_1 =$	3.42	$X_2 =$	3.21	$X_3 =$	2.97	$X_4 =$	3.96	
$n_1 =$	9	$n_2 =$	10	$n_3 =$	9	$n_4 =$	8	$N = 36$

The calculation is given in Table I.2. The first step in computing an F-ratio on most ANOVA procedures is to calculate the correction term designated as computation factor 1 in Table I.2. This is simply the sum of all the scores across groups, squared and divided by the total number of observations (N). The second term in this procedure is calculated by squaring each score and then taking the sums across groups; this term is designated computational factor 2 in Table I.2. The third computational term is the sum of all the scores in each group, squared, divided by the number of subjects in that group (n_i), and then summed across groups; this term is designated computational factor 3 in Table I.2. These calculations are summarized in part a of Table I.2.

Table I.2

---

a)
$$1. = \{\Sigma(\Sigma X_i)\}^2/N = (121.40)^2/36 = 409.38$$
$$2. = \Sigma(\Sigma X^2) = (3.5^2 + 3.6^2 + 4.0^2 + \ldots + 3.6^2 + 3.9^2) = 418.52$$
$$3. = \Sigma(\Sigma X_i)^2/n_i = (30.8)^2/9 + (32.1)^2/10 + (26.8)^2/9$$
$$+ (31.7)^2/8 = 413.86$$

---

b)
$$\text{Sum of squares}_{(\text{between})} = (3) - (1) = 413.86 - 409.38 = 4.48$$
$$\text{Sum of squares}_{(\text{within})} = (2) - (3) = 418.52 - 413.86 = 4.66$$
$$\text{(error)}$$
$$\text{Sum of squares}_{(\text{total})} = (2) - (1) = 418.52 - 409.38 = 9.14$$

---

c)
$$df_{(\text{between})} = k - 1 = 4 - 1 = 3$$
$$df_{(\text{within})} = N - k = 36 - 4 = 32$$
$$df_{(\text{total})} = N - 1 = 36 - 1 = 35$$

Once you have calculated the three terms just described, the sum of squares can easily be calculated as shown in part b of Table I.2. Next the mean square is calculated by dividing the sum of squares by its appropriate degrees of freedom. Degrees of freedom, as you may recall from Chapter 7, for the between groups variance, are the number of groups minus one, while the degrees of freedom for the within groups variance are the total number of subjects minus the number of groups. These procedures are summarized in part c of Table I.2 and the final ANOVA summary including the value of F ($MS_{\text{between}}/MS_{\text{error}}$) is given in Table I.3. Note that the between group SS and the within group SS should add up to the total SS.

The value of F obtained from the data is 10.64 for 3 and 32 degrees of freedom. To determine the probability of obtaining an F value this large, we need to examine Table F in Appendix B. Since our value of F far exceeds the value needed for even $\alpha = .001$, we accept the hypothesis that

Table I.3 ANOVA Summary

Source of variation	SS	df	MS	F-ratio
Drug Level (between groups)	4.48	3	1.49	10.64
Experimental Error (within groups)	4.66	32	.14	
Total	9.14	35		

injection of different amounts of the drug resulted in a reliable change in responding, $F(3, 32) = 10.64, p < .05$.

What the foregoing statement indicates is that differences in dosage level of the drug produce some differential behavior; however, the ANOVA procedure does not tell us if any of the differences between groups might be reliable. In order to determine this, further analysis must be done.

The first step in getting some idea of where differences might be found is to plot the data. The data from the drug experiment are plotted in Fig. I.1. Inspection of Fig. I.1 should reveal some rather interesting trends in the data. It appears that as we increase dosage of the drug from a zero level (placebo) up to a medium dose, latency tends to decrease. However, a high dosage of the drug results in longer latencies than a zero dose. Now the question is, are any of these differences significant, that is, do any of the means in Fig. I.1 significantly differ from each other? To determine the reliability of other differences, we must use a **Multiple Comparison Test.**

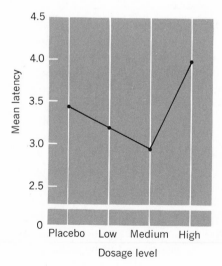

Fig. I.1 Latency as a function of drug dosage.

Multiple Comparison Tests

We have just said that the overall F-ratio, though significant, is not the end of our statistical analysis. In order to find out which group means are reliably different, we need one more analysis. The analysis is a Multiple Comparison Test. **A Multiple Comparison Test is a test that enables us to compare any and all mean differences in terms of their reliability.** There are many such tests available, and we list some of the most frequently used ones:

1. Scheffé Test
2. Tukey (a) Test
3. Tukey (b) Test
4. Newman-Keuls Test
5. Duncan's Multiple Range Test
6. t-test

These tests may be used to obtain a variety of results depending on the questions being asked. Generally speaking, the Newman-Keuls procedure and the Duncan test are not recommended by mathematical statisticians. The Scheffé test is not recommended for making all possible comparisons between means. The most useful test for making comparisons is the Tukey (a) Test. We have outlined the use of the Tukey (a) Test for making comparisons between means in the following section.

Tukey's (a) test

The Tukey (a) Test is a useful statistic for comparing each group to every other group (pairwise) to determine which group means are significantly different from each other. The test involves the calculation of a range statistic (HSD) for each rank that separates one mean from the next. If the difference between these means is larger than the range statistic then the means are reliably different from each other. The computation of the range statistic is given by the following formula:

$$HSD = q(\alpha, df)\sqrt{\frac{MS_{error}}{n}}$$

where $q(\alpha, df)$ = a range statistic for the actual significance level of the F value, and

df = the degrees of freedom for the MS_{error}.

In the event the n's in each group are unequal, we can use an approximation method for determining HSD. This method uses a harmonic mean (n) for the group size which is given by the following formula:

$$\tilde{n} = \frac{k}{\left[\dfrac{1}{\tilde{n}_1} + \dfrac{1}{n_2} + \cdots \dfrac{1}{n_j}\right]}$$

This harmonic group size is then used in place of n in the general HSD formula. This procedure *should not* be used if the n's differ greatly from each other.

The use of this procedure can be illustrated by considering the data in Table I.1 and the resulting ANOVA given in Table I.3. The first step is to rank order the means from smallest to largest. For the present data the rank order of means would be Dose 2 (2.97), Dose 1 (3.21), Placebo (3.45), and Dose 3 (3.92). We arrange these means as in Table I.4 and find the difference between each pair of means. Each Row 1 difference is each of the group means minus the Dose 2 mean, while the Row 2 differences are each of the remaining group means minus the Dose 1 mean, etc.

Table I.4 Summary of Tukey Procedure

	Treatments		Dose 2	Dose 1	Placebo	Dose 3
		Mean	2.97	3.21	3.42	3.96
	Dose 2	2.97		.24	.45	.99
a)	Dose 1	3.21			.24	.71
	Placebo	3.42				.54
	Dose 3	3.96				

Tabled q value $= 4.78$
$df = 32, \alpha = .01$

b) $\quad \tilde{n} = \dfrac{4}{(1/9) + (1/10) + (1/9) + (1/8)} = 8.94$

$HSD = q\sqrt{MS_{error}/\tilde{n}}$

$\quad\quad\quad = q\sqrt{.14/8.94}$

$\quad\quad\quad = .12q = (.12)(4.78)$

$\quad\quad\quad = .57$

		Dose 2	Dose 1	Placebo	Dose 3
	Dose 2		—	—	*
c)	Dose 1			—	*
	Placebo				
	Dose 3				

Once we have obtained these differences between means we need to calculate HSD. We do this by looking up in Table G in Appendix B q (α, df) for the maximum number of steps (r) the means are apart. If there are two means $r = 2$, if there are three means $r = 3$, five means $r = 5$, and so on. For our data $r = 4$ and the corresponding value of q (.01, 32) for $r = 4$ is 4.78. Next we calculate HSD as in part b of Table I.4. If any of our mean differences given in part a of Table I.4 exceed HSD (.57), then these means are significantly different. The easiest method for determining which differences are significant is as follows:

1. Enter row 1 of part a of Table I.4. Look at the difference score at the extreme right end of the row. This is the difference between the largest and smallest mean (the largest difference score). If it exceeds HSD then consider the difference immediately to the left which is the second largest difference score in that row. If it exceeds HSD repeat the procedure until a difference is found which doesn't exceed HSD. Stop for that row at that point since all differences to the left of that point are smaller than HSD.

2. Repeat this procedure for each row until a row is entered where the extreme right difference is smaller than HSD. Stop, for there cannot be any significant differences to the left of this one or below it, since they are all smaller.

The summary of the multiple comparisons using this procedure is given in Part c of Table I.4. Only the means of the Dose 3 group vs. the Dose 2 group and the means of the Dose 3 group vs. Dose 1 group are significant using this procedure.

We can say that as a result of the injection of the drug that Dose 3 resulted in reliably ($p < .01$) higher response latencies in comparison to Dose 2 or Dose 1, but not the placebo condition. Notice that the results of the study are most accurately described through the use of this procedure.

A Note on the *t*-test

Before leaving the one-way classification ANOVA, we should mention an alternative but more limited procedure, namely, the *t*-test. Through a procedure analogous to the one-way ANOVA, it is possible to compute a statistic known as *t*. The *t* procedure is more limited than the one-way ANOVA in that *t* can be calculated on only **two** independent groups, whereas F can be calculated on **any number** of independent groups. They are alternatives in the sense that, for a two-group design, $F = t^2$. It makes little sense to us to demonstrate both procedures, since the one-way ANOVA can be used in place of *t* when there are two groups or it can only be used for more than two groups. For those who are interested, the t procedure is outlined in most introductory statistics texts.

ANOVA MODEL II

The two-way ANOVA procedure for independent groups is similar to the one-way procedure except that here we are dealing with two independent variables. Since there are two independent variables, there must be three F-ratios, one for each main variable and one for the interaction.

A numerical example

Like the one-way, in the two-way procedure we must calculate the correction term, computational factor 1, which is similar to that in the one-way procedure. We must also calculate the sum of each score squared, computational factor 2, plus three other computational terms. In order to calculate the last three computational terms, we must arrange the data into an

Table I.5 Data from Anxiety Study

		Raw Data		
			B—Task	
		motor task b_1	verbal task b_2	memory task b_3
		12	15	16
		10	14	14
	a_1 = High Anxiety	15	13	17
		9	17	20
a)		7	20	22
		8	19	19
	A — Anxiety Level			
		12	12	10
		15	11	9
	a_2 = Low Anxiety	14	9	6
		17	18	10
		9	13	11
		10	10	8

Table I.5 (Continued)   Totals

AB Summary Table		b_1	b_2	b_3	
b)	a_1	61	98	108	267
A	a_2	77	73	54	204
		138	171	162	471

c)
1. $= (\Sigma X_i)^2/n\mathrm{AB} = (471)^2/6 \times 2 \times 3 = 6162.25$
2. $= \Sigma X_i^2 = (12^2 + 10^2 + 15^2 + \ldots + 10^2 + 11^2 + 8^2) = 6765.00$
3. $= \Sigma(\mathrm{A}_i)^2/n\mathrm{B} = (267^2 + 204^2)/6 \times 3 = 6272.50$
4. $= \Sigma(\mathrm{B}_i)^2/n\mathrm{A} = (138^2 + 171^2 + 162^2)/6 \times 2 = 6210.75$
5. $= \Sigma(\mathrm{AB}_i)^2/n = (61^2 + 98^2 + \ldots + 73^2 + 54^2)/6 = 6527.17$

d)
$\mathrm{SS_A} = (3) - (1) = 6272.50 - 6162.25 = 110.25$
$\mathrm{SS_B} = (4) - (1) = 6210.75 - 6162.25 = 48.50$
$\mathrm{SS_{AB}} = (5) - (3) - (4) + (1)$
$\quad\quad = 6527.17 - 6272.50 - 6210.75 + 6162.25 = 206.17$
$\mathrm{SS_{within\ error}} = (2) - (5) = 6765.00 - 6527.17 = 237.83$
$\mathrm{SS_{total}} = (2) - (1) = 6765.00 - 6162.25 = 602.75$

e)
$df_\mathrm{A} = \mathrm{A} - 1 = 2 - 1 = 1$
$df_\mathrm{B} = \mathrm{B} - 1 = 3 - 1 = 2$
$df_\mathrm{AB} = (\mathrm{A} - 1)(\mathrm{B} - 1) = (2 - 1)(3 - 1) = 2$
$df_\mathrm{error} = \mathrm{AB}(n - 1) = 2 \times 3 \times 5 = 30$
$df_\mathrm{total} = n\mathrm{AB} - 1 = 6 \times 2 \times 3 - 1 = 35$

AB summary table which summarizes each cell with the sum of all the observations in that cell. The data from a hypothetical experiment which reports the effects of anxiety on different performance tasks are presented in Table I.5. The scores in each cell are errors made by the various subjects in each group under the conditions indicated. The AB summary table is given in part b of Table I.5 for these data. The values in each cell are the total number of errors made by each group. The scores are then summed across rows and columns to get row and column totals.

The computational formulas for the various computational terms are given in part c of Table I.5. Computational factor 3 is each row sum squared and all added, then divided by n and multiplied by the number of B levels (B). Computational factor 4 is similar to 3 except that it deals with the column totals. Computational factor 5 is the value of each cell in the AB summary table squared, summed, and divided by n.

The methods for calculation of the various sums of squares is given in part d of Table I.5 and the method for determination of the various df is given in part e of Table I.5.

Table I.6 gives a summary of the results of the ANOVA and the corresponding F values for each variable and the interaction. The values of F for each of these was obtained by dividing each mean square by the mean square error.

Table I.6 Summary of ANOVA Procedure

Source of variation	SS	df	MS	F-ratio
A–Anxiety	110.25	1	110.25	13.92
B–Type of Test	48.50	2	24.25	3.06
A × B–Anxiety × Type of Test	206.17	2	103.09	13.01
Error	237.83	30	7.92	
Total	602.75	35		

The next step is to determine if any of these F values are significant. Reference to Table F in Appendix B indicates that for 1 and 30 degrees of freedom and $\alpha = .05$, an F value of 4.17 is required. Hence, we would conclude the level of anxiety (variable A) was reliably affecting the performance of the subjects, $F(1, 30) = 13.92, p < .05$. An F value of 3.32 is required for 2 and 30 degrees of freedom and $\alpha = .05$. The value of F for the B variable (type of Test) in our experiment is below this value so we conclude that the subjects' performance was not reliably different on the various tests, $F(2, 30) = 3.06, p > .05$. However, the value of F for the interaction is significant, $F(2, 30) = 13.01, p < .05$, which means that anxiety level and Test Type are differentially affecting the subject's performance.

To gain a clue as to the nature of this interaction, we need to plot the data presented in Table I.5. The data given in Table 5 are plotted in Fig. I.2. This figure indicates that if anxiety is high, performance is worse on verbal and memory tasks, whereas under low anxiety, performance on these two tasks improves. This means that the Anxiety Level and Type of Task interact to affect performance.

ANOVA MODEL III

The three-way classification ANOVA is very similar to the two-way except for one additional main effect (C factor) and the possibility of several dif-

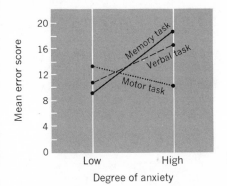

Fig. I.2 Plot of data given in Table I.5.

ferent interactions including a triple interaction. Hence, in the three-way ANOVA we need to estimate the variance for three main effects (A, B, and C), three double interactions (A × B, A × C, and B × C), and one triple interaction (A × B × C). For this analysis we need to compute nine computational terms, the correction term (1), the sum of the squares (2), three terms associated with the main effects (3, 4, 5), three terms associated with the second order interactions (6, 7, 8), and one associated with the triple interaction (9). In order to facilitate the computation of these terms, we need to reduce the data into several smaller tables.

Computational procedures and numerical example

A set of unpublished data from a clinical psychology experiment designed according to a three factor independent design is given in Table I.7. The three variables studied in this experiment were several treatment techniques for juvenile delinquents. Factor A was the Maturity Level of the youngsters—High or Low. Factor B was the Quality of the Counseling program administered to the youngsters (defined by the counselor's supervisors)—High Quality, Medium, or Poor. The third factor was the Type of Counseling Treatment that was used—Behavior Modification or Transactional Analysis. Hence, the design of the experiment was a 2 × 3 × 2 factorial independent group design. It was hypothesized by the investigators that Transactional Analysis would be a more effective type of Counseling for High Maturity subjects, while Behavior Modification would be a more effective Type of Treatment for Low Maturity subjects. The degree of effectiveness would vary as a direct function of the Quality of Counseling. The dependent variable was the mean amount of change on a large number of personality factors between reception and release. Positive values represent improvement; negative values represent impairment.

Table I.7 Data From a Juvenile Delinquency Study

a)

	Behavior modification (c_1)			Transactional analysis (c_2)		
	b_1 Q.C.	b_2 M.C.	b_3 P.C.	b_1 Q.C.	b_2 M.C.	b_3 P.C.
	.25	.21	−.62	1.30	.51	−.08
	.26	−.10	−1.33	1.18	.40	−.01
	.30	−.21	−.99	.08	−.99	.15
a_1–Hi Maturity	−.10	−.31	.18	.98	−.08	−.21
	.50	.08	.56	1.01	.16	.10
	−.25	.22	−.51	.98	.18	−.26
A–Maturity Level	.96	−.11	−2.71	5.53	.18	−.31
	.99	.08	−.02	−.08	−.08	−1.01
	.76	.01	−.07	−.22	−.64	−.91
	.05	.04	.10	−.46	−.42	−2.01
a_2–Low Maturity	.16	.21	.16	−.18	.03	−.76
	.23	−.16	.03	−.19	.08	−.81
	.41	−.01	−.72	−.31	−.91	−.04
	2.60	.17	−.52	−1.44	−1.94	−5.54

$G = -3.13$

b)

ABC Summary Table

	c_1			c_2		
	b_1	b_2	b_3	b_1	b_2	b_3
a_1	.96	−.11	−2.71	5.53	.18	−.31
a_2	2.60	.17	−.52	−1.44	−1.94	−5.54

AB Summary Table

	b_1	b_2	b_3	
a_1	6.49	.07	−3.02	3.54
a_2	1.16	−1.77	−6.06	−6.67
	7.65	−1.70	−9.08	

AC Summary Table

	c_1	c_2	
a_1	−1.86	5.40	3.54
a_2	2.25	−8.92	6.67
	.39	−3.52	

BC Summary Table

	c_1	c_2		
b_1	3.56	4.09	7.65	15.30
b_2	.06	−1.76	−1.70	−3.40
b_3	−3.23	−5.85	−9.08	−18.16
	−.39	−3.52	−3.13	

Table I.7 (Continued)

---

1. $= (\Sigma X_i)^2/n\text{ABC} = -3.13^2/6 \times 2 \times 3 \times 2 = .14$
2. $= \Sigma X_i^2 = (.25^2 + .26^2 + .30^2 + \ldots + -.04^2) = 23.72$
3. $= (\Sigma A_i^2)/n\text{BC} = (3.54)^2 + (-6.67)^2/6 \times 3 \times 2 = 51.02/36 = 1.58$
4. $= (\Sigma B_i^2)/n\text{AC} = (7.65)^2 + (-1.70)^2 + (-9.08)^2/6 \times 2 \times 2 = 143.85/24 = 5.99$

c) 5. $= (\Sigma C_i^2)/n\text{BC} = (.39)^2 + (-3.52)^2/6 \times 3 \times 2 = 12.54/36 = .35$
6. $= \{\Sigma(AB)^2\}/n\text{C} = \{(6.49)^2 + (.07)^2 + \ldots + (-6.06)^2\}/6 \times 2 = 92.45/12 = 7.70$
7. $= \{\Sigma(AC)^2\}/n\text{B} = \{(-1.86)^2 + \ldots + (-8.92)^2\}/6 \times 3 = 117.25/18 = 6.51$
8. $= \{\Sigma(BC)^2\}/n\text{A} = \{(3.56)^2 + \ldots + (-5.85)^2\}/6 \times 2 = 77.16/12 = 6.43$
9. $= \{\Sigma(ABC)^2\}/n = \{(.96)^2 + (-.11)^2 + \ldots + (-5.54)^2\}/6 = 82.57/6 = 13.76$

$SS_A = 3 - 1 = 1.58 - .14 = 1.34$
$SS_B = 4 - 1 = 5.99 - .14 = 5.85$
$SS_C = 5 - 1 = .35 - .14 = .21$
$SS_{AB} = 6 - 3 - 4 + 1 = 7.63 - 1.58 - 5.99 + .14 = .20$

d) $SS_{AC} = 7 - 3 - 5 + 1 = 6.51 - 1.58 - .35 + .14 = 4.72$
$SS_{BC} = 8 - 4 - 5 + 1 = 6.43 - 5.99 - .35 + .14 = .23$
$SS_{ABC} = 9 - 6 - 7 - 8 + 3 + 4 + 5 - 1 = 13.76 - 7.63 - 6.51 - 6.43$
$\qquad + 1.58 + 5.99 + .35 - .14 = 2.40$
$SS_{error} = 2 - 9 = 23.72 - 13.76 = 9.96$
$SS_{total} = 2 - 1 = 23.72 - .14 = 23.17$

$df_A = A - 1 = 2 - 1 = 1$
$df_B = B - 1 = 3 - 1 = 2$
$df_C = C - 1 = 2 - 1 = 1$
$df_{AB} = (A - 1)(B - 1) = (2 - 1)(3 - 1) = 2$

e) $df_{AC} = (A - 1)(C - 1) = (2 - 1)(2 - 1) = 1$
$df_{BC} = (B - 1)(C - 1) = (3 - 1)(2 - 1) = 2$
$df_{ABC} = (A - 1)(B - 1)(C - 1) = (2 - 1)(3 - 1)(2 - 1) = 2$
$df_{error} = ABC(n - 1) = 2 \times 3 \times 2(6 - 1) = 60$
$df_{total} = N - 1 = 72 - 1 = 71$

The raw data from this experiment are given in part a of Table I.7. The grand total of all the scores is given below the table. This total is used to calculate the correction term (1) in part c of Table I.7. Part b of Table I.7 gives the various summary tables needed to facilitate calculation of the various computational terms. The ABC summary table is the sum of all the observations in each cell and is used to calculate term (9). Summary table AB is the sum across c levels in the ABC summary table. This means that a_1b_1 under c_1 is added to a_1b_1 under c_2, a_1b_1 under c_1 is added to a_1b_2 under c_2, and so forth. For example, cell a_1b_1 is 6.49. This value was obtained by adding cell $a_1b_1c_1$ (.96) with cell $a_1b_1c_2$ (5.53). Likewise cell a_2b_2 is -1.77. This was obtained by adding cell $a_2b_2c_1$ (.17) with cell $a_2b_2c_2$ (-1.94). The other cells in the AB summary table were derived in a like manner. The cell entries in this table are used to calculate computational term (6) and the row totals to calculate computational term (3). The AC and BC summary tables are similar to the AB summary table except the AC summary table has entries added across B levels while the BC table has entries added across A levels. The AC cell entries are used to calculate computational term (7) and the column totals to calculate computational term (5). The BC cell entries are used to calculate computational term (8) and the row totals computational term (4). The calculation of these various computational terms is given in part c of Table I.7.

The calculation of the various sums of the squares from the computational terms is given in part d of Table I.7. The calculation of the degrees of freedom for each source of variance are given in part e of Table I.7.

The summary of the ANOVA results on the data given in part a of Table I.7 is presented in Table I.8. Table F in Appendix B indicates that Factor A (Maturity Level) had a significant affect on the dependent variable, $F (1, 60) = 7.88$, $p < .05$. Factor B (Quality of Counseling) also had a significant affect on the dependent measure, $F (2, 60) = 16.0$, $p < .05$; while Factor C (Type of Counseling) did not have a reliable affect on the dependent variable, $F (1, 60) = 1.24$, $p > .05$.

The AB interaction was not significant. Here the sum of squares was near zero, indicating that a plot of this interaction should result in lines that are nearly parallel. A plot of this interaction is presented in Fig. I-3.

Table I.8 Summary Table

Source of variation	SS	df	MS	F-ratio
A	1.34	1	1.34	7.88
B	5.85	2	2.72	16.00
C	.21	1	.21	1.24
AB	.20	2	.10	1.18
AC	4.52	1	4.52	26.59
BC	.23	2	.12	.71
ABC	2.40	2	1.20	7.06
Error	9.96	60	.17	
Total	23.17	71		

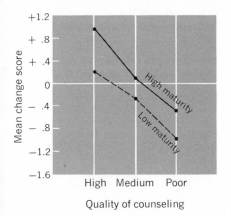

Fig. I.3 Plot of the AB interaction.

The AC interaction is significant, $F(1, 60) = 26.59$, $p < .05$. In order to determine the nature of this interaction we must plot it. A plot of this interaction is given in Fig. I.4. It can be seen from Fig. I.4 that High Maturity subjects do better under Transactional Type of Counseling while Low Maturity subjects do better under a Behavior Modification program. In fact, it appears that Transactional Analysis has a negative effect on Low Maturity subjects, while Behavior Modification had a slight negative effect on High Maturity subjects.

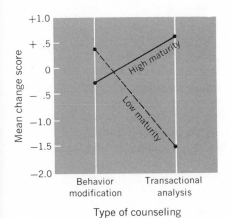

Fig. I.4 Plot of the AC interaction.

The Quality of Counseling × Type of Counseling interaction was not significant, $F < 1$, but the triple Maturity Level × Quality of Counseling × Type of Counseling interaction was significant, $F(2, 60) = 7.06$, $p < .05$. To gain some insight into this interaction, we must plot it. The plot of this

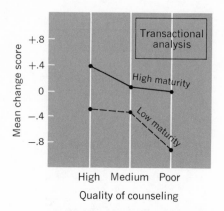

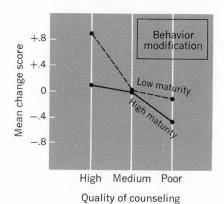

Fig. I.5 Plot of triple interaction.

interaction is given in Fig. I.5. Inspection of Fig. I.5 indicates that this interaction was in part due to the tendency of Low Maturity subjects to show a greater decrement as the Quality of Counseling declined under Transactional Analysis and the tendency under Behavior Modification of the high maturity subjects to decline as Quality of Counseling decreased.

repeated measures designs

Repeated measures designs are those which incorporate several observations on the same subject. That is, each subject may contribute **more than one score to the analysis.** The repeated measure dimension usually is a time variable, meaning that measures on subjects are taken across time.

There are three main types of repeated measures designs which enjoy some popularity, the most common of which are the **mixed designs.** These are designs which combine both repeated measures and independent groups within the same study. The simplest repeated measures design (T × S design), which you may recall involves all subjects being observed under all treatment conditions, is considerably less frequently employed because, in its simplicity, it can provide only very limited information. Another type of repeated measures designs is known as Latin Square designs, in which sequential or ordering effects may be evaluated. There is a host of Latin Square designs available to the researcher and, since their use seems to be somewhat restricted, we recommend that you consult other texts for these designs (Bruning and Kintz, 1968; Winer, 1971).

ANOVA MODEL R-I

The ANOVA MODEL R-I is typically referred to as a Treatment $\times$ Subjects (T $\times$ S) design. If an experiment is conducted according to a T $\times$ S design, then all subjects should experience all levels of the treatment variable, presumably in the same order. The following points should be carefully noted:

1. There is only *one* independent variable in a T $\times$ S design, although this treatment condition may have as many levels (t_1, t_2, . . . t_n) as you wish.

2. Each subject in the experiment experiences *all* levels of the treatment. If the various levels of the treatment may be administered in any order, you must make a decision as to the order. If you believe that the order of the levels of the treatment is important, you should attempt to evaluate this order effect by using a Latin Square design.* Should you decide that the order is unimportant, or as is more often the case, that the levels of the treatment may be experienced in *only one* order such as in measurements over time, then the T $\times$ S design is most appropriate.

Computational procedures and numerical example

The first step in the T $\times$ S ANOVA procedure is to arrange the data in a table with the experimental or independent variable conditions represented by columns and the subjects represented by rows. A set of hypothetical data collected according to the rationale of the T $\times$ S design is given in part a of Table II.1. Here the experimental question is: Does test taking ability improve with practice? Each treatment level in part a of Table II.1 represents a test of general knowledge and the independent variable is practice.

Four computational terms need to be calculated from the data in order to get estimates of the various sources of variance. The first of these terms is computed as follows: (1) sum all the scores, (2) square this total, and (3) divide this squared total by the total number of observations. Computational factor 2 is the sum of each observation squared. The third computational factor is each column total squared, summed across groups, and divided by the number of subjects (n). The last computational factor is the sum of the observations for each subject squared, summed across subjects, and divided by the number of levels of the independent variable (k). The calculation of these computation terms are summarized in part b of Table II.1. Procedures for calculation of the sum of the squares for each source

*Note this procedure is not effective if there are interactions involving order effects present.

Table II.1 Development of Test-Taking Skill—Each Level of T Represents a Test on General Knowledge

	Subject	t_1	t_2	t_3	t_4	t_5	Total (R)
	1	50	45	65	80	85	325
	2	73	74	80	86	90	403
	3	47	63	65	64	70	309
	4	61	72	88	85	83	389
a)	5	37	44	45	51	55	232
	6	86	83	80	78	75	402
	7	83	90	92	92	94	451
	8	77	80	80	78	88	403
	9	58	60	73	79	84	354
		572	611	668	693	724	$\Sigma X = 3268$

b)
1. $= (\Sigma X)^2/N = (3268)^2/45 = 237{,}329.42$
2. $= \Sigma X^2 = (50^2 + 73^2 + \ldots + 88^2 + 84^2) = 247{,}488$
3. $= \Sigma(X)^2/n = (572^2 + 611^2 + \ldots + 724^2)/9 = 239{,}017.11$
4. $= (\Sigma R^2)/k = (325^2 + 403^2 + \ldots + 354^2)/5 = 244{,}278$

c)
$SS_{\text{between subjects}} = (4) - (1) = 244{,}278 - 237{,}329.42 = 6948.58$
$SS_{\text{within subjects}} = (2) - (4) = 247{,}488 - 244{,}278 = 3210$
$SS_{\text{treatments}} = (3) - (1) = 239{,}017.11 - 237{,}329.42 = 1687.69$
$SS_{\text{error (T}\times\text{S)}} = (2) - (3) - (4) + (1) = 247{,}488 - 239{,}017.11 - 244{,}278$
$$+ 237{,}329.42 = 1522.31$$

d)
$df_{\text{between subjects}} = n - 1 = 9 - 1 = 8$
$df_{\text{within subjects}} = n(k - 1) = 9(5 - 1) = 36$
$df_{\text{treatments}} = k - 1 = 5 - 1 = 4$
$df_{\text{error}} = (n - 1)(k - 1) = (9 - 1)(5 - 1) = 32$

of variance are given in part c of Table II.1, while procedures for determining the df are given in part d of Table II.1.

You should note that the Treatments $\times$ Subjects interaction is usually taken as the estimate of error variance in this design. This is reasonable if you think about it for a moment. In the independent groups ANOVA designs reviewed in the previous chapter, error variance was estimated on the basis of variability observed within each cell of the design matrix. **In the T $\times$ S design, however, there is exactly one score in each of the cells; the within-cell variance must therefore be exactly equal to zero.** It follows, therefore, that experimental effects cannot meaningfully be tested with respect to within-cell variance.

What, then, may be used as an estimate of error variance? Well, to the extent that a particular level of the treatment variable affected all subjects in the same way, each subject should perform comparably to every other subject in each treatment condition. To the extent that subjects reacted *differentially* across treatment levels, we must assume that many factors were uncontrolled. This differential behavior over treatment levels is another way of saying that there is an interaction of Treatments by Subjects. This T × S interaction is therefore taken to be the most appropriate estimate of error variance in a T × S design.*

$$F_{\text{Treatment}} = \frac{MS_{\text{Treatment}}}{MS_{\text{TxS}}}$$

The summary of the ANOVA procedure and the resulting F-ratio are given in Table II.2. Inspection of Table F in Appendix B indicates the obtained *F*-ratio is reliable, $F(4, 32) = 8.87$, $p < .05$. To find out if the means differ significantly from each other, a further analysis must be done. To gain some insight into the nature of the observed differences we can plot the data given in Table 1 as in Fig. II.1. Inspection of Fig. II.1 indicates that with increased practice the test scores go up. In order to test to see if any of the means depicted in Fig. II.1 are reliably different, we must apply a multiple comparison procedure such as the Tukey Test.

Table II.2 ANOVA Summary

Source of variance	SS	df	MS	F-ratio
Treatments	1687.69	4	421.92	8.87
Subjects	6948.58	8	868.58	
Treatment X Subjects Interaction (estimate of error)	1522.31	32	47.57	
Total	10158.58	44		

Comparisons among means

Following the application of the ANOVA technique to a T × S experiment, it is possible to determine which means are significantly different

---

*Although it is logically possible to calculate a main effect of subjects, it turns out, for a variety of reasons, that sometimes it is not possible to meaningfully interpret this effect (see Winer, 1971).

using a multiple comparison technique. Such a comparison technique must incorporate the fact that observations were taken on the same subjects or on matched subjects. One such multiple comparison test is the Tukey Test which utilizes the same procedures as given in the previous chapter.

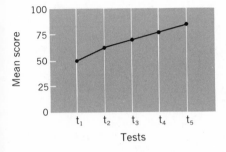

Fig. II.1 Test scores average as a function of practice.

ANOVA MODEL R-II

This ANOVA model is the first of three mixed ANOVA procedures to be presented. It is a mixed design in that we are dealing with both independent groups and repeated measures. Model R-II is composed of one fixed factor and one repeated measure. In the example given below, rats had been rewarded either on a portion of the total trials during acquisition—which is known as partial reinforcement—or rewarded every trial—which is called continuous reinforcement. All animals were then run in an extinction procedure over a period of four days, that is, all trials resulted in nonreinforcement. This design, then, is a two-way mixed factorial design with the independent groups factor being Schedule of Reward in acquisition (continuous reward versus partial reward) and the repeated measure factor being the subject's performance across days of extinction. The speed with which the subjects completed the response is presented in part of Table II.3.

The data in part a of Table II.3 are arranged with the B variable representing repeated measure and the A variable representing independent groups. This is a matter of convention and in this book we will always have the variable that is repeated as the last variable in the design—in this case, B. Once the data have been arranged as in part a of Table II.3, a number of smaller summary tables which will facilitate computations need to be constructed. The AB summary table is simply the sum of the entries in each cell and is given in part b of Table II.3. This table is used to calculate computational terms 3, 4, and 5 in part c of Table II.3. The first two computational terms are derived from the raw data and computation term 6 is computed from the sum of the observations for each subject. The summary of these various computational terms is given in part c of Table II.3.

The calculation of the sum of squares for each source of variance is given in part d of Table II.3, while the *df* for these sources of variance are given in part e of Table II.3.

Table II.3 Calculational Tables for Model R-II

<table>
<tr><td rowspan="2"></td><td rowspan="2"></td><td rowspan="2"></td><td rowspan="2">S</td><td colspan="4">(Days)
B</td><td rowspan="2">Total
(R)</td></tr>
<tr><td>b_1</td><td>b_2</td><td>b_3</td><td>b_4</td></tr>
<tr><td rowspan="10">a)</td><td rowspan="5">a_1</td><td rowspan="5">Partial reward</td><td>1</td><td>2.3</td><td>2.0</td><td>1.6</td><td>1.0</td><td>6.9</td></tr>
<tr><td>2</td><td>1.7</td><td>1.5</td><td>1.2</td><td>.7</td><td>5.1</td></tr>
<tr><td>3</td><td>2.0</td><td>1.7</td><td>1.1</td><td>.5</td><td>5.3</td></tr>
<tr><td>4</td><td>3.1</td><td>2.8</td><td>2.2</td><td>1.3</td><td>9.4</td></tr>
<tr><td>5</td><td>2.8</td><td>2.3</td><td>1.8</td><td>.9</td><td>7.8</td></tr>
<tr><td rowspan="5">a_2</td><td rowspan="5">Continuous
reward</td><td>6</td><td>2.8</td><td>.3</td><td>.1</td><td>.0</td><td>3.2</td></tr>
<tr><td>7</td><td>3.2</td><td>1.4</td><td>1.0</td><td>.4</td><td>6.0</td></tr>
<tr><td>8</td><td>1.4</td><td>.2</td><td>.0</td><td>.0</td><td>1.6</td></tr>
<tr><td>9</td><td>2.5</td><td>1.7</td><td>.8</td><td>.2</td><td>5.2</td></tr>
<tr><td>10</td><td>3.0</td><td>2.2</td><td>1.4</td><td>.4</td><td>7.0</td></tr>
</table>

AB Summary Table

b)		b_1	b_2	b_3	b_4	Total
	a_1	11.9	10.3	7.9	4.4	34.5
	a_2	12.9	5.8	3.3	1.0	23.0
	Total	24.8	16.1	11.2	5.4	57.5

c)

1. $= (\Sigma X_i)^2/nAB = (57.5)^2/5 \times 2 \times 4 = 82.66$
2. $= \Sigma X_i^2 = (2.3^2 + 1.7^2 + \ldots + .2^2 + .4^2) = 118.51$
3. $= (\Sigma A^2)/nB = (34.5^2 + 23.0^2)/5 \times 4 = 85.96$
4. $= (\Sigma B^2)/nA = (24.8^2 + 16.1^2 + 11.2^2 + 5.4^2)/5 \times 2 = 102.88$
5. $= \{\Sigma(AB)^2\}/n = (11.9^2 + 10.3^2 + \ldots + 3.3^2 + 1.0^2)/5 = 108.28$
6. $= (\Sigma R^2)/B = (6.9^2 + 5.1^2 + \ldots + 5.2^2 + 7.0^2)/4 = 93.94$

d)

$SS_{\text{between subjects}} = (6) - (1) = 93.94 - 82.66 = 11.28$

$SS_{\text{A factor}} = (3) - (1) = 85.96 - 82.66 = 3.30$

$SS_{\text{Error A}} = (6) - (3) = 93.94 - 85.96 = 7.98$

$SS_{\text{within subjects}} = (2) - (6) = 118.51 - 93.94 = 24.57$

$SS_{\text{B factor}} = (4) - (1) = 102.88 - 82.66 = 20.22$

$SS_{\text{A} \times \text{B interaction}} = (5) - (3) - (4) + (1) = 108.28 - 85.96 - 102.88 + 82.66 = 2.10$

$SS_{\text{Error B}} = (2) - (5) - (6) + (3) = 118.51 - 108.28 - 93.94 + 85.96 = 2.31$

Table II.3   (Continued)

e)

$$df_{\text{between subjects}} = An - 1 = 2 \times 5 - 1 = 9$$
$$df_{\text{A factor}} = A - 1 = 2 - 1 = 1$$
$$df_{\text{Error A}} = A(n - 1) = 2(5 - 1) = 8$$
$$df_{\text{within subjects}} = An(B - 1) = 2 \times 5(4 - 1) = 30$$
$$df_{\text{B factor}} = B - 1 = 4 - 1 = 3$$
$$df_{\text{A}\times\text{B interaction}} = (A - 1)(B - 1) = (2 - 1)(4 - 1) = 3$$
$$df_{\text{Error B}} = A(n - 1)(B - 1) = 2(5 - 1)(4 - 1) = 24$$
$$df_{\text{total}} = nAB - 1 = 5 \times 2 \times 4 - 1 = 39$$

The summary of the analysis of variance is given in Table II.4. Notice that there are two error terms—error for A and error for B.* The first error term, error A, is used as the error estimate in calculating the F-ratio associated with the A variable or reward schedule. The second error term, error B, is used as the error estimate in calculating the F-ratio associated with the repeated B variable and the A $\times$ B interaction. Hence, the df for the A variable F-ratio is different from the df for the B variable and interaction F-ratios.

Table II.4   ANOVA Summary

Source of variance	SS	df	MS	F-ratio
Between subjects	11.28	9		
Variable A	3.30	1	3.30	3.30
Error for A	7.98	8	1.00	
Within subjects	24.57	30		
Variable B	20.22	3	6.74	74.88
A $\times$ B Interaction	2.10	3	.70	7.77
Error for B	2.31	24	.09	

In this set of results, we find that the F for the A variable was not significant, $F(1, 8) = 3.30$, $p > .05$. This means that the type of reward schedule did not affect the subjects performance overall, The B variable, days of extinction, was significant, $F(3, 24) = 74.88$, $p < .05$. This means the groups run increasingly slower during extinction. The Type of Reward Schedule $\times$ Days of Extinction interaction was also reliable, $F(3, 24) = 7.77$, $p < .05$. This indicates that the groups are reducing their speed—extinguishing—at different rates. As can be seem from Fig. II.2, the partially reinforced group is more persistent over extinction days than the continuously reinforced group.

*Notice also the total variance is divided into two main sources of variance—within subject and between subject variance. These two major sources of variance are then subdivided into their various components for calculation of F-ratios.

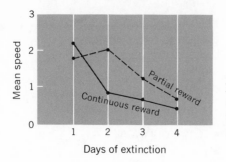

Fig. II.2 Extinction speeds of a group of partially rewarded subjects compared to those of continuously rewarded subjects.

ANOVA MODEL R-III

This ANOVA model is a three-way mixed design with one repeated factor, factor C, and two fixed factors represented by independent groups. For this analysis we must construct a number of smaller tables from the raw data to obtain the various computational terms. This particular ANOVA model is probably the most prevalent model employed.

Computational procedures and numerical example

Let us assume that an experiment has been run in which college students were required to learn how to "run through" a maze. Students are seated at a desk, blindolded, given a pencil and a metal sheet containing grooves in the pattern of a maze. The student is placed in the starting position, told to GO!, and must get to the end of the maze. Typically, one would measure either or both the number of errors committed and the time to traverse the maze. In this particular example, we wish to examine maze performance as a function of the complexity (simple vs. complex) of the maze, whether the trials are massed, that is, follow each other closely or spaced, and the extent to which familiarity with the maze influences relearning at a later time, in this example one week later. We would naturally expect the subjects to make more errors on the complex maze than the simple one, because there is more opportunity to do so, and so the main effect of Type of Maze should be significant. The number of errors made by the subjects in the course of learning the two mazes under the various conditions is given in Table II.5.

The various summary tables we need to calculate from these data are given in part b of Table II.5. The ABC summary table is the sum of all the cell entries for each cell. The AB summary table is the ABC entries summed across C levels. This means that for entry a_1b_1 we add c_1 and c_2 (148 + 55 = 203) to get that cell entry. The other entries in this table and the other tables are derived in a similar manner (the AC table has entries summed

Table II.5 Calculational Tables for Model R-III

			Subjects	Learning c_1	Relearning c_2	Total (R)
			1	32	11	43
	Massed		2	41	15	56
	b_1		3	40	12	52
			4	35	17	52
Simple Maze A (a_1)			5	45	6	51
	Spaced		6	52	10	62
	b_2		7	55	8	63
			8	50	4	54
			9	103	42	145
	Massed		10	90	30	120
	b_1		11	120	48	168
			12	112	45	157
Complex Maze B (a_2)			13	72	25	97
	Spaced		14	80	31	111
	b_2		15	83	35	118
			16	70	27	97

a)

b)

ABC Summary Table

		c_1	c_2	Total
a_1	b_1	148	55	203
	b_2	202	28	230
a_2	b_1	425	165	590
	b_2	305	118	423
	Total	1080	366	1446

AB Summary Table

	b_1	b_2	Total
a_1	203	230	433
a_2	590	423	1013
Total	793	653	1446

AC Summary Table

	c_1	c_2	Total
a_1	350	83	433
a_2	730	283	1013
Total	1080	366	1446

BC Summary Table

	c_1	c_2	Total
b_1	573	220	793
b_2	507	146	653
Total	1080	366	1446

Table II.5 (Continued)

c)

1. $= (\Sigma x)^2/nABC = (1446)^2/4 \times 2 \times 2 \times 2 = 65341.13$
2. $= \Sigma x^2 = 96338$
3. $= \Sigma A^2/nBC = (433)^2 + (1013)^2/4 \times 2 \times 2 = 75853.63$
4. $= \Sigma B^2/nAC = (793)^2 + (653)^2/4 \times 2 \times 2 = 65953.63$
5. $= \Sigma C^2/nAB = (1080)^2 + (366)^2/4 \times 2 \times 2 = 81272.25$
6. $= \Sigma(AB^2)/nC = (203)^2 + (230)^2 + (590)^2 + (423)^2/4 \times 2 = 77642.25$
7. $= \Sigma(AC^2)/nB = (350)^2 + (83)^2 + (730)^2 + (283)^2/4 \times 2 = 92797.25$
8. $= \Sigma(BC^2)/nA = (573)^2 + (220)^2 + (507)^2 + (146)^2/4 \times 2 = 81886.75$
9. $= \Sigma(ABC^2)/n = (148)^2 + \ldots + (118)^2/4 = 95329$
10. $= \Sigma R^2/C = (43)^2 \ldots + (97)^2/2 = 78542$

$SS_{\text{between subjects}} = (10) - (1) = 78542 - 65341.13 = 13200.87$
$SS_{\text{A factor}} = (3) - (1) = 75853.63 - 65341.13 = 10512.50$
$SS_{\text{B factor}} = (4) - (1) = 65953.63 - 65341.13 = 612.50$
$SS_{\text{A}\times\text{B interaction}} = (6) - (3) - (4) + (1) = 77642.25 - 75853.63 - 65953.63$
$\qquad\qquad\qquad\qquad\qquad + 65341.13 = 1176.12$
$SS_{\text{Error A}} = (10) - (6) = 78542 - 77642.25 = 899.75$
$SS_{\text{within subjects}} = (2) - (10) = 96338 - 78542 = 17796.00$
$SS_{\text{C factor}} = (5) - (1) = 81272.25 - 65341.13 = 15931.12$

d)

$SS_{\text{A}\times\text{C interaction}} = (7) - (3) - (5) + (1) = 92797.25 - 75853.63 - 81272.25$
$\qquad\qquad\qquad\qquad\qquad + 65341.13 = 1012.50$
$SS_{\text{B}\times\text{C interaction}} = (8) - (4) - (5) + (1) = 81886.75 - 65953.63 - 81272.25$
$\qquad\qquad\qquad\qquad\qquad + 65341.13 = 2.00$
$SS_{\text{A}\times\text{B}\times\text{C interaction}} = (9) - (6) - (7) - (8) + (3) + (4) + (5) - (1) = 95329$
$\qquad\qquad\qquad\qquad\qquad - 77642.25 - 92797.25 - 81886.75 + 75853.63$
$\qquad\qquad\qquad\qquad\qquad + 65953.63 + 81272.25 - 65341.13 = 741.13$
$SS_{\text{Error C}} = (2) - (9) - (10) + (6) = 96338 - 95329 - 78542 + 77642.25$
$\qquad\qquad\qquad = 109.25$

e)

$df_{\text{between subjects}} = nAB - 1 = 4 \times 2 \times 2 - 1 = 15$
$df_{\text{A variable}} = A - 1 = 2 - 1 = 1$
$df_{\text{B variable}} = B - 1 = 2 - 1 = 1$
$df_{\text{A}\times\text{B interaction}} = (A - 1)(B - 1) = (2 - 1)(2 - 1) = 1$
$df_{\text{Error A}} = AB(n - 1) = 2 \times 2(4 - 1) = 12$
$df_{\text{within subjects}} = nAB(C - 1) = 4 \times 2 \times 2(2 - 1) = 16$
$df_{\text{C variable}} = C - 1 = 2 - 1 = 1$
$df_{\text{A}\times\text{C interaction}} = (A - 1)(C - 1) = (2 - 1)(2 - 1) = 1$
$df_{\text{B}\times\text{C interaction}} = (B - 1)(C - 1) = (2 - 1)(2 - 1) = 1$
$df_{\text{A}\times\text{B}\times\text{C interaction}} = (A - 1)(B - 1)(C - 1) = (2 - 1)(2 - 1)(2 - 1) = 1$
$df_{\text{Error C}} = AB(n - 1)(C - 1) = 2 \times 2(4 - 1)(2 - 1) = 12$

across B levels, while the BC table has entries summed across A levels). Also included are row and column totals which are used in calculating some of the computational terms given in part c of Table II.5.

A summary of all the computational terms needed to estimate the various sums of squares are given in part c of Table II.5 and the derivation of the various sums of squares is given in part d of Table II.5. The calculation of the various *df* for the sums of squares is given in part e of Table II.5.

The summary of the ANOVA procedure is given in Table II.6. Notice there are two error terms—one concerned with the *F*-ratios associated with the A and B factors and one concerned with the *F*-ratios associated with the C factor and interactions involving the C factor. The sources of variance A, B, and A × B are tested against error for A in the *F*-ratio; all other sources of variance are tested against error for C.

Table II.6 ANOVA Summary

Source of variance	SS	df	MS	F-ratio
Between subjects	13200.87	15		
A	10512.50	1	10512.50	140.20
B	612.50	1	612.50	8.17
A × B	1176.12	1	1176.12	15.69
Error for A	899.75	12	74.98	
Within subjects	17796.00	16		
C	15931.12	1	15931.12	1750.67
A × C	1012.50	1	1012.50	111.26
B × C	2.00	1	2.00	.22
A × B × C	741.13	1	741.13	81.44
Error for C	109.25	12	9.10	

The analysis indicated, as expected, that the more complex maze (factor A) resulted in significantly more errors, $F(1, 12) = 140.20, p < .05$. Overall, if trials were spaced rather than massed, significantly more errors tended to occur, $F(1, 12) = 8.17, p < .05$. The interaction of Maze Type × Type of Acquisition was also reliable, $F(1, 12) = 15.69, p < .05$. In order to gain some insight into the nature of this interaction, we have plotted this interaction in Fig. II.3. Examination of this figure indicates that fewer errors are made under spaced training if the maze was simple, whereas if training was massed, fewer errors were made if the maze was complex. Thus, both type of maze and type of acquisition training are acting together to determine performance.

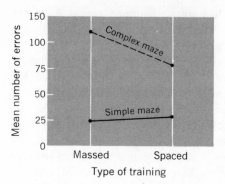

Fig. II.3 Mean number of errors made on learning two types of mazes as a function of type of training—massed or spaced.

The mazes were easier to learn the second time (C factor), $F(1, 12) =$ 1750.67, $p < .05$. This relearning of the maze also reliably interacted with the type of maze (A — C interaction), $F(1, 12) = 111.26$, $p < .05$. The plot of this interaction is shown in Fig. II.4. Examination of this figure indicates relearning of the complex maze was much easier than the relearning of the simple maze.

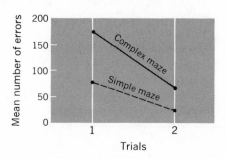

Fig. II.4 Mean number of errors on learning and relearning two different mazes.

The triple interaction of Type of Maze × Type of Acquisition × Trials was also significant, $F(1, 12) = 81.44$, $p < .05$. A plot of this interaction is given in Fig. II.5. This figure indicates that this interaction is probably due to the tendency of subjects to make more errors in relearning the simple maze under massed training.

ANOVA MODEL R-IV

This ANOVA procedure is one for a complex three-way mixed design where one variable represents independent groups and the other two variables

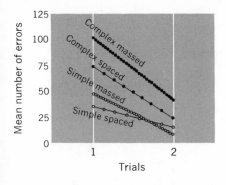

Fig. II.5 Learning and relearning two
different types of mazes under two
practice conditions.

represent repeated measures. Model R-IV is similar to other complex
ANOVA procedures in that a number of summary tables need to be derived
from the original data to facilitate calculation of the computational factors
used to estimate the various sources of variance.

Computational procedures and numerical example

Consider the experiment cited in the previous section concerning maze
learning. Suppose we wished to look at the course of acquisition (learning)
in the simple maze rather than just looking at overall learning. To do this,
we can break the acquisition period into thirds. The design of the experiment would now consist of two groups of subjects learning a simple maze
under massed or spaced trials. In addition, we would be interested in the
course of learning during acquisition (three Blocks of Trials) and the original
learning and relearning of the maze. In other words, the design would be a
$2 \times 3 \times 2$ factorial with one variable represented by independent groups
and the others by repeated measures, that is, measures taken on the same
group of subjects.

The data from the above experiment are presented in part a of Table II.7.
The various subtables needed to be derived from the data are given in
part b of Table II.7. The ABC summary table is the sum of each set of cell
entries. The AB summary table is the scores in the ABC table summed
across the C factor, hence the first entry in the AB table (a_1b_1) is $c_1 + c_2 + c_3$
under a_1b_1 or $74 + 46 + 28 = 148$. Other entries in the AB, AC, and BC
summary tables are derived in an analogous manner (AC table entries are
summed across B, and BC summary table entries are summed across A).
Two other tables also need to be calculated. These are the subject tables.

The B $\times$ subject within groups is the sum of each subject's score across
C levels. Hence, the entry for Subject #1 under b_1 is the $c_1 + c_2 + c_3$ scores
for that subject under b_1, while the b_2 entry is $c_1 + c_2 + c_3$ under b_2 for that
subject. This is done for all eight subjects. The next table is similar except

Table II.7 Calculational Tables for Model R-IV

a)

		B					
		b_1 Learning			b_2 Relearning		
A		first 1/3 c_1	second 1/3 c_2	last 1/3 c_3	first 1/3 c_1	second 1/3 c_2	last 1/3 c_3
Massed a_1	S_1	17	10	5	4	4	3
	S_2	20	14	7	7	5	3
	S_3	23	9	8	4	5	3
	S_4	14	13	8	5	5	7
Spaced a_2	S_5	26	12	7	3	1	2
	S_6	28	17	7	2	4	4
	S_7	21	26	8	3	4	1
	S_8	19	20	11	1	2	1

ABC Summary Table

	b_1			b_2		
	c_1	c_2	c_3	c_1	c_2	c_3
a_1	74	46	28	20	19	16
a_2	94	75	33	9	11	8
Total	168	121	61	29	30	24

433

AB Summary Table

	b^1	b^2	Total
a_1	148	55	203
a_2	202	28	230
Total	350	83	433

b)

AC Summary Table

	c_1	c_2	c_3	Total
a_1	94	65	44	203
a_2	103	86	41	230
Total	197	151	85	433

BC Summary Table

	c_1	c_2	c_3	Total
b_1	168	121	61	350
b_2	29	30	24	83
Total	197	151	85	433

B × Subjects Within Groups Summary Table

	b_1	b_2	Pb
S_1	32	11	43
S_2	41	15	56
S_3	40	12	52
S_4	35	17	52
S_5	45	6	51
S_6	52	10	62
S_7	55	8	63
S_8	50	4	54

C × Subjects Within Groups Summary Table

	c_1	c_2	c_3	Pc
S_1	21	14	8	43
S_2	27	19	10	56
S_3	27	14	11	52
S_4	19	18	15	52
S_5	29	13	9	51
S_6	30	21	11	62
S_7	24	30	9	63
S_8	20	22	12	54

Table II.7 (Continued)

1. $= (\Sigma X_i)^2/nABC = (433)^2/4 \times 2 \times 2 \times 3 = (433)^2/48 = 187489/48 = 3906.02$

2. $= \Sigma X^2 = 6591$

3. $= (\Sigma A^2)/nBC = (203)^2 + (233)^2/4 \times 2 \times 3 = 41209 + 52960/24 = 74109/24 = 3921.21$

4. $= (\Sigma B^2)/nAC = (350)^2 + (83)^2/4 \times 2 \times 3 = 122500 + 6889/24 = 129389/24 = 5391.21$

5. $= (\Sigma C^2)/nAB = (197)^2 + (151)^2 + (85)^2/4 \times 2 \times 2 = 68835/16 = 4302.19$

c)
6. $= \Sigma(AB)^2/nC = (148)^2 + (55)^2 + (202)^2 + (28)^2/4 \times 3 = 66517/12 = 5543.08$

7. $= \Sigma(AC)^2/nB = (94)^2 + (65)^2 + (44)^2 + (103)^2 + (86)^2 + (41)^2/4 \times 2 = 34683/8 = 4335.38$

8. $= \Sigma(BC)^2/nA = (168)^2 + (121)^2 + (61)^2 + (29)^2 + (30)^2 + (24)^2/4 \times 2 = 48903/8 = 6112.88$

9. $= \Sigma(ABC)^2/n = (74)^2 + \ldots + (8)^2/4 = 25209/4 = 6302.25$

10. $= \Sigma P^2/BC = (43)^2 + \ldots + (54)^2/2 \times 3 = 23723/6 = 3953.83$

11. $= \Sigma(BP)^2/C = (32)^2 + \ldots + (4)^2/3 = 16779/3 = 5593$

12. $= \Sigma(CP)^2/B = (21)^2 + \ldots + (12)^2/2 = 8985/2 = 4492.5$

$SS_{\text{between subjects}} = (10) - (1) = 3953.83 - 3906.02 = 47.81$

$SS_{\text{A factor}} = (3) - (1) = 3921.21 - 3906.02 = 15.19$

$SS_{\text{subjects within groups error}} = (10) - (3) = 3953.83 - 3921.21 = 32.62$

$SS_{\text{within subjects}} = (2) - (10) = 6571 - 3953.83 = 2617.17$

$SS_{\text{B factor}} = (4) - (1) = 5391.21 - 3906.02 = 1485.19$

$SS_{\text{AB factor}} = (6) - (3) - (4) + (1) = 5543.08 - 3921.21 - 5391.21 + 3906.02 = 136.68$

d)
$SS_{\text{B} \times \text{within groups error}} = (11) - (6) - (10) + (3) = 5593 - 5543.08 - 3953.83 + 3921.21 = 17.30$

$SS_{\text{C factor}} = (5) - (1) = 4302.19 - 3906.02 = 396.17$

$SS_{\text{AC factor}} = (7) - (3) - (5) + (1) = 4335.38 - 3921.21 - 4302.19 + 3906.02 = 18$

$SS_{\text{C} \times \text{within groups error}} = (12) - (7) - (10) + (3) = 4492.5 - 4335.38 - 3953.83 + 3921.21 = 124.50$

$SS_{\text{BC factor}} = (8) - (4) - (5) + (1) = 6112.88 - 5391.21 - 4302.19 + 3906.02 = 325.50$

$SS_{\text{ABC factor}} = (9) - (6) - (7) - (8) + (3) + (4) + (5) - (1) = 6302.25 - 5543.08 - 4335.38 - 6112.88 + 3921.21 + 4302.19 + 5391.21 - 3906.02 = 19.49$

$SS_{\text{BC} \times \text{within groups}} = (2) - (9) - (11) - (12) + (6) + (7) + (10) - (3) = 6571 - 6302.25 - 5593 - 4492.5$
$\qquad + 5543.08 + 4335.38 + 3953.83 - 3921.21 = 94.33$

e)

$$df_{\text{between subjects}} = An - 1 = 2 \times 4 - 1 = 7$$

$$df_{\text{A factor}} = A - 1 = 2 - 1 = 1$$

$$df_{\text{error A}} = A(n - 1) = 2 \times (4 - 1) = 6$$

$$df_{\text{within subjects}} = nA(BC - 1) = 4 \times 2 (2 \times 3 - 1) = 40$$

$$df_{\text{B factor}} = B - 1 = 2 - 1 = 1$$

$$df_{\text{AB factor}} = (A - 1)(B - 1) = (2 - 1)(2 - 1) = 1$$

$$df_{\text{error B}} = A(n - 1)(B - 1) = 2(4 - 1)(2 - 1) = 6$$

$$df_{\text{C factor}} = C - 1 = 3 - 1 = 2$$

$$df_{\text{AC factor}} = (A - 1)(C - 1) = (2 - 1)(3 - 1) = 2$$

$$df_{\text{error C}} = A(n - 1)(C - 1) = 2(4 - 1)(3 - 1) = 12$$

$$df_{\text{BC factor}} = (B - 1)(C - 1) = (2 - 1)(3 - 1) = 2$$

$$df_{\text{ABC factor}} = (A - 1)(B - 1)(C - 1) = (2 - 1)(2 - 1)(3 - 1) = 2$$

$$df_{\text{error BC}} = A(n - 1)(B - 1)(C - 1) = 2(4 - 1)(2 - 1)(3 - 1) = 12$$

we now sum $b_1 + b_2$ for each subject under c_1. The totals are P_b and P_c, respectively. The summary of the calculation of the various computational terms is given in part c of Table II.7. The calculation of the sums of squares for the various sources of variance are given in part d of Table II.7 and the calculation of the df associated with the sources of variance are given in part e of Table II.7.

The summary of the ANOVA procedure is given in Table II.8. The appropriate error term to use in testing each of the main effects and interactions is given just below these effects in Table II.8. Thus, error for B is used to test B and AB effects, error for C is used to test C and AC effects,

Table II.8 ANOVA Summary

Source of variance	SS	df	MS	F-ratio
Between subjects	47.81	7		
A	15.19	1	15.19	2.79
Error for A	32.62	6	5.44	
Within subjects	2617.17	40		
B	1485.19	1	1485.19	515.69
A × B	136.68	1	136.68	47.46
Error for B	17.30	6	2.88	
C	396.17	2	198.09	19.08
A × C	18.00	2	9.00	.87
Error for C	124.50	12	10.38	
B × C	325.50	2	162.75	20.71
A × B × C	19.49	2	9.75	1.24
Error for BC	94.33	12	7.86	

and so on. The effect of type of acquisition, spaced or massed, did not affect the subjects performance, $F(1, 6) = 2.79, p > .05$. The relearning effect was significant, $F(1, 6) = 575.69, p < .05$, indicating that the subjects made fewer errors in relearning the maze. The interaction of type of acquisition × relearning was significant, $F(1, 6) = 47.46, p < .05$. A plot of this interaction is given in Fig. II.6. Fig. II.6 indicates that subjects relearned the maze faster if their original acquisition training was spaced rather than massed.

The trials factor was significant, $F(2, 12) = 19.08, p < .05$, indicating that the subjects did indeed learn the maze. The interaction of Type of Acquisition × Trials was not significant, $F(2, 12) = .87, p > .05$. The Relearning × Trials interaction was significant, $F(2, 12) = 20.71, p < .05$. A plot of this interaction is given in Fig. II.7. Fig. II.7 indicates that this is

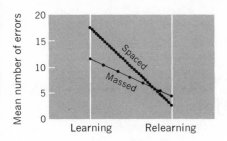

Fig. II.6 A plot of the type of acquisition × relearning interaction.

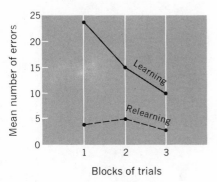

Fig. II.7 A plot of the relearning × trials interaction.

due to the tendency of subjects to make the same number of errors in each block of trials in relearning, whereas there was a marked decrease in errors across trials in the original learning.

nonparametric statistics based on qualitative data

It will be recalled from earlier discussion that qualitative data reflect a nominal scale of measurement which means we have employed some kind of classification device. **Research involving this type of data consists of counting the number of cases falling within each category, or, if you will, the frequency of cases falling within each category.** Our dependent variable for such research, then, will always be **frequency data.**

Chi Square

Perhaps the most widely used of the nonparametric statistics is chi square, symbolized by χ^2. The chi square design permits an evaluation to be made of the distribution of frequencies over categories. Specifically, it is constructed to determine if the distribution of frequencies across categories can reasonably be attributed to random variation. The chi square statistic may be calculated on qualitative data which have been classified along either one or two dimensions. We will treat each of these in turn.

One-way classification chi square

Consider the hypothetical set of data presented in Table III.1. Table III.1 gives data obtained from a dice experiment in which 100 persons participated who claimed to have telekenetic powers. These persons tried to obtain sevens and elevens by attempting to control the toss of the dice with their thoughts. Each person was allowed one toss of the dice. We can see from Table III.1 that these people obtained seven or eleven on 21 and 13 tosses, respectively, out of 100 total tosses of the dice. Is this significantly different from what we would expect if only chance factors were operating?

Table III.1 Observed Frequency of Numbers Obtained in 100 Tosses of Two Dice

	seven	eleven	others
Observed Frequency	21	13	66

How many sevens and elevens would we **expect on the basis of chance?** We know that the probability of obtaining a seven on one toss of the dice is 6/36; therefore, the number of sevens we would expect in 100 tosses would be 100 × 6/36 or 16.7. By similar reasoning the number of elevens expected would be 2/36 × 100 or 5.5, and the expected frequency of all other numbers would be 28/36 × 100 or 77.8. We may record these expected values of each category under the observed value in parentheses as in Table III.2.

Table III.2 Observed and Expected Frequencies in the Dice Experiment

	seven	eleven	others
Observed Frequency	21	13	66
Expected Frequency	(16.7)	(5.5)	(77.8)

We may now calculate the value of χ^2 by means of the following formula:

$$\chi^2 = \sum \frac{(O - E)^2}{E}$$

where: O = the frequency of occurrences **observed** in each category

E = the **expected** frequency of cases in each category if only chance factors were operating.

One simple way to do this calculation is to arrange the data as in Table III.3. The value of our χ^2 calculated from these data using the above formula is 12.0.

Table III.3 Calculated Example

k	O	E	O − E	$(O - E)^2$	$\dfrac{(O - E)^2}{E}$	
1 (seven)	21	16.7	4.3	18.5	18.5/16.7	= 1.1
2 (eleven)	13	5.5	7.5	56.3	56.3/5.5	= 10.2
3 (other)	66	77.8	−11.8	139.2	139.2/77.8	= 1.7
	100	100			$\chi^2 = \Sigma \dfrac{(O - E)^2}{E}$	$\chi^2 = 12.0$

Having obtained the value of χ^2, we are now in a position to determine if these observed frequencies are distributed as would be expected on the basis of chance. Stated another way, we wish to know if our calculated value of χ^2 has reached an acceptable level of *significance*. To do this, we must enter the appropriate appendixed table with the proper number of *df*. Generally, the *df* for a one-way classification chi square is $k - 1$ or the number of categories minus one; the *df* for our example would be $3 - 1$ or 2.

Next we look up the value of χ^2 in Appendix B, Table C (which provides the sampling distribution of the χ^2 statistic) under the appropriate *df* and decide what significance level our value of χ^2 has achieved. If $\alpha < .05$, we may accept the hypothesis that these observed frequencies were not distributed over categories as would be expected by chance. In our example, if we achieve $\alpha \leq .05$, we would say that our sampled persons could, in fact, control the dice so that they performed above chance level. The value of χ^2 needed to attain significance at $\alpha = .05$ for 2 *df* is 5.99. Since our calculated value of χ^2 is greater than 5.99, we conclude that these persons could, in fact, obtain more sevens and elevens in this hypothetical study than would be expected on the basis of chance alone, $\chi^2 (2) = 12.00, p < .05$.

Let us take one more example. This time our example is a school that is looking for a name for its newly formed football team. After long debate, the student government came up with two names: Muskats and Stormers. The dean agreed to put the matter to a vote of the entire student body and to accept the vote, provided a *clear preference* was demonstrated by the voters. The tabulated vote showed that of 150 total votes, 85 favored the Muskats and 65 favored Stormers. Was there a clear preference for the name Muskats? We provide the solution to this question in Table III.4.

Table III.4 Calculated Example

	O	E	O − E	(O − E)²	$\dfrac{(O - E)^2}{E}$	
Muskats	85	75	10	100	100/75	= 1.33
Stormers	65	75	− 10	100	100/75	= 1.33
	150				$\Sigma \dfrac{(O - E)^2}{E}$	$\chi^2 = 2.66$

$\chi^2 = 2.66$
$df = k - 1 = 2 - 1 = 1$
Results: $\chi^2(1) = 2.66, p > .05$

Notice two points contained in Table III.4:

1. If only chance were operating, we would expect half of the voters to prefer one name and half to prefer the other. Hence, the *expected* frequencies are each 75 (1/2 of 150 = 75).

2. The value of χ^2 indicates there is no reason to believe one name is preferred over another.

What should the Dean conclude from these results? Simply that no "clear preference"—or "significant difference" in our language—was observed between the two names.

Two-way classification chi square

Just as it is possible to analyze the joint effects of two independent factors upon performance, it is also possible to examine how individuals—represented by frequency scores—distribute themselves within two different categorical classifications. What is tested here is whether or not these variables as defined by the classes are **independent** of one another. Look at the 2 × 2 matrix presented in Fig. III.1, in which frequency data would be recorded. We have, in fact, supplied each column frequency; that is, of 100 people sampled, 75 were male and 25 female. We may say that of the sample as a whole 75/100 were male and 25/100 female. Is the sex of the individuals **independent** of the choice of political party affiliation? If it were, of all those claiming to be Democrats, 75/100 of them should be male and 25/100 should be female. The same should be true for all those claiming to be Republicans. If this feature of independence is borne out by the data, we

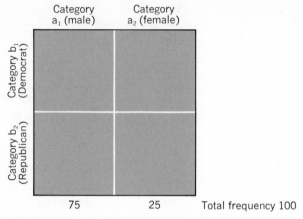

Fig. III.1 2 × 2 matrix of frequency data.

should then *expect* the frequencies obtained from the sample to be approximately represented by Fig. III.2. To the extent that the observed frequencies depart from independence, the calculated value of χ^2 should tend to be significant. Thus, **a significant χ^2 suggests relatedness while a nonsignificant χ^2 suggests independence of the classification.**

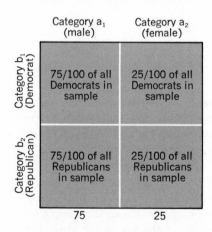

Fig. III.2 The case of independence in a 2 × 2 matrix of frequency data.

Let us apply this discussion to the results of a hypothetical survey of the preference for mini-skirts by males and females (sex variable) presented in the top portion of Table III.5. The expected cell frequencies are calculated as indicated in part b of Table III.5 and χ^2 is computed by the same formula as we used in the one-way classification example.

Table III.5 A Worked Example for a 2 × 2 χ^2 Matrix

		Observed frequencies		
		Mini-Skirt Preference		
		Prefer	Not Prefer	
a)	Male	90	10	100
	Female	120	80	200
		210	90	300

Expected frequencies on basis of independence

		Prefer	Not Prefer			Prefer	Not Prefer
	Male	210/300 of all 100 males	90/300 of all 100 males	=	Male	$\frac{210}{300} \times 100$	$\frac{90}{300} \times 100$
b)	Female	210/300 of all 200 females	90/300 of all 200 females		Female	$\frac{210}{300} \times 200$	$\frac{90}{300} \times 200$

		Prefer	Not Prefer	
	Male	70	30	100
=	Female	140	60	200
		210	90	

Calculation of χ^2

	Cell	O	E	O − E	$(O - E)^2$	$\dfrac{(O - E)^2}{E}$	
	Male, Prefer	90	70	20	400	400/70	= 5.71
c)	Male, Not Prefer	10	30	−20	400	400/30	= 2.86
	Female, Prefer	120	140	−20	400	400/140	= 13.33
	Female, Not Prefer	80	60	20	400	400/60	= 6.67

$$\Sigma \frac{(O - E)^2}{E} = \chi^2 = 28.57$$

The example in Table III.5 yielded an χ^2 of 28.57. In order to determine whether or not this χ^2 is significant, we need to enter the Chi Square Table with the proper number of df. For any matrix containing r number of rows and c number of columns,

$$df = (r - 1)(c - 1).$$

For an example, $r = 2$ and $c = 2$, therefore

$$df = (r - 1)(c - 1)$$
$$df = (2 - 1)(2 - 1)$$
$$df = 1.*$$

The χ^2 Table (Table C, Appendix B) should be entered at $df = 1$. Because the calculated value of 28.57 is greater than the largest tabled value, we may write:

$$\chi^2 (1) = 28.57, p < .05.$$

The conclusion would then be that preference for mini-skirts is related to the sex of the person, that is, the two variables are *not* independent of one another.

We may go even one step further by asking about the strength of this observed significant relationship. To answer this question, we may calculate ϕ^2 (read as phi square).† Phi square is really the Pearson r^2 and is interpreted as such.

$$\phi^2 = \chi^2/N$$

where: N is the total frequency

For our example:

$$\phi^2 = \chi^2/N$$
$$\phi^2 = 28.57/300$$
$$\phi^2 = .095$$

The interpretation of ϕ^2 is that $9\frac{1}{2}\%$ of the variance of mini-skirt preference is accounted for on the basis of sex. Hence, although preference is significantly related to sex (χ^2), it is not strongly related to sex (ϕ^2).

---

*Our df in a 2 × 2 matrix may be understood by inventing your own matrix and inserting each row and column total. Then pick *any* cell and fill in *any* number. You will see that the other cell frequencies are now completely determined (i.e., you were *free to choose* only *one* cell value).

†You should note that ϕ^2 can be calculated only on data contained in a 2 × 2 matrix. For more complex two-way classification matrices, you should use Cramer's ϕ statistic:

$$\phi^2 = \chi^2/N(k - 1) \quad \text{where } k \text{ is the } smaller \text{ of } r \text{ and } c.$$

Table III.6 An Alternative Calculational Formula for χ^2 in a 2 × 2 Matrix

Schema

a)

A	B	A + B
C	D	C + D

A + C   B + D

$$\chi^2 = \frac{N(AD - BC)^2}{(A+B)(C+D)(A+C)(B+D)}$$

Data and calculation

b)

	Prefer	Not Prefer	
Male	90	10	100
Female	120	80	200
	210	90	300

$$\chi^2 = \frac{300\{(90)(80) - (10)(120)\}^2}{(100)(200)(210)(90)}$$

$$\chi^2 = \frac{300(7200 - 1200)^2}{378,000,000}$$

$$\chi^2 = \frac{10,800,000,000}{378,000,000}$$

$$\chi^2 = 28.58$$

Before leaving the calculation of χ^2, we should mention that there is an alternative computational formula for a 2 × 2 matrix. This alternative is recommended if a desk calculator is available. We have recalculated the data given in Table III.5 and present this method in Table III.6. You should note that the two methods are mathematically equivalent and should supply identical answers. That we are .01 off of our values in Table III.5 is a result of rounding off errors.

Some limitations of chi square

Chi square should be used under the following conditions only:

1. The categories are independent and mutually exclusive, meaning that a subject can contribute **only one** score to the study. That is, N summarizes

both the total number of subjects **and,** at the same time, the total number of observations.

2. No expected cell frequency should be less than 5.

3. As a general rule, your sample should consist of more than 20 subjects.

If condition 1 cannot be met, a chi square design is incorrect and a McNemar test—which we will discuss—should be used. If one of the other two conditions cannot be met, the use of the Fisher Exact Probability Test —described next—is dictated when the data are arranged in a 2 × 2 matrix.

Fisher Exact Probability Test

The Fisher Exact Probability Test is an extremely valuable statistic to evaluate frequency data in which the sample size is very small and where you have a 2 × 2 contingency matrix. The calculation associated with the Fisher Exact Probability Test gives the actual p value of the observed differences. For illustrative purposes, we will calculate the value of p for the hypothetical data given in Table III.7. The steps that we need to go through are as follows:

1. Arrange the data into a 2 × 2 contingency table and calculate row and column totals as shown in part a of Table III.7.

2. Calculate the value of p. Do this by taking the product of all the factorials represented by the row and column totals and divide by each cell factorial and the total N factorial. This is shown in part b of Table III.7.

3. The calculated one-tailed value of p in part b of Table III.7 is equal to .09. This is the actual probability of obtaining cell frequencies distributed as observed in part a of Table III.7; therefore we conclude that these frequencies are distributed as we would expect on the basis of chance. If p had been equal to .05 or less, then we could entertain the alternative hypothesis, that is, that other factors than chance ones might have been operating.

McNemar Test

The McNemar Test allows us to determine if changes in categorical data occur as a function of time. This test is particularly suited to a pre-test post-test design in which frequency data has been collected. For this test, a χ^2 is calculated.

Table III.7 Hypothetical Data Analyzed Via the Fisher Exact Probability Test

a)

A	B	
8	5	13 (A + B)
C	D	
4	9	13 (C + D)

12	14
(A + C)	(B + D)

b)

$$p = \frac{(A + B)!\ (C + D)!\ (A + C)!\ (B + D)!}{N!\ A!\ B!\ C!\ D!}$$

$$= \frac{13!\ 13!\ 12!\ 14!}{26!\ 8!\ 5!\ 4!\ 9!}$$

$$p = .09$$

The general procedure for calculating a χ^2 for McNemar test is as follows:

1. Arrange your data into a 2 × 2 table where the rows represent the pre-test and the columns represent the post-test as shown in Table III.8. Note that if changes in classification occur between the pre-test and post-test that these changes are reflected in cells A and D.

2. The value of χ^2 is given by the following formula:

$$\chi^2 = \frac{(|A - D| - 1)^2}{A + D}$$

where: A and D are the frequencies of those cell entries.

$(|A - D| - 1)^2$ means to subtract 1 from the absolute difference of

Table III.8 2 × 2 Table For a McNemar Test

		Post-Test	
		Category Y	Category X
Pre-Test	Category X	A	B
	Category Y	C	D

$A - D$ (ignore the sign of subtraction) prior to squaring. The df for this test is always 1.

NUMERICAL EXAMPLE   A McNemar Test calculated from a set of hypothetical data is given in Table III.9. Part a of Table III.9 gives the raw frequency data in a 2×2 table and part b of the Table shows the calculation of x^2. The value of x^2 from these data is 1.35. An examination of Table C in Appendix B indicates that for 1 df a x^2 of at least 3.84 is needed for $\alpha = .05$ for a two-tailed test since we were not predicting the direction of the difference. Our value of x^2 falls short of this tabled value and we must conclude that there were no reliable changes between the pre- and post-test, $x^2 (1) = 1.35, p > .05$.

Table III.9 Example of the Calculation of an x^2 for the McNemar Test

		Post-Test	
		No	Yes
a)	Yes Pre-Test	25	22
	No	12	35

b)
$$x^2 = \frac{(|A - D| - 1)^2}{A + D} = \frac{(|25 - 35| - 1)^2}{25 + 35}$$
$$= \frac{(|10| - 1)^2}{60} = \frac{(9)^2}{60}$$
$$x^2 = 1.35$$

Cochran Q Test

The Cochran Q Test is an extension of the McNemar Test to include more than two repeated measures. Hence, this test provides a way of testing differences between several groups of matched subjects on dichotomous data. There are a large number of uses to which this test can be handily put. For example, with this test, you can determine the effect of various categories of information on the same subject's responses, or determine whether the various stages of certain politicians' campaigns were influencing the way people were planning to vote.

The method for calculating Q, which approximates the distribution of x^2, is as follows:

1. Arrange the data in a table with the rows representing subjects and the columns representing the repeated factor.

2. Categories are coded and each subject's response across time is listed in the appropriate place. By coding we mean that we can represent classes of responses by numbers. Hence, yes could equal 0 and no could equal 1 (or 0 is failure and 1 is success).

3. The value of *Q* is then given by the following formula:

$$Q = \frac{(k-1)\{k\Sigma G^2 - (\Sigma G)^2\}}{k\Sigma L - \Sigma L^2}$$

where: G = the sum of the codes in each of the columns
L = the sum of the codes across rows
k = the number of columns or repeated measures

The *df* for this test are $k - 1$.

NUMERICAL EXAMPLE   The calculation of the value of *Q* is given in Table III.10 and is based upon results from a hypothetical experiment on the influence of various types of experimenters. In part a, the rows represent subjects and the columns represent various types of experimenters. If the subject liked a particular type of experimenter, a 1 was recorded, if not, a 0. Part b gives the calculation of *Q* from these data. The value of *Q* here is 8.7. We then treat *Q* as though it were an χ^2 in order to test its significance, since the sampling distribution of *Q* is very similar to that of χ^2, especially when $N > 5$.

Table III.10   Numerical Example of a Cochran *Q* Test

Subject No.	Experimenter 1 (warm)	Experimenter 2 (indifferent)	Experimenter 3 (hostile)	Experimenter 4 (tape recorder)	L	L^2
1	1	1	0	0	2	4
2	1	1	0	0	2	4
3	1	0	1	0	2	4
4	1	0	0	0	1	1
5	1	0	0	0	1	1
6	1	0	0	1	2	4
7	1	1	1	0	3	9
8	1	0	0	1	2	4
9	1	0	0	1	2	4
10	1	1	1	0	3	9
11	0	1	1	0	2	4
	$G_1 = 10$	$G_2 = 5$	$G_3 = 4$	$G_4 = 3$	$\Sigma L = 22$	$\Sigma L^2 = 48$

a)

Table III.10 (Continued)

$$Q = (k-1)\{k\Sigma G^2 - (\Sigma G)^2\}/k\Sigma L - \Sigma L^2$$
b) $$Q = (4-1)\{4[(10)^2 + (5)^2 + (4)^2 + (3)^2] - (10 + 5 + 4 + 3)^2\}/4(22)(48)$$
$$Q = 8.7$$
$$df = k - 1 = 4 - 1 = 3$$

Examining Table C in Appendix B we find that a value of χ^2 for $df = 3$ and $\alpha = .05$ is 7.82. Our value is larger than this tabled value; therefore we can conclude that the type of experimenter reliably influenced whether the subject liked him or not, $Q(3) = 8.7\ p < .05$.

nonparametric statistics based on quantitative data

Now we will cover some of the more frequently used nonparametric procedures for analyzing data based on quantitative measurement which has been transformed into ranks. Each of these tests has its parametric analogue and should only be used when any of the parametric assumptions cannot be met. We present these analogues in Table IV.1.

Table IV.1 Parametric and Analogous Nonparametric Procedures for Four Designs

Design	Parametric procedure	Nonparametric procedure
Two independent groups	ANOVA MODEL I	Mann-Whitney U-test
Two matched groups	ANOVA MODEL R-I	Wilcoxon Signed Ranks Test
Simple randomized (several independent groups)	ANOVA MODEL I	Kruskal-Wallis Test
T $\times$ S	T $\times$ S ANOVA	Friedman Test

Mann-Whitney U-Test

The Mann-Whitney U-test can be used to determine if there are any reliable differences between two independent groups of scores. The parametric analogue of the U-test is the ANOVA MODEL I for two independent groups; the U-test is, by the way, nearly as "powerful" as the ANOVA MODEL I.

Calculation of U involves ranking the scores in each group, but since tables are available which give p values associated with the *sum of the ranks of either group*, U need not be calculated. Hence, only the sum of the ranks are calculated. The steps for calculation of the sum of the ranks (T') are outlined below (see Table IV.2):

1. Rank all scores combining both groups from smallest to largest (for this step, treat the scores as belonging to one large group).

2. Sum the ranks of the scores for either group.

3. Look up the sum of the ranks (T') in Table H in Appendix B for the appropriate size of the two groups. The T' on the left is the larger sum of ranks while that on the right is the smaller sum of ranks. It does not make any difference which T' is used—the larger or the smaller. Either will give the proper answer.

NUMERICAL EXAMPLE   An example of calculation of T' is given in Table IV.2. Notice that some of the scores in Table IV.2 have the same value (their ranks are tied). In cases of tied ranks, we assign the *average rank* to each score. For example, there are three scores of 50 in the example which should occupy ranks 9, 10, and 11. So we assign a rank of $(9 + 10 + 11)/3$ or 10 to each score of 50 and the next largest score following 50 (i.e., 55) then has a rank of 12 because we have already used up ranks 9, 10, and 11. The smaller sum of ranks is 59.5 or, rounding off, 60. We next look this value up in Table H in Appendix B where $n_1 = 8$ and $n_2 = 9$. We find that the probability of obtaining a sum of the ranks this small is .138. Consequently we can say that these two groups of scores are not significantly different from each other ($p > .05$).

Some of the advantages of using the U-test to evaluate differences between two independent groups are:

1. It is easy to compute.

2. It can only be used on quantitative data.

3. It will usually result in the same decision as to the reliability of differences as the ANOVA MODEL I.

Table IV.2 Calculation of the Sum of Ranks for a
Mann-Whitney U-test

Group 1 scores	Rank	Group 2 scores	Rank
50	10	49	8
62	16.5	35	2
36	3.5	56	13
42	7	55	12
61	15	50	10
57	14	40	6
62	16.5	36	3.5
50	10	37	5
		32	1
$\Sigma_{\text{ranks}} = T' = \overline{82.5}$		$\Sigma_{\text{ranks}} = T' = \overline{59.5}$	
Number of scores in Group 1 $= n_1$		Number of scores in Group 2 $= n_2$	
$n_1 = 8$		$n_2 = 9$	

The Wilcoxon Matched Pairs Signed-Ranks Test

The Wilcoxon Signed-Ranks Test provides a powerful test of whether any differences between scores collected on two groups of matched subjects exist or not. Its parametric analogue is the ANOVA MODEL R-I.

The Wilcoxon Test is fairly simple to use. The calculation for the Wilcoxon Test proceeds as follows (see Table IV.3):

1. List the pairs of scores according to the way they matched.

2. Obtain a difference score for each pair (e.g., subtract the score of Subject #1 in Group #2 from the score of Subject #1 in Group #1). Let us call these difference scores d_i.

3. Rank all of the difference scores without regard to their sign from smallest to largest. This means that for ranking purposes, we ignore the direction of the differences between the pairs of scores.

4. Affix the sign of the difference to the rank. Hence, a minus d_i now has a minus rank whereas a plus d_i has a positive rank.

5. Occasionally ties between scores may occur, i.e., their difference is zero. If this occurs, these scores are dropped from the analysis.

6. If ties between non-zero d_is occur, then these d_is are assigned average ranks.

7. The sum of the ranks of the less frequent sign is calculated. This sum is designated as T.

8. Finally, look up T in Table I of Appendix B. Enter Table I in the row for the appropriate N or total number of pairs. The values of T for various significance levels are listed. Your T must be *less than or equal to* this tabled value of T to achieve significance at the appropriate level.

Table IV.3 Calculation of T for a Wilcoxon Signed-Ranks Test

Subject	Group 1	Group 2	d_i	Rank	Rank with less frequent sign
1	75	70	5	6	
2	86	44	42	8	
3	81	83	−2	3	−3
4	79	76	3	5	
5	70	71	−1	1	−1
6	69	50	19	7	
7	53	51	2	3	
8	54	56	−2	3	−3
					$\Sigma = T = 7$

NUMERICAL EXAMPLE The calculation of d_i and T for a set of scores obtained from two groups of matched subjects is given in Table IV.3. For this set of data $T = 6$ and $N = 8$. An examination of Table I in Appendix B indicates that for this size sample, T must be *less than or equal to* 4 for significance at $\alpha = .05$. The value of T we calculated was 6 and larger than the value needed for significance; hence, we must conclude on the basis of these data that the experimental treatment did not result in reliable differences between our two groups ($p > .05$).

The Kruskal-Wallis One-Way ANOVA

The Kruskal-Wallis One-Way ANOVA can be used to determine if overall differences between independent groups exist.

The calculation of the statistic H associated with the Kruskal-Wallis One-Way ANOVA is as follows (see Table IV.4):

1. The data are arranged by group and ranked from smallest to largest as though they belonged to one huge group.

2. The sum of the ranks (R_i) is obtained for each group by adding the ranks for each group. These sums are then squared.

3. The value of H is obtained according to the following formula:

$$H = \frac{12}{N(N+1)} \Sigma \left[\frac{R_i^2}{n_i} \right] - 3(N+1)$$

where: k = the number of groups in the experiment
N = the total sample size
R_i = the sum of the ranks for a group
n_i = size of a particular group
Σ = directs us to sum these across all groups.

4. Look up the value of H in Table C in Appendix B under the appropriate df where $df = k - 1$.

5. In the event of ties, we assign these tied scores the average rank for the involved ranks. We must then correct H for ties. This is done as follows:

$$\text{Divide } H \text{ by } 1 - \frac{(t^3 - t)}{N^3 - N}$$

where t = the total number of tied scores.

Table IV.4 Calculation of H from Three Groups

	Group A	Rank	Group B	Rank	Group C	Rank
	56	1	69	5	71	6
	62	2	80	7.5	80	7.5
	64	3	82	10	87	12
a)	67	4	85	11	92	16.5
	81	9	91	14	94	20
	90	13	92	16.5	94	20
			94	20	94	20
					94	20

$$n_1 = 6 \qquad\qquad n_2 = 7 \qquad\qquad n_3 = 8$$
$$\Sigma R_1 = 32 \qquad\qquad \Sigma R_2 = 84 \qquad\qquad \Sigma R_3 = 122$$
$$R_1^2 = 1024 \qquad\qquad R_2^2 = 7056 \qquad\qquad R_3^2 = 14884$$

b) $H = \dfrac{12}{21(21+1)} \left[\dfrac{(32)^2}{6} + \dfrac{(84)^2}{7} + \dfrac{(122)^2}{8} \right] - 3(31+1) = 12.93$

$$\text{Correction for ties: } H = \frac{12.93}{1 - \dfrac{(6^3 - 6)}{(21^3 - 21)}} = 13.23$$

NUMERICAL EXAMPLE   The calculation of H from the scores obtained on groups of independent subjects is given in Table IV.4. The calculated value of H for this example after correcting for ties is 13.23. The df are $k - 1$ or 2. Examination of Table C in Appendix B shows that for 2 df the value of H needed to achieve significance is $H = 5.99$ for $\alpha = .05$ or $H = 9.21$ for $\alpha = .01$. We can now state that our experimental treatment results in a reliable effect on the behavior of our subjects.

Friedman Two-Way ANOVA by Ranks

This test is used to evaluate data collected according to the rationale of a T $\times$ S design where the data are quantitative or ranked. Hence, one dimension of the design is represented by Subjects and the other dimension by Treatments (rows and columns, respectively). The various treatment conditions may be represented by the same subject or matched subjects.

The calculation of the Friedman test yields a statistic called χ_r^2 which has the same distribution as χ^2 providing:

1. $k = 3$, $N > 9$, or,
2. $k = 4$, $N \geq 5$.

Where $k =$ number of treatment conditions, and
$N =$ number of subjects (or sets of scores).

If your experimental values of either k or n do not meet these requirements, then the Chi Square table cannot be used to determine probability levels and the reader is referred to Segal (1956).

The general procedure to follow in calculation of χ_r^2 for the Friedman Two-Way ANOVA is outlined below (see Table IV.5):

1. Arrange your data into a table where the rows represent subjects and the columns represent the various treatment conditions. Enter the subjects' scores in the appropriate places.

2. Rank the scores in *each row* from 1 to k, i.e., the scores for each subject or set of matched subjects are *ranked across conditions*.

3. These ranks are then summed down the columns to obtain a sum of the ranks for each condition.

4. The value of χ_r^2 is then given by the following formula:

$$\chi_r^2 = \frac{12}{Nk(k + 1)} \sum (R_i^2 - 3N(k + 1))$$

where: k = the number of treatment conditions

N = total number of subjects or the number of k sets of matched subjects

R_i = the sum of the ranks for a treatment condition

Σ = directs you to add up the sum of the ranks for each treatment condition, following squaring, across k treatments.

Table IV.5 Numerical Example of a Friedman Two-Way ANOVA by Ranks

Subject		Treatments							
		1	(rank)	2	(rank)	3	(rank)	4	(rank)
	1	10	1.5	41	4	10	1.5	11	2
	2	12	1	62	4	15	3	13	2
	3	14	1	72	4	17	3	16	2
	4	16	1	86	4	18	2	19	3
	5	22	1	101	4	19	2	21	3
a)	6	27	3	102	4	25	1	26	2
	7	32	3	103	4	31	2	30	1
	8	46	3	109	4	42	2	41	1
	9	81	3	110	4	60	2	53	1
	10	96	3	116	4	61	1	71	2
		$\Sigma R_1 = 20.5$		$\Sigma R_2 = 40$		$\Sigma R_3 = 19.5$		$\Sigma R_4 = 19$	

b)
$$\chi_r^2 = \frac{12}{10(4)(4+1)}\left[(20.5)^2 + (40)^2 + (19.5)^2 + (19)^2\right] - 3(10)(4+1)$$
$$= 15.69$$
$$df = k - 1 = 4 - 1 = 3$$

NUMERICAL EXAMPLE The actual calculation of an X_r^2 is summarized in Table IV.5. Part a of Table IV.5 gives the raw data for 10 subjects on four treatment conditions, so that N for this sample is 10 and $K = 4$. The rank of each score across rows is placed adjacent to each score and the sum of these ranks is given at the bottom of the columns. Calculation of X_r^2 from these data is given in part b of Table IV.5.

The χ_r^2 obtained from these data is 15.69 for 3 df. From examination of Table C in Appendix B it can be seen that for $df = 3$, a value of $\chi^2 = 11.34$ is needed for $\alpha = .01$. Our value falls below this value and consequently we would conclude that our treatment reliability affected the behavior of our subjects, $\chi_r^2 (3) = 15.69$, $p < .05$.

appendix B

tables

Table A Ordinates and Areas of the Normal Curve (In Terms of σ Units)

$\frac{x}{\sigma}$	Area	Ordinate	$\frac{x}{\sigma}$	Area	Ordinate	$\frac{x}{\sigma}$	Area	Ordinate
.00	.0000	.3989	.20	.0793	.3910	.40	.1554	.3683
.01	.0040	.3989	.21	.0832	.3902	.41	.1591	.3668
.02	.0080	.3989	.22	.0871	.3894	.42	.1628	.3653
.03	.0120	.3988	.23	.0910	.3885	.43	.1664	.3637
.04	.0160	.3986	.24	.0948	.3876	.44	.1700	.3621
.05	.0199	.3984	.25	.0987	.3867	.45	.1736	.3605
.06	.0239	.3982	.26	.1026	.3857	.46	.1772	.3589
.07	.0279	.3980	.27	.1064	.3847	.47	.1808	.3572
.08	.0319	.3977	.28	.1103	.3836	.48	.1844	.3555
.09	.0359	.3973	.29	.1141	.3825	.49	.1879	.3538
.10	.0398	.3970	.30	.1179	.3814	.50	.1915	.3521
.11	.0438	.3965	.31	.1217	.3802	.51	.1950	.3503
.12	.0478	.3961	.32	.1255	.3790	.52	.1985	.3485
.13	.0517	.3956	.33	.1293	.3778	.53	.2019	.3467
.14	.0557	.3951	.34	.1331	.3765	.54	.2054	.3448
.15	.0596	.3945	.35	.1368	.3752	.55	.2088	.3429
.16	.0636	.3939	.36	.1406	.3739	.56	.2123	.3410
.17	.0675	.3932	.37	.1443	.3725	.57	.2157	.3391
.18	.0714	.3925	.38	.1480	.3712	.58	.2190	.3372
.19	.0753	.3918	.39	.1517	.3697	.59	.2224	.3352

Table A (Continued)

$\frac{x}{\sigma}$	Area	Ordinate	$\frac{x}{\sigma}$	Area	Ordinate	$\frac{x}{\sigma}$	Area	Ordinate
.60	.2257	.3332	1.00	.3413	.2420	1.40	.4192	.1497
.61	.2291	.3312	1.01	.3438	.2396	1.41	.4207	.1476
.62	.2324	.3292	1.02	.3461	.2371	1.42	.4222	.1456
.63	.2357	.3271	1.03	.3485	.2347	1.43	.4236	.1435
.64	.2389	.3251	1.04	.3508	.2323	1.44	.4251	.1415
.65	.2422	.3230	1.05	.3531	.2299	1.45	.4265	.1394
.66	.2451	.3209	1.06	.3554	.2275	1.46	.4279	.1374
.67	.2486	.3187	1.07	.3577	.2251	1.47	.4292	.1354
.68	.2517	.3166	1.08	.3599	.2227	1.48	.4306	.1334
.69	.2549	.3144	1.09	.3621	.2203	1.49	.4319	.1315
.70	.2580	.3123	1.10	.3643	.2179	1.50	.4332	.1295
.71	.2611	.3101	1.11	.3665	.2155	1.51	.4345	.1276
.72	.2642	.3079	1.12	.3686	.2131	1.52	.4357	.1257
.73	.2673	.3056	1.13	.3708	.2107	1.53	.4370	.1238
.74	.2703	.3034	1.14	.3729	.2083	1.54	.4382	.1219
.75	.2734	.3011	1.15	.3749	.2059	1.55	.4394	.1200
.76	.2764	.2989	1.16	.3770	.2036	1.56	.4406	.1182
.77	.2794	.2966	1.17	.3790	.2012	1.57	.4418	.1163
.78	.2823	.2943	1.18	.3810	.1989	1.58	.4429	.1145
.79	.2852	.2920	1.19	.3830	.1965	1.59	.4441	.1127

.1109	.4452	1.60	.1942	.3849	1.20	.2897	.2881	.80
.1092	.4463	1.61	.1919	.3869	1.21	.2874	.2910	.81
.1074	.4474	1.62	.1895	.3888	1.22	.2850	.2939	.82
.1057	.4484	1.63	.1872	.3907	1.23	.2827	.2967	.83
.1040	.4495	1.64	.1849	.3925	1.24	.2803	.2995	.84
.1023	.4505	1.65	.1826	.3944	1.25	.2780	.3023	.85
.1006	.4515	1.66	.1804	.3962	1.26	.2756	.3051	.86
.0989	.4525	1.67	.1781	.3980	1.27	.2732	.3078	.87
.0973	.4535	1.68	1.758	.3997	1.28	.2709	.3106	.88
.0957	.4545	1.69	.1736	.4015	1.29	.2685	.3133	.89
.0940	.4554	1.70	.1714	.4032	1.30	.2661	.3159	.90
.0925	.4564	1.71	.1691	.4049	1.31	.2637	.3186	.91
.0909	.4573	1.72	.1669	.4066	1.32	.2613	.3212	.92
.0893	.4582	1.73	.1647	.4082	1.33	.2589	.3238	.93
.0878	.4591	1.74	.1626	.4099	1.34	.2565	.3264	.94
.0863	.4599	1.75	.1604	.4115	1.35	.2541	.3289	.95
.0848	.4608	1.76	.1582	.4131	1.36	.2516	.3315	.96
.0833	.4616	1.77	.1561	.4147	1.37	.2492	.3340	.97
.0818	.4625	1.78	.1539	.4162	1.38	.2468	.3365	.98
.0804	.4633	1.79	.1518	.4177	1.39	.2444	.3389	.99

Table A (Continued)

$\frac{x}{\sigma}$	Area	Ordinate	$\frac{x}{\sigma}$	Area	Ordinate	$\frac{x}{\sigma}$	Area	Ordinate
1.80	.4641	.0790	2.20	.4861	.0355	2.60	.4953	.0136
1.81	.4649	.0775	2.21	.4864	.0347	2.61	.4955	.0132
1.82	.4656	.0761	2.22	.4868	.0339	2.62	.4956	.0129
1.83	.4664	.0748	2.23	.4871	.0332	2.63	.4957	.0126
1.84	.4671	.0734	2.24	.4875	.0325	2.64	.4959	.0122
1.85	.4678	.0721	2.25	.4878	.0317	2.65	.4960	.0119
1.86	.4686	.0707	2.26	.4881	.0310	2.66	.4961	.0116
1.87	.4693	.0694	2.27	.4884	.0303	2.67	.4962	.0113
1.88	.4699	.0681	2.28	.4887	.0297	2.68	.4963	.0110
1.89	.4706	.0669	2.29	.4890	.0290	2.69	.4964	.0107
1.90	.4713	.0656	2.30	.4893	.0283	2.70	.4965	.0104
1.91	.4719	.0644	2.31	.4896	.0277	2.71	.4966	.0101
1.92	.4726	.0632	2.32	.4898	.0270	2.72	.4967	.0099
1.93	.4732	.0620	2.33	.4901	.0264	2.73	.4968	.0096
1.94	.4738	.0608	2.34	.4904	.0258	2.74	.4969	.0093
1.95	.4744	.0596	2.35	.4906	.0252	2.75	.4970	.0091
1.96	.4750	.0584	2.36	.4909	.0246	2.76	.4971	.0088
1.97	.4756	.0573	2.37	.4911	.0241	2.77	.4972	.0086
1.98	.4761	.0562	2.38	.4913	.0235	2.78	.4973	.0084
1.99	.4767	.0551	2.39	.4916	.0229.	2.79	.4974	.0081

2.00	.4772	.0540	2.40	.4918	.0224	2.80	.4974	.0079
2.01	.4778	.0529	2.41	.4920	.0219	2.81	.4975	.0077
2.02	.4783	.0519	2.42	.4922	.0213	2.82	.4976	.0075
2.03	.4788	.0508	2.43	.4925	.0208	2.83	.4977	.0073
2.04	.4793	.0498	2.44	.4927	.0203	2.84	.4977	.0071
2.05	.4798	.0488	2.45	.4929	.0198	2.85	.4978	.0069
2.06	.4803	.0478	2.46	.4931	.0194	2.86	.4979	.0067
2.07	.4808	.0468	2.47	.4932	.0189	2.87	.4979	.0065
2.08	.4812	.0459	2.48	.4934	.0184	2.88	.4980	.0063
2.09	.4817	.0449	2.49	.4936	.0180	2.89	.4981	.0061
2.10	.4821	.0440	2.50	.4938	.0175	2.90	.4981	.0060
2.11	.4826	.0431	2.51	.4940	.0171	2.91	.4982	.0058
2.12	.4830	.0422	2.52	.4941	.0167	2.92	.4982	.0056
2.13	.4834	.0413	2.53	.4943	.0163	2.93	.4983	.0055
2.14	.4838	.0404	2.54	.4945	.0158	2.94	.4984	.0053
2.15	.4842	.0395	2.55	.4946	.0154	2.95	.4984	.0051
2.16	.4846	.0387	2.56	.4948	.0151	2.96	.4985	.0050
2.17	.4850	.0379	2.57	.4949	.0147	2.97	.4985	.0048
2.18	.4854	.0371	2.58	.4951	.0143	2.98	.4986	.0047
2.19	.4857	.0363	2.59	.4952	.0139	2.99	.4986	.0046
						3.00	.4987	.0044

Source: From J. E. Wert, *Educational Statistics.* Used with permission of McGraw-Hill Book Company.

Table B Listing of Random Numbers

09 18 82 00 97	32 82 53 95 27	04 22 08 63 04	83 38 98 73 74	64 27 85 80 44
90 04 58 54 97	51 98 15 06 54	94 93 88 19 97	91 87 07 61 50	68 47 66 46 59
73 18 95 02 07	47 67 72 62 69	62 29 06 44 64	27 12 46 70 18	41 36 18 27 60
75 76 87 64 90	20 97 18 17 49	90 42 91 22 72	95 37 50 58 71	93 82 34 31 78
54 01 64 40 56	66 28 13 10 03	00 68 22 73 98	20 71 45 32 95	07 70 61 78 13
08 35 86 99 10	78 54 24 27 85	13 66 15 88 73	04 61 89 75 53	31 22 30 84 20
28 30 60 32 64	81 33 31 05 91	40 51 00 78 93	32 60 46 04 75	94 11 90 18 40
53 84 08 62 33	81 59 41 36 28	51 21 59 02 90	28 46 66 87 95	77 76 22 07 91
91 75 75 37 41	61 61 36 22 69	50 26 39 02 12	55 78 17 65 14	83 48 34 70 55
89 41 59 26 94	00 39 75 83 91	12 60 71 76 46	48 94 97 23 06	94 54 13 74 08
77 51 30 38 20	86 83 42 99 01	68 41 48 27 74	51 90 81 39 80	72 89 35 55 07
19 50 23 71 74	69 97 92 02 88	55 21 02 97 73	74 28 77 52 51	65 34 46 74 15
21 81 85 93 13	93 27 88 17 57	05 68 67 31 56	07 08 28 50 46	31 85 33 84 52
51 47 46 64 99	68 10 72 36 21	94 04 99 13 45	42 83 60 91 91	08 00 74 54 49
99 55 96 83 31	62 53 52 41 70	69 77 71 28 30	74 81 97 81 42	43 86 07 28 34
33 71 34 80 07	93 58 47 28 69	51 92 66 47 21	58 30 32 98 22	93 17 49 39 72
85 27 48 68 93	11 30 32 92 70	28 83 43 41 37	73 51 59 04 00	71 14 84 36 43
84 13 38 96 40	44 03 55 21 66	73 85 27 00 91	61 22 26 05 61	62 32 71 84 23
56 73 21 62 34	17 39 59 61 31	10 12 39 16 22	85 49 65 75 60	81 60 41 88 80
65 13 85 68 06	87 64 88 52 61	34 31 36 58 61	45 87 52 10 69	85 64 44 72 77
38 00 10 21 76	81 71 91 17 11	71 60 29 29 37	74 21 96 40 49	65 58 44 96 98
37 40 29 63 97	01 30 47 75 86	56 27 11 00 86	47 32 46 26 05	40 03 03 74 38
97 12 54 03 48	87 08 33 14 17	21 81 53 92 50	75 23 76 20 47	15 50 12 95 78
21 82 64 11 34	47 14 33 40 72	64 63 88 59 02	49 13 90 64 41	03 85 65 45 52
73 13 54 27 42	95 71 90 90 35	85 79 47 42 96	08 78 98 81 56	64 69 11 92 02
07 63 87 79 29	03 06 11 80 72	96 20 74 41 56	23 82 19 95 38	04 71 36 69 94
60 52 88 34 41	07 95 41 98 14	59 17 52 06 95	05 53 35 21 39	61 21 20 64 55
83 59 63 56 55	06 95 89 29 83	05 12 80 97 19	77 43 35 37 83	92 30 15 04 98
10 85 06 27 46	99 59 91 05 07	13 49 90 63 19	53 07 57 18 39	06 41 01 93 62
39 82 09 89 52	43 62 26 31 47	64 42 18 08 14	43 80 00 93 51	31 02 47 31 67
59 58 00 64 78	75 56 97 88 00	88 83 55 44 86	23 76 80 61 56	04 11 10 84 08
38 50 80 73 41	23 79 34 87 63	90 82 29 70 22	17 71 90 42 07	95 95 44 99 53
30 69 27 06 68	94 68 81 62 27	56 19 68 00 91	82 06 76 34 00	05 46 26 92 00
65 44 39 56 59	18 28 82 74 37	49 63 22 40 41	08 33 76 56 76	96 29 99 08 36
27 26 75 02 64	13 19 27 22 94	07 47 74 46 06	17 98 54 89 11	97 34 13 03 58

Table B (Continued)

91 30 70 69 91	19 07 22 42 10	36 69 95 37 28	28 82 53 57 93	28 97 66 62 52
68 43 49 46 88	84 47 31 36 22	62 12 69 84 08	12 84 38 25 90	09 81 59 31 46
48 90 81 58 77	54 74 52 45 91	35 70 00 47 54	83 82 45 26 92	54 13 05 51 60
06 91 34 51 97	42 67 27 86 01	11 88 30 95 28	63 01 19 89 01	14 97 44 03 44
10 45 51 60 19	14 21 03 37 12	91 34 23 78 21	88 32 58 08 51	43 66 77 08 83
12 88 39 73 43	65 02 76 11 84	04 28 50 13 92	17 97 41 50 77	90 71 22 67 69
21 77 83 09 76	38 80 73 69 61	31 64 94 20 96	63 28 10 20 23	08 81 64 74 49
19 52 35 95 15	65 12 25 96 59	86 28 36 82 58	69 57 21 37 98	16 43 59 15 29
67 24 55 26 70	35 58 31 65 63	79 24 68 66 86	76 46 33 42 22	26 65 59 08 02
60 58 44 73 77	07 50 03 79 92	45 13 42 65 29	26 76 08 36 37	41 32 64 43 44
53 85 34 13 77	36 06 69 48 50	58 83 87 38 59	49 36 47 33 31	96 24 04 36 42
24 63 73 87 36	74 38 48 93 42	52 62 30 79 92	12 36 91 86 01	03 74 28 38 73
83 08 01 24 51	38 99 22 28 15	07 75 95 17 77	97 37 72 75 85	51 97 23 78 67
16 44 42 43 34	36 15 19 90 73	27 49 37 09 39	85 13 03 25 52	54 84 65 47 59
60 79 01 81 57	57 17 86 57 62	11 16 17 85 76	45 81 95 29 79	65 13 00 48 60
03 99 11 04 61	93 71 61 68 94	66 08 32 46 53	84 60 95 82 32	88 61 81 91 61
38 55 59 55 54	32 88 65 97 80	08 35 56 08 60	29 73 54 77 62	71 29 92 38 53
17 54 67 37 04	92 05 24 62 15	55 12 12 92 81	59 07 60 79 36	27 95 45 89 09
32 64 35 28 61	95 81 90 68 31	00 91 19 89 36	76 35 59 37 79	80 86 30 05 14
69 57 26 87 77	39 51 03 59 05	14 06 04 06 19	29 54 96 96 16	33 56 46 07 80
24 12 26 65 91	27 69 90 64 94	14 84 54 66 72	61 95 87 71 00	90 89 97 57 54
61 19 63 02 31	92 96 26 17 73	41 83 95 53 82	17 26 77 09 43	78 03 87 02 67
30 53 22 17 04	10 27 41 22 02	39 68 52 33 00	10 06 16 88 29	55 98 66 64 85
03 78 89 75 99	75 86 72 07 17	74 41 65 31 66	35 20 83 33 74	87 53 90 88 23
48 22 86 33 79	85 78 34 76 19	53 15 26 74 33	35 66 35 29 72	16 81 86 03 11
60 36 59 46 53	35 07 53 39 49	42 61 42 92 97	01 91 82 83 16	98 95 37 32 31
83 79 94 24 02	56 62 33 44 42	34 99 44 13 74	70 07 11 47 36	09 95 81 80 65
32 96 00 74 05	36 40 98 32 32	99 38 54 16 00	11 13 30 75 86	15 91 70 62 53
19 32 25 38 45	57 62 05 26 06	66 49 76 86 46	78 13 86 65 59	19 64 09 94 13
11 22 09 47 47	07 39 93 74 08	48 50 92 39 29	27 48 24 54 76	85 24 43 51 59
31 75 15 72 60	68 98 00 53 39	15 47 04 83 55	88 65 12 25 96	03 15 21 91 21
88 49 29 93 82	14 45 40 45 04	20 09 49 89 77	74 84 39 34 13	22 10 97 85 08
30 93 44 77 44	07 48 18 38 28	73 78 80 65 33	28 59 72 04 05	94 20 52 03 80
22 88 84 88 93	27 49 99 87 48	60 53 04 51 28	74 02 28 46 17	82 03 71 02 68
78 21 21 69 93	35 90 29 13 86	44 37 21 54 86	65 74 11 40 14	87 48 13 72 20

Table B (Continued)

41 84 98 45 47	46 85 05 23 26	34 67 75 83 60	74 91 06 43 45	19 32 58 15 49
46 35 23 30 49	69 24 89 34 60	45 30 50 75 21	61 31 83 18 55	14 41 37 09 51
11 08 79 62 94	14 01 33 17 92	59 74 76 72 77	76 50 33 45 13	39 66 37 75 44
52 70 10 83 37	56 30 38 73 15	16 52 06 96 76	11 65 49 98 93	02 18 16 81 61
57 27 53 68 98	81 30 44 85 85	68 65 22 73 76	92 85 25 58 66	88 44 80 35 84
20 85 77 31 56	70 28 42 43 26	79 37 59 52 20	01 15 96 32 67	10 62 24 83 91
15 63 38 49 24	90 41 59 36 14	33 52 12 66 65	55 82 34 76 41	86 22 53 17 04
92 69 44 82 97	39 90 40 21 15	59 58 94 90 67	66 82 14 15 75	49 76 70 40 37
77 61 31 90 19	88 15 20 00 80	20 55 49 14 09	96 27 74 82 57	50 81 60 76 16
38 68 83 24 86	45 13 46 35 45	59 40 47 20 59	43 94 75 16 80	43 85 25 96 93
25 16 30 18 89	70 01 41 50 21	41 29 06 73 12	71 85 71 59 57	68 97 11 14 03
65 25 10 76 29	37 23 93 32 95	05 87 00 11 19	92 78 42 63 40	18 47 76 56 22
36 81 54 36 25	18 63 73 75 09	82 44 49 90 05	04 92 17 37 01	14 70 79 39 97
64 39 71 16 92	05 32 78 21 62	20 24 78 17 59	45 19 72 53 32	83 74 52 25 67
04 51 52 56 24	95 09 66 79 46	48 46 08 55 58	15 19 11 87 82	16 93 03 33 61
83 76 16 08 73	43 25 38 41 45	60 83 32 59 83	01 29 14 13 49	20 36 80 71 26
14 38 70 63 45	80 85 40 92 79	43 52 90 63 18	38 38 47 47 61	41 19 63 74 80
51 32 19 22 46	80 08 87 70 74	88 72 25 67 36	66 16 44 94 31	66 91 93 16 78
72 47 20 00 08	80 89 01 80 02	94 81 33 19 00	54 15 58 34 36	35 35 25 41 31
05 46 65 53 06	93 12 81 84 64	74 45 79 05 61	72 84 81 18 34	79 98 26 84 16
39 52 87 24 84	82 47 42 55 93	48 54 53 52 47	18 61 91 36 74	18 61 11 92 41
81 61 61 87 11	53 34 24 42 76	75 12 21 17 24	74 62 77 37 07	58 31 91 59 97
07 58 61 61 20	82 64 12 28 20	92 90 41 31 41	32 39 21 97 63	61 19 96 79 40
90 76 70 42 35	13 57 41 72 00	69 90 26 37 42	78 46 42 25 01	18 62 79 08 72
40 18 82 81 93	29 59 38 86 27	94 97 21 15 98	62 09 53 67 87	00 44 15 89 97
34 41 48 21 57	86 88 75 50 87	19 15 20 00 23	12 30 28 07 83	32 62 46 86 91
63 43 97 53 63	44 98 91 68 22	36 02 40 08 67	76 37 84 16 05	65 96 17 34 88
67 04 90 90 70	93 39 94 55 47	94 45 87 42 84	05 04 14 98 07	20 28 83 40 60
79 49 50 41 46	52 16 29 02 86	54 15 83 42 43	46 97 83 54 82	59 36 29 59 38
91 70 43 05 52	04 73 72 10 31	75 05 19 30 29	47 66 56 43 82	99 78 29 34 78
94 01 54 68 74	32 44 44 82 77	59 82 09 61 63	64 65 42 58 43	41 14 54 28 20
74 10 88 82 22	88 57 07 40 15	25 70 49 10 35	01 75 51 47 50	48 96 83 86 03
62 88 08 78 73	95 16 05 92 21	22 30 49 03 14	72 87 71 73 34	39 28 30 41 49
11 74 81 21 02	80 58 04 18 67	17 71 05 96 21	06 55 40 78 50	73 95 07 95 52
17 94 40 56 00	60 47 80 33 43	25 85 25 89 05	57 21 63 96 18	49 85 69 93 26

Table B (Continued)

66 06 74 27 92	95 04 35 26 80	46 78 05 64 87	09 97 15 94 81	37 00 62 21 86
54 24 49 10 30	45 54 77 08 18	59 84 99 61 69	61 45 92 16 47	87 41 71 71 98
30 94 55 75 89	31 73 25 72 60	47 67 00 76 54	46 37 62 53 66	94 74 64 95 80
69 17 03 74 03	86 99 59 03 07	94 30 47 18 03	26 82 50 55 11	12 45 99 13 14
08 34 58 89 75	35 84 18 57 71	08 10 55 99 87	87 11 22 14 76	14 71 37 11 81
27 76 74 35 84	85 30 18 89 77	29 49 06 97 14	73 03 54 12 07	74 69 90 93 10
13 02 51 43 38	54 06 61 52 43	47 72 46 67 33	47 43 14 39 05	31 04 85 66 99
80 21 73 62 92	98 52 52 43 35	24 43 22 48 96	43 27 75 88 74	11 46 61 60 82
10 87 56 20 04	90 39 16 11 05	57 41 10 63 68	53 85 63 07 43	08 67 08 47 41
54 12 75 73 26	26 62 91 90 87	24 47 28 87 79	30 54 02 78 86	61 73 27 54 54
60 31 14 28 24	37 30 14 26 78	45 99 04 32 42	17 37 45 20 03	70 70 77 02 14
49 73 97 14 84	92 00 39 80 86	76 66 87 32 09	59 20 21 19 73	02 90 23 32 50
78 62 65 15 94	16 45 39 46 14	39 01 49 70 66	83 01 20 98 32	25 57 17 76 28
66 69 21 39 86	99 83 70 05 82	81 23 24 49 87	09 50 49 64 12	90 19 37 95 68
44 07 12 80 91	07 36 29 77 03	76 44 74 25 37	98 52 49 78 31	65 70 40 95 14
41 46 88 51 49	49 55 41 79 94	14 92 43 96 50	95 29 40 05 56	70 48 10 69 05
94 55 93 75 59	49 67 85 31 19	70 31 20 56 82	66 98 63 40 99	74 47 42 07 40
41 61 57 03 60	64 11 45 86 60	90 85 06 46 18	80 62 05 17 90	11 43 63 80 72
50 27 39 31 13	41 79 48 68 61	24 78 18 96 83	55 41 18 56 67	77 53 59 98 92
41 39 68 05 04	90 67 00 82 89	40 90 20 50 69	95 08 30 67 83	28 10 25 78 16
25 80 72 42 60	71 52 97 89 20	72 68 20 73 85	90 72 65 71 66	98 88 40 85 83
06 17 09 79 65	88 30 29 80 41	21 44 34 18 08	68 98 48 36 20	89 74 79 88 82
60 80 85 44 44	74 41 28 11 05	01 17 62 88 38	36 42 11 64 89	18 05 95 10 61
80 94 04 48 93	10 40 83 62 22	80 58 27 19 44	92 63 84 03 33	67 05 41 60 67
19 51 69 01 20	46 75 97 16 43	13 17 75 52 92	21 03 68 28 08	77 50 19 74 27
49 38 65 44 80	26 60 42 35 54	21 78 54 11 01	91 17 81 01 74	29 42 09 04 38
06 31 28 89 40	15 99 56 93 21	47 45 86 48 09	98 18 98 18 51	29 65 18 42 15
60 94 20 03 07	11 89 79 26 74	40 40 56 80 32	96 71 75 42 44	10 70 14 13 93
92 32 99 89 32	78 28 44 63 47	71 20 99 20 61	39 44 89 31 36	25 72 20 85 64
77 93 66 35 74	31 38 34 19 24	85 56 12 96 71	58 13 71 78 20	22 75 13 65 18
38 10 17 77 56	11 65 71 38 97	95 88 95 70 67	47 64 81 38 85	70 66 99 34 06
39 64 16 94 57	91 33 92 25 02	92 61 38 97 19	11 94 75 62 03	19 32 42 05 04
84 05 44 04 55	99 39 66 36 80	67 66 76 06 31	69 18 19 68 45	38 52 51 16 00
47 46 80 35 77	57 64 96 32 66	24 70 07 15 94	14 00 42 31 53	69 24 90 57 46
43 32 13 13 70	28 97 72 38 96	76 47 96 85 62	62 34 20 75 89	08 89 90 59 85

302

Table B (Continued)

```
64 28 16 18 26   18 55 56 49 37   13 17 33 33 65   78 85 11 64 99   87 06 41 30 75
66 84 77 04 95   32 35 00 29 85   86 71 63 87 46   26 31 37 74 63   55 38 77 26 81
72 46 13 32 30   21 52 95 34 24   92 58 10 22 62   78 43 86 62 76   18 39 67 35 38
21 03 29 10 50   13 05 81 62 18   12 47 05 65 00   15 29 27 61 39   59 52 65 21 13
95 36 26 70 11   06 65 11 61 36   01 01 60 08 57   55 01 85 63 74   35 82 47 17 08

49 71 29 73 80   10 40 45 54 52   34 03 06 07 26   75 21 11 02 71   36 63 36 84 24
58 27 56 17 64   97 58 65 47 16   50 25 94 63 45   87 19 54 60 92   26 78 76 09 39
89 51 41 17 88   68 22 42 34 17   73 95 97 61 45   30 34 24 02 77   11 04 97 20 49
15 47 25 06 69   48 13 93 67 32   46 87 43 70 88   73 46 50 98 19   58 86 93 52 20
12 12 08 61 24   51 24 74 43 02   60 88 35 21 09   21 43 73 67 86   49 22 67 78 37

19 61 21 84 30   11 66 19 47 70   77 60 36 56 69   86 86 81 26 65   30 01 27 59 89
39 14 17 74 00   28 00 06 42 38   73 25 87 17 94   31 34 02 62 56   66 45 33 70 16
64 75 68 04 57   08 74 71 28 36   03 46 95 06 78   03 27 44 34 23   66 67 78 25 56
92 90 15 18 78   56 44 12 29 98   29 71 83 84 47   06 45 32 53 11   07 56 55 37 71
03 55 19 00 70   09 48 39 40 50   45 93 81 81 35   36 90 84 33 21   11 07 35 18 03

98 88 46 62 09   06 83 05 36 56   14 66 35 63 46   71 43 00 49 09   19 81 80 57 07
27 36 98 68 82   53 47 30 75 41   53 63 37 08 63   03 74 81 28 22   19 36 04 90 88
59 06 67 59 74   63 33 52 04 83   43 51 43 74 81   58 27 82 69 67   49 32 54 39 51
91 64 79 37 83   64 16 94 90 22   98 58 80 94 95   49 82 95 90 68   38 83 10 48 38
83 60 59 24 19   39 54 20 77 72   71 56 87 56 73   35 18 58 97 59   44 90 17 42 91

24 89 58 85 30   70 77 43 54 39   46 75 87 04 72   70 20 79 26 75   91 62 36 12 75
15 72 02 65 56   95 59 62 00 94   73 75 08 57 88   34 26 40 17 03   46 83 36 52 48
14 14 15 34 10   38 64 90 63 43   57 25 66 13 42   72 70 97 53 18   90 37 93 75 62
27 41 67 56 70   92 17 67 25 35   93 11 95 60 77   06 88 61 82 44   92 34 43 13 74
32 07 10 74 29   81 00 74 77 49   40 74 45 69 74   23 33 68 88 21   53 84 11 05 36

11 44 58 27 93   24 83 19 32 41   14 19 97 62 68   70 88 36 80 02   03 82 91 74 43
32 51 37 64 00   52 22 59 23 48   62 30 89 84 81   29 74 43 31 65   33 14 16 10 20
51 47 94 50 27   76 16 05 74 11   13 78 01 36 32   52 30 87 77 62   88 87 43 36 97
43 21 05 14 66   09 08 85 03 95   26 74 30 53 06   21 70 67 00 01   99 43 98 07 67
28 74 99 51 48   94 89 77 86 36   96 75 00 90 24   94 53 89 11 43   96 69 36 18 86

15 18 47 57 63   47 07 58 81 58   05 31 35 34 39   14 90 80 88 30   60 09 62 15 51
23 65 16 25 46   96 89 22 52 40   47 51 15 84 83   87 34 27 88 18   07 85 53 92 69
30 56 62 12 20   00 29 22 40 69   25 07 22 95 19   52 54 85 40 91   21 28 22 12 96
60 95 81 76 95   58 07 26 89 90   60 32 99 59 55   71 58 66 34 17   35 94 76 78 07
17 62 16 45 47   46 85 03 79 81   38 52 70 90 37   64 75 60 33 24   04 98 68 36 66
```

Table B (Continued)

99 28 22 58 44	79 13 97 84 35	35 42 84 35 61	69 79 96 33 14	12 99 19 35 16
41 39 49 42 06	93 43 23 78 36	94 91 92 68 46	02 55 57 44 10	94 91 54 81 99
55 28 03 74 70	93 62 20 43 45	15 09 21 95 10	18 09 41 66 13	78 23 45 00 01
65 49 19 79 76	38 30 63 21 92	82 63 95 46 24	72 43 49 26 06	23 19 17 46 93
81 52 10 01 04	18 24 87 55 83	90 32 65 07 85	54 03 46 62 51	35 77 41 46 92
92 34 54 45 79	85 93 24 40 53	75 70 42 08 40	86 58 38 39 44	52 45 67 37 66
13 96 33 11 51	32 36 49 16 91	47 35 74 03 38	23 43 52 40 65	08 45 89 53 66
16 52 01 12 94	23 23 80 17 48	41 69 06 73 28	54 81 43 77 77	10 05 74 23 32
59 42 30 23 09	70 70 38 57 36	46 14 81 42 58	29 23 61 21 52	05 08 86 58 25
47 46 36 55 33	21 19 96 05 55	33 92 80 18 17	07 39 68 92 15	30 72 22 21 02
81 88 09 22 61	17 29 28 81 90	61 78 14 88 98	92 52 52 12 83	88 58 16 00 98
91 92 60 08 19	59 14 40 02 24	30 57 09 01 94	18 32 90 69 99	26 85 71 92 38
12 42 52 81 08	16 55 41 60 16	00 04 28 32 29	10 33 33 61 68	65 61 79 48 34
01 78 22 39 24	49 44 03 04 32	81 07 73 15 43	95 21 66 48 65	13 65 85 10 81
09 33 77 45 38	44 55 36 46 72	90 96 04 18 49	93 86 54 46 08	93 17 63 48 51
10 24 92 93 29	19 71 59 40 82	14 73 88 66 67	43 70 86 63 54	93 69 22 55 27
73 46 39 93 80	38 79 38 57 74	19 05 61 39 39	46 06 22 76 47	66 14 66 32 10
37 29 63 31 21	54 19 63 41 08	75 81 48 59 86	71 17 11 51 02	28 99 26 31 65
62 38 03 62 69	60 01 40 72 01	62 44 84 63 85	42 17 58 83 50	46 18 24 91 26
19 56 76 43 50	16 31 55 39 69	80 39 58 11 14	54 35 86 45 78	47 26 91 57 47
05 49 89 08 30	25 95 59 92 36	43 28 69 10 64	99 96 99 51 44	64 42 47 73 77
27 55 32 42 41	08 15 08 95 35	08 70 39 10 41	77 32 38 10 79	45 12 79 36 86
62 15 10 70 75	83 15 51 02 52	73 10 08 86 18	23 89 18 74 18	45 41 72 02 68
71 31 45 03 63	26 86 02 77 99	49 41 68 35 34	19 18 70 80 59	76 67 70 21 10
12 36 47 12 10	87 05 25 02 41	90 78 59 78 89	81 39 95 81 30	64 43 90 56 14

Table C Values of Chi-square (χ^2) at the 5% and 1%
Levels of Significance

Degrees of freedom (df)	5%	1%
1	3.84	6.64
2	5.99	9.21
3	7.82	11.34
4	9.49	13.28
5	11.07	15.09
6	12.59	16.81
7	14.07	18.48
8	15.51	20.09
9	16.92	21.67
10	18.31	23.21
11	19.68	24.72
12	21.03	26.22
13	22.36	27.69
14	23.68	29.14
15	25.00	30.58
16	26.30	32.00
17	27.59	33.41
18	28.87	34.80
19	30.14	36.19
20	31.41	37.57
21	32.67	38.93
22	33.92	40.29
23	35.17	41.64
24	36.42	42.98
25	37.65	44.31
26	38.88	45.64
27	40.11	46.96
28	41.34	48.28
29	42.56	49.59
30	43.77	50.89

Source: Abridged from Table IV of Fisher and Yates,
Statistical Tables for Biological, Agricultural and Medical Research,
Longman Group Ltd., London (previously published by Oliver &
Boyd, Edinburgh), 6th ed., 1973, by permission of the authors
and publishers.

Table D Critical Values of the Pearson Product Moment Correlation Coefficient (*r*)

N − 2	.10	.05	.02	.01	.001
1	.98769	.99692	.999507	.999877	.9999988
2	.90000	.95000	.98000	.990000	.99900
3	.8054	:8783	.93433	.95873	.99116
4	.7293	.8114	.8822	.91720	.97406
5	.6694	.7545	.8329	.8745	.95074
6	.6215	.7067	.7887	.8343	.92493
7	.5822	.6664	.7498	.7977	.8982
8	.5494	.6319	.7155	.7646	.8721
9	.5214	.6021	.6851	.7348	.8471
10	.4973	.5760	.6581	.7079	.8233
11	.4762	.5529	.6339	.6835	.8010
12	.4575	.5324	.6120	.6614	.7800
13	.4409	.5139	.5923	.6411	.7603
14	.4259	.4973	.5742	.6226	.7420
15	.4124	.4821	.5577	.6055	.7246
16	.4000	.4683	.5425	.5897	.7084
17	.3887	.4555	.5285	.5751	.6932
18	.3783	.4438	.5155	.5614	.6787
19	.3687	.4329	.5034	.5487	.6652
20	.3598	.4227	.4921	.5368	.6524
25	.3233	.3809	.4451	.4869	.5974
30	.2960	.3494	.4093	.4487	.5541
35	.2746	.3246	.3810	.4182	.5189
40	.2573	.3044	.3578	.3932	.4896
45	.2428	.2875	.3384	.3721	.4648
50	.2306	.2732	.3218	.3541	.4433
60	.2108	.2500	.2948	.3248	.4078
70	.1954	.2319	.2737	.3017	.3799
80	.1829	.2172	.2565	.2830	.3568
90	.1726	.2050	.2422	.2673	.3375
100	.1638	.1946	.2301	.2540	.3211

Source: Taken from Table VI of Fisher and Yates, *Statistical Tables for Biological, Agricultural and Medical Research*, Longman Group Ltd., London (previously published by Oliver & Boyd, Edinburgh), 6th ed., 1973, by permission of the authors and publishers.

Table E Values of ρ (Rank-order Correlation Coefficient) at the 5% and 1% Levels of Significance

Number of pairs	5%	1%
5	1.000	—
6	.886	1.000
7	.786	.929
8	.738	.881
9	.683	.833
10	.648	.794
12	.591	.777
14	.544	.714
16	.506	.665
18	.475	.625
20	.450	.591
22	.428	.562
24	.409	.537
26	.392	.515
28	.377	.496
30	.364	.478

Source: Computed from E. G. Olds, "Distribution of the sum of squares of rank differences for small number of individuals," *Ann Math. Statist.* (1938), 9:133–148; and "The 5% significance levels for sums of squares of rank differences and a correction," *Ann. Math. Statist.* (1949), 20:117–118.

Table F Per Cent Points in the F Distribution

df_2		df_1 1	2	3	4	5	6	8	12	24	∞
1	0.1%	405284	500000	540379	562500	576405	585937	598144	610667	623497	636619
	0.5%	16211	20000	21615	22500	23056	23437	23925	24426	24940	25465
	1 %	4052	4999	5403	5625	5764	5859	5981	6106	6234	6366
	2.5%	647.79	799.50	864.16	899.58	921.85	937.11	956.66	976.71	997.25	1018.30
	5 %	161.45	199.50	215.71	224.58	230.16	233.99	238.88	243.91	249.05	254.32
	10 %	39.86	49.50	53.59	55.83	57.24	58.20	59.44	60.70	62.00	63.33
	20 %	9.47	12.00	13.06	13.73	14.01	14.26	14.59	14.90	15.24	15.58
2	0.1	998.5	999.0	999.2	999.2	999.3	999.3	999.4	999.4	999.5	999.5
	0.5	198.50	199.00	199.17	199.25	199.30	199.33	119.37	199.42	199.46	199.51
	1	98.49	99.00	99.17	99.25	99.30	99.33	99.36	99.42	99.46	99.50
	2.5	38.51	39.00	39.17	39.25	39.30	39.33	39.37	39.42	39.46	39.50
	5	18.51	19.00	19.16	19.25	19.30	19.33	19.37	19.41	19.45	19.50
	10	8.53	9.00	9.16	9.24	9.29	9.33	9.37	9.41	9.45	9.49
	20	3.56	4.00	4.16	4.24	4.28	4.32	4.36	4.40	4.44	4.48
3	0.1	167.5	148.5	141.1	137.1	134.6	132.8	130.6	128.3	125.9	123.5
	0.5	55.55	49.80	47.47	46.20	45.39	44.84	44.13	43.39	42.62	41.83
	1	34.12	30.81	29.46	28.71	28.24	27.91	27.49	27.05	26.60	26.12
	2.5	17.44	16.04	15.44	15.10	14.89	14.74	14.54	14.34	14.12	13.90
	5	10.13	9.55	9.28	9.12	9.01	8.94	8.84	8.74	8.64	8.53
	10	5.54	5.46	5.39	5.34	5.31	5.28	5.25	5.22	5.18	5.13
	20	2.68	2.89	2.94	2.96	2.97	2.97	2.98	2.98	2.98	2.98

Table F (Continued)

df_2		df_1, 1	2	3	4	5	6	8	12	24	∞
4	0.1%	74.14	61.25	56.18	53.44	51.71	50.53	49.00	47.41	45.77	44.05
	0.5%	31.33	26.28	24.26	23.16	22.46	21.98	21.35	20.71	20.03	19.33
	1 %	21.20	18.00	16.69	15.98	15.52	15.21	14.80	14.37	13.93	13.46
	2.5%	12.22	10.65	9.98	9.60	9.36	9.20	8.98	8.75	8.51	8.26
	5 %	7.71	6.94	6.59	6.39	6.26	6.16	6.04	5.91	5.77	5.63
	10 %	4.54	4.32	4.19	4.11	4.05	4.01	3.95	3.90	3.83	3.76
	20 %	2.35	2.47	2.48	2.48	2.48	2.47	2.47	2.46	2.44	2.43
5	0.1	47.04	36.61	33.20	31.09	29.75	28.84	27.64	26.42	25.14	23.78
	0.5	22.79	18.31	16.53	15.56	14.94	14.51	13.96	13.38	12.78	12.14
	1	16.26	13.27	12.06	11.39	10.97	10.67	10.29	9.89	9.47	9.02
	2.5	10.01	8.43	7.76	7.39	7.15	6.98	6.76	6.52	6.28	6.02
	5	6.61	5.79	5.41	5.19	5.05	4.95	4.82	4.68	4.53	4.36
	10	4.06	3.78	3.62	3.52	3.45	3.40	3.34	3.27	3.19	3.10
	20	2.18	2.26	2.25	2.24	2.23	2.22	2.20	2.18	2.16	2.13
6	0.1	35.51	27.00	23.70	21.90	20.81	20.03	19.03	17.99	16.89	15.75
	0.5	18.64	14.54	12.92	12.03	11.46	11.07	10.57	10.03	9.47	8.88
	1	13.75	10.92	9.78	9.15	8.75	8.47	8.10	7.72	7.31	6.88
	2.5	8.81	7.26	6.60	6.23	5.99	5.82	5.60	5.37	5.12	4.85
	5	5.99	5.14	4.76	4.53	4.39	4.28	4.15	4.00	3.84	3.67
	10	3.78	3.46	3.29	3.18	3.11	3.05	2.98	2.90	2.82	2.72
	20	2.07	2.13	2.11	2.09	2.08	2.06	2.04	2.02	1.99	1.95

7	0.1	29.22	21.69	18.77	17.19	16.21	15.52	14.63	13.71	12.73	11.69
	0.5	16.24	12.40	10.88	10.05	9.52	9.16	8.68	8.18	7.65	7.08
	1	12.25	9.55	8.45	7.85	7.46	7.19	6.84	6.47	6.07	5.65
	2.5	8.07	6.54	5.89	5.52	5.29	5.12	4.90	4.67	4.42	4.14
	5	5.59	4.74	4.35	4.12	3.97	3.87	3.73	3.57	3.41	3.23
	10	3.59	3.26	3.07	2.96	2.88	2.83	2.75	2.67	2.58	2.47
	20	2.00	2.04	2.02	1.99	1.97	1.96	1.93	1.91	1.87	1.83
8	0.1	25.42	18.49	15.83	14.39	13.49	12.86	12.04	11.19	10.30	9.34
	0.5	14.69	11.04	9.69	8.81	8.30	7.95	7.50	7.01	6.50	5.95
	1	11.26	8.65	7.59	7.01	6.63	6.37	6.03	5.67	5.28	14.86
	2.5	7.57	6.06	5.42	5.05	4.82	4.65	4.43	4.20	3.95	3.67
	5	5.32	4.46	4.07	3.84	3.69	3.58	3.44	3.28	3.12	2.93
	10	3.46	3.11	2.92	2.81	2.73	2.67	2.59	2.50	2.40	2.29
	20	1.95	1.98	1.95	1.92	1.90	1.88	1.86	1.83	1.79	1.74
9	0.1	22.86	16.39	13.90	12.56	11.71	11.13	10.37	9.57	8.72	7.81
	0.5	13.61	10.11	8.72	7.96	7.47	7.13	6.69	6.23	5.73	5.19
	1	10.56	8.02	6.99	6.42	6.06	5.80	5.47	5.11	4.73	4.31
	2.5	7.21	5.71	5.08	4.72	4.48	4.32	4.10	3.87	3.61	3.33
	5	5.12	4.26	3.86	3.63	3.48	3.37	3.23	3.07	2.90	2.71
	10	3.36	3.01	2.81	2.69	2.61	2.55	2.47	2.38	2.28	2.16
	20	1.91	1.94	1.90	1.87	1.85	1.83	1.80	1.76	1.72	1.67
10	0.1	21.04	14.91	12.55	11.28	10.48	9.92	9.20	8.45	7.64	6.76
	0.5	12.83	9.43	8.08	7.34	6.87	6.54	6.12	5.66	5.17	4.64
	1	10.04	7.56	6.55	5.99	5.64	5.39	5.06	4.71	4.33	3.91

Table F (Continued)

df_2		df_1 1	2	3	4	5	6	8	12	24	∞
	2.5%	6.94	5.46	4.83	4.47	4.24	4.07	3.85	3.62	3.37	3.08
	5 %	4.96	4.10	3.71	3.48	3.33	3.22	3.07	2.91	2.74	2.54
	10 %	3.28	2.92	2.73	2.61	2.52	2.46	3.28	2.28	2.18	2.06
	20 %	1.88	1.90	1.86	1.83	1.80	1.78	1.75	1.72	1.67	1.62
11	0.1	19.69	13.81	11.56	10.35	9.58	9.05	8.35	7.63	6.85	6.00
	0.5	12.23	8.91	7.60	6.88	6.42	6.10	5.68	5.24	4.76	4.23
	1	9.65	7.20	6.22	5.67	5.32	5.07	4.74	4.40	4.02	3.60
	2.5	6.72	5.26	4.63	4.28	4.04	3.88	3.66	3.43	3.17	2.88
	5	4.84	3.98	3.59	3.36	3.20	3.09	2.95	2.79	2.61	2.40
	10	3.23	2.86	2.66	2.54	2.45	2.39	2.30	2.21	2.10	1.97
	20	1.86	1.87	1.83	1.80	1.77	1.75	1.72	1.68	1.63	1.57
12	0.1	18.64	12.97	10.80	9.63	8.89	8.38	7.71	7.00	6.25	5.42
	0.5	11.75	8.51	7.23	6.52	6.07	5.76	5.35	4.91	4.43	3.90
	1	9.33	6.93	5.95	5.41	5.06	4.82	4.50	4.16	3.78	3.36
	2.5	6.55	5.10	4.47	4.12	3.89	3.73	3.51	3.28	3.02	2.72
	5	4.75	3.88	3.49	3.26	3.11	3.00	2.85	2.69	2.50	2.30
	10	3.18	2.81	2.61	2.48	2.39	2.33	2.24	2.15	2.04	1.90
	20	1.84	1.85	1.80	1.77	1.74	1.72	1.69	1.65	1.60	1.54
13	0.1	17.81	12.31	10.21	9.07	8.35	7.86	7.21	6.52	5.78	4.97
	0.5	11.37	8.19	6.93	6.23	5.79	5.48	5.08	4.64	4.17	3.65
	1	9.07	6.70	5.74	5.20	4.86	4.62	4.30	3.96	3.59	3.16

2.5	6.41	4.97	4.35	4.00	3.77	3.60	3.39	3.15	2.89	2.60
5	4.67	3.80	3.41	3.18	3.02	2.92	2.77	2.60	2.42	2.21
10	3.14	2.76	2.56	2.43	2.35	2.28	2.20	2.10	1.98	1.85
20	1.82	1.83	1.78	1.75	1.72	1.69	1.66	1.62	1.57	1.51
14 0.1	17.14	11.78	9.73	8.62	7.92	7.43	6.80	6.13	5.41	4.60
0.5	11.06	7.92	6.68	6.00	5.56	5.26	4.86	4.43	3.96	3.44
1	8.86	6.51	5.56	5.03	4.69	4.46	4.14	3.80	3.43	3.00
2.5	6.30	4.86	4.24	3.89	3.66	3.50	3.29	3.05	2.79	2.49
5	4.60	3.74	3.34	3.11	2.96	2.85	2.70	2.53	2.35	2.13
10	3.10	2.73	2.52	2.39	2.31	2.24	2.15	2.05	1.94	1.80
20	1.81	1.81	1.76	1.73	1.70	1.67	1.64	1.60	1.55	1.48
15 0.1	16.59	11.34	9.34	8.25	7.57	7.09	6.47	5.81	5.10	4.31
0.5	10.80	7.70	6.48	5.80	5.37	5.07	4.67	4.25	3.79	3.26
1	8.68	6.36	5.42	4.89	4.56	4.32	4.00	3.67	3.29	2.87
2.5	6.20	4.77	4.15	3.80	3.58	3.41	3.20	2.96	2.70	2.40
5	4.54	3.68	3.29	3.06	2.90	2.79	2.64	2.48	2.29	2.07
10	3.07	2.70	2.49	2.36	2.27	2.21	2.12	2.02	1.90	1.76
20	1.80	1.79	1.75	1.71	1.68	1.66	1.62	1.58	1.53	1.46
16 0.1	16.12	10.97	9.00	7.94	7.27	6.81	6.19	5.55	4.85	4.06
0.5	10.58	7.51	6.30	5.64	5.21	4.91	4.52	4.10	3.64	3.11
1	8.53	6.23	5.29	4.77	4.44	4.20	3.89	3.55	3.18	2.75
2.5	6.12	4.69	4.08	3.73	3.50	3.34	3.12	2.89	2.63	2.32
5	4.49	3.63	3.24	3.01	2.85	2.74	2.59	2.42	2.24	2.01
10	3.05	2.67	2.46	2.33	2.24	2.18	2.09	1.99	1.87	1.72
20	1.79	1.78	1.74	1.70	1.67	1.64	1.61	1.56	1.51	1.43

Table F (Continued)

df_2		df_1 1	2	3	4	5	6	8	12	24	∞
17	0.1%	15.72	10.66	8.73	7.68	7.02	6.56	5.96	5.32	4.63	3.85
	0.5%	10.38	7.35	6.16	5.50	5.07	4.78	4.39	3.97	3.51	2.98
	1 %	8.40	6.11	5.18	4.67	4.34	4.10	3.79	3.45	3.08	2.65
	2.5%	6.04	4.62	4.01	3.66	3.44	3.28	3.06	2.82	2.56	2.25
	5 %	4.45	3.59	3.20	2.96	2.81	2.70	2.55	2.38	2.19	1.96
	10 %	3.03	2.64	2.44	2.31	2.22	2.15	2.06	1.96	1.84	1.69
	20 %	1.78	1.77	1.72	1.68	1.65	1.63	1.59	1.55	1.49	1.42
18	0.1	15.38	10.39	8.49	7.46	6.81	6.35	5.76	5.13	4.45	3.67
	0.5	10.22	7.21	6.03	5.37	4.96	4.66	4.28	3.86	3.40	2.87
	1	8.28	6.01	5.09	4.58	4.25	4.01	3.71	3.37	3.00	2.57
	2.5	5.98	4.56	3.95	3.61	3.38	3.22	3.01	2.77	2.50	2.19
	5	4.41	3.55	3.16	2.93	2.77	2.66	2.51	2.34	2.15	1.92
	10	3.01	2.62	2.42	2.29	2.20	2.13	2.04	1.93	1.81	1.66
	20	1.77	1.76	1.71	1.67	1.64	1.62	1.58	1.53	1.48	1.40
19	0.1	15.08	10.16	8.28	7.26	6.61	6.18	5.59	4.97	4.29	3.52
	0.5	10.07	7.09	5.92	5.27	4.85	4.56	4.18	3.76	3.31	2.78
	1	8.18	5.93	5.01	4.50	4.17	3.94	3.63	3.30	2.92	2.49
	2.5	5.92	4.51	3.90	3.56	3.33	3.17	2.96	2.72	2.45	2.13
	5	4.38	3.52	3.13	2.90	2.74	2.63	2.48	2.31	2.11	1.88
	10	2.99	2.61	2.40	2.27	2.18	2.11	2.02	1.91	1.79	1.63
	20	1.76	1.75	1.70	1.66	1.63	1.61	1.57	1.52	1.46	1.39

20	0.1	14.82	9.95	8.10	7.10	6.46	6.02	5.44	4.82	4.15	3.38
	0.5	9.94	6.99	5.82	5.17	4.76	4.47	4.09	3.68	3.22	2.69
	1	8.10	5.85	4.94	4.43	4.10	3.87	3.56	3.23	2.86	2.42
	2.5	5.87	4.46	3.86	3.51	3.29	3.13	2.91	2.68	2.41	2.09
	5	4.35	3.49	3.10	2.87	2.71	2.60	2.45	2.28	2.08	1.84
	10	2.97	2.59	2.38	2.25	2.16	2.09	2.00	1.89	1.77	1.61
	20	1.76	1.75	1.70	1.65	1.62	1.60	1.56	1.51	1.45	1.37
21	0.1	14.59	9.77	7.94	6.95	6.32	5.88	5.31	4.70	4.03	3.26
	0.5	9.83	6.89	5.73	5.09	4.68	4.39	4.01	3.60	3.15	2.61
	1	8.02	5.78	4.87	4.37	4.04	3.81	3.51	3.17	2.80	2.36
	2.5	5.83	4.42	3.82	3.48	3.25	3.09	2.87	2.64	2.37	2.04
	5	4.32	3.47	3.07	2.84	2.68	2.57	2.42	2.25	2.05	1.81
	10	2.96	2.57	2.36	2.23	2.14	2.08	1.98	1.88	1.75	1.59
	20	1.75	1.74	1.69	1.65	1.61	1.59	1.55	1.50	1.44	1.36
22	0.1	14.38	9.61	7.80	6.81	6.19	5.76	5.19	4.58	3.92	3.15
	0.5	9.73	6.81	5.65	5.02	4.61	4.32	3.94	3.54	3.08	2.55
	1	7.94	5.72	4.82	4.31	3.99	3.76	3.45	3.12	2.75	2.31
	2.5	5.79	4.38	3.78	3.44	3.22	3.05	2.84	2.60	2.33	2.00
	5	4.30	3.44	3.05	2.82	2.66	2.55	2.40	2.23	2.03	1.78
	10	2.95	2.56	2.35	2.22	2.13	2.06	1.97	1.86	1.73	1.57
	20	1.75	1.73	1.68	1.64	1.61	1.58	1.54	1.49	1.43	1.35
23	0.1	14.19	9.47	7.67	6.69	6.08	5.65	5.09	4.48	3.82	3.05
	0.5	9.63	6.73	5.58	4.95	4.54	4.26	3.88	3.47	3.02	2.48
	1	7.88	5.66	4.76	4.26	3.94	3.71	3.41	3.07	2.70	2.26

Table F (Continued)

df_2		df_1 1	2	3	4	5	6	8	12	24	∞
	2.5%	5.75	4.35	3.75	3.41	3.18	3.02	2.81	2.57	2.30	1.97
	5 %	4.28	3.42	3.03	2.80	2.64	2.53	2.38	2.20	2.00	1.76
	10 %	2.94	2.55	2.34	2.21	2.11	2.05	1.95	1.84	1.72	1.55
	20 %	1.74	1.73	1.68	1.63	1.60	1.57	1.53	1.49	1.42	1.34
24	0.1	14.03	9.34	7.55	6.59	5.98	5.55	4.99	4.39	3.74	2.97
	0.5	9.55	6.66	5.52	4.89	4.49	4.20	3.83	3.42	2.97	2.43
	1	7.82	5.61	4.72	4.22	3.90	3.67	3.36	3.03	2.66	2.21
	2.5	5.72	4.32	3.72	3.38	3.15	2.99	2.78	2.54	2.27	1.94
	5	4.26	3.40	3.01	2.78	2.62	2.51	2.36	2.18	1.98	1.73
	10	2.93	2.54	2.33	2.19	2.10	2.04	1.94	1.83	1.70	1.53
	20	1.74	1.72	1.67	1.63	1.59	1.57	1.53	1.48	1.42	1.33
25	0.1	13.88	9.22	7.45	6.49	5.88	5.46	4.91	4.31	3.66	2.89
	0.5	9.48	6.60	5.46	4.84	4.43	4.15	3.78	3.37	2.92	2.38
	1	7.77	5.57	4.68	4.18	3.86	3.63	3.32	2.99	2.62	2.17
	2.5	5.69	4.29	3.69	3.35	3.13	2.97	2.75	2.51	2.24	1.91
	5	4.24	3.38	2.99	2.76	2.60	2.49	2.34	2.16	1.96	1.71
	10	2.92	2.53	2.32	2.18	2.09	2.02	1.93	1.82	1.69	1.52
	20	1.73	1.72	1.66	1.62	1.59	1.56	1.52	1.47	1.41	1.32
26	0.1	13.74	9.12	7.36	6.41	5.80	5.38	4.83	4.24	3.59	2.82
	0.5	9.41	6.54	5.41	4.79	4.38	4.10	3.73	3.33	2.87	2.33

	1	7.72	5.53	4.64	4.14	3.82	3.59	3.29	2.96	2.58	2.13
	2.5	5.66	4.27	3.67	3.33	3.10	2.94	2.73	2.49	2.22	1.88
	5	4.22	3.37	2.98	2.74	2.59	2.47	2.32	2.15	1.95	1.69
	10	2.91	2.52	2.31	2.17	2.08	2.01	1.92	1.81	1.68	1.50
	20	1.73	1.71	1.66	1.62	1.58	1.56	1.52	1.47	1.40	1.31
27	0.1	13.61	9.02	7.27	6.33	5.73	5.31	4.76	4.17	3.52	2.75
	0.5	9.34	6.49	5.36	4.74	4.34	4.06	3.69	3.28	2.83	2.29
	1	7.68	5.49	4.60	4.11	3.78	3.56	3.26	2.93	2.55	2.10
	2.5	5.63	4.24	3.65	3.31	3.08	2.92	2.71	2.47	2.19	1.85
	5	4.21	3.35	2.96	2.73	2.57	2.46	2.30	2.13	1.93	1.67
	10	2.90	2.51	2.30	2.17	2.07	2.00	1.91	1.80	1.67	1.49
	20	1.73	1.71	1.66	1.61	1.58	1.55	1.51	1.46	1.40	1.30
28	0.1	13.50	8.93	7.19	6.25	5.66	5.24	4.69	4.11	3.46	2.70
	0.5	9.28	6.44	5.32	4.70	4.30	4.02	3.65	3.25	2.79	2.25
	1	7.64	5.45	4.57	4.07	3.75	3.53	3.23	2.90	2.52	2.06
	2.5	5.61	4.22	3.63	3.29	3.06	2.90	2.69	2.45	2.17	1.83
	5	4.20	3.34	2.95	2.71	2.56	2.44	2.29	2.12	1.91	1.65
	10	2.89	2.50	2.29	2.16	2.06	2.00	1.90	1.79	1.66	1.48
	20	1.72	1.71	1.65	1.61	1.57	1.55	1.51	1.46	1.39	1.30
29	0.1	13.39	8.85	7.12	6.19	5.59	5.18	4.64	4.05	3.41	2.64
	0.5	9.23	6.40	5.28	4.66	4.26	3.98	3.61	3.21	2.76	2.21
	1	7.60	5.42	4.54	4.04	3.73	3.50	3.20	2.87	2.49	2.03
	2.5	5.59	4.20	3.61	3.27	3.04	2.88	2.67	2.43	2.15	1.81
	5	4.18	3.33	2.93	2.70	2.54	2.43	2.28	2.10	1.90	1.64

Table F (Continued)

df_2	%	df_1 1	2	3	4	5	6	8	12	24	∞
	10 %	2.89	2.50	2.28	2.15	2.06	1.99	1.89	1.78	1.65	1.47
	20 %	1.72	1.70	1.65	1.60	1.57	1.54	1.50	1.45	1.39	1.29
30	0.1	13.29	8.77	7.05	6.12	5.53	5.12	4.58	4.00	3.36	2.59
	0.5	9.18	6.35	5.24	4.62	4.23	3.95	3.58	3.18	2.73	2.18
	1	7.56	5.39	4.51	4.02	3.70	3.47	3.17	2.84	2.47	2.01
	2.5	5.57	4.18	3.59	3.25	3.03	2.87	2.65	2.41	2.14	1.79
	5	4.17	3.32	2.92	2.69	2.53	2.42	2.27	2.09	1.89	1.62
	10	2.88	2.49	2.28	2.14	2.05	1.98	1.88	1.77	1.64	1.46
	20	1.72	1.70	1.64	1.60	1.57	1.54	1.50	1.45	1.38	1.28
40	0.1	12.61	8.25	6.60	5.70	5.13	4.73	4.21	3.64	3.01	2.23
	0.5	8.83	6.07	4.98	4.37	3.99	3.71	3.35	2.95	2.50	1.93
	1	7.31	5.18	4.31	3.83	3.51	3.29	2.99	2.66	2.29	1.80
	2.5	5.42	4.05	3.46	3.13	2.90	2.74	2.53	2.29	2.01	1.64
	5	4.08	3.23	2.84	2.61	2.45	2.34	2.18	2.00	1.79	1.51
	10	2.84	2.44	2.23	2.09	2.00	1.93	1.83	1.71	1.57	1.38
	20	1.70	1.68	1.62	1.57	1.54	1.51	1.47	1.41	1.34	1.24
60	0.1	11.97	7.76	6.17	5.31	4.76	4.37	3.87	3.31	2.69	1.90
	0.5	8.49	5.80	4.73	4.14	3.76	3.49	3.13	2.74	2.29	1.69
	1	7.08	4.98	4.13	3.65	3.34	3.12	2.82	2.50	2.12	1.60
	2.5	5.29	3.93	3.34	3.01	2.79	2.63	2.41	2.17	1.88	1.48

	5	4.00	3.15	2.76	2.52	2.37	2.25	2.10	1.92	1.70	1.39
	10	2.79	2.39	2.18	2.04	1.95	1.87	1.77	1.66	1.51	1.29
	20	1.68	1.65	1.59	1.55	1.51	1.48	1.44	1.38	1.31	1.18
120	0.1	11.38	7.31	5.79	4.95	4.42	4.04	3.55	3.02	2.40	1.56
	0.5	8.18	5.54	4.50	3.92	3.55	3.28	2.93	2.54	2.09	1.43
	1	6.85	4.79	3.95	3.48	3.17	2.96	2.66	2.34	1.95	1.38
	2.5	5.15	3.80	3.23	2.89	2.67	2.52	2.30	2.05	1.76	1.31
	5	3.92	3.07	2.68	2.45	2.29	2.17	2.02	1.83	1.61	1.25
	10	2.75	2.35	2.13	1.99	1.90	1.82	1.72	1.60	1.45	1.19
	20	1.66	1.63	1.57	1.52	1.48	1.45	1.41	1.35	1.27	1.12
∞	0.1	10.83	6.91	5.42	4.62	4.10	3.74	3.27	2.74	2.13	1.00
	0.5	7.88	5.30	4.28	3.72	3.35	3.09	2.74	2.36	1.90	1.00
	1	6.64	4.60	3.78	3.32	3.02	2.80	2.51	2.18	1.79	1.00
	2.5	5.02	3.69	3.12	2.79	2.57	2.41	2.19	1.94	1.64	1.00
	5	3.84	2.99	2.60	2.37	2.21	2.09	1.94	1.75	1.52	1.00
	10	2.71	2.30	2.08	1.94	1.85	1.77	1.67	1.55	1.38	1.00
	20	1.64	1.61	1.55	1.50	1.46	1.43	1.38	1.32	1.23	1.00

Source: Taken from Table V of Fisher and Yates, *Statistical Tables for Biological, Agricultural and Medical Research*, Longman Group Ltd., London (previously published by Oliver & Boyd, Edinburgh), 6th ed., 1973, by permission of the authors and publishers. This abridgement is from E. F. Lindquist, *Design and Analysis of Experiments in Psychology and Education*, 1953. Boston: Houghton Mifflin Company. Reprinted by permission.

Table G Distribution of the Studentized Range Statistic

df for error variance	1 − α	\(r\) — number of steps between ordered means													
		2	3	4	5	6	7	8	9	10	11	12	13	14	15
1	.95	18.0	27.0	32.8	37.1	40.4	43.1	45.4	47.4	49.1	50.6	52.0	53.2	54.3	55.4
	.99	90.0	135	164	186	202	216	227	237	246	253	260	266	272	277
2	.95	6.09	8.3	9.8	10.9	11.7	12.4	13.0	13.5	14.0	14.4	14.7	15.1	15.4	15.7
	.99	14.0	19.0	22.3	24.7	26.6	28.2	29.5	30.7	31.7	32.6	33.4	34.1	34.8	35.4
3	.95	4.50	5.91	6.82	7.50	8.04	8.48	8.85	9.18	9.46	9.72	9.95	10.2	10.4	10.5
	.99	8.26	10.6	12.2	13.3	14.2	15.0	15.6	16.2	16.7	17.1	17.5	17.9	18.2	18.5
4	.95	3.93	5.04	5.76	6.29	6.71	7.05	7.35	7.60	7.83	8.03	8.21	8.37	8.52	8.66
	.99	6.51	8.12	9.17	9.96	10.6	11.1	11.5	11.9	12.3	12.6	12.8	13.1	13.3	13.5
5	.95	3.64	4.60	5.22	5.67	6.03	6.33	6.58	6.80	6.99	7.17	7.32	7.47	7.60	7.72
	.99	5.70	6.97	7.80	8.42	8.91	9.32	9.67	9.97	10.2	10.5	10.7	10.9	11.1	11.2
6	.95	3.46	4.34	4.90	5.31	5.63	5.89	6.12	6.32	6.49	6.65	6.69	6.92	7.03	7.14
	.99	5.24	6.33	7.03	7.56	7.97	8.32	8.61	8.87	9.10	9.30	9.49	9.65	9.81	9.95
7	.95	3.34	4.16	4.69	5.06	5.36	5.61	5.82	6.00	6.16	6.30	6.43	6.55	6.66	6.76
	.99	4.95	5.92	6.54	7.01	7.37	7.68	7.94	8.17	8.37	8.55	8.71	8.86	9.00	9.12
8	.95	3.26	4.04	4.53	4.89	5.17	5.40	5.60	5.77	5.92	6.05	6.18	6.29	6.39	6.48
	.99	4.74	5.63	6.20	6.63	6.96	7.24	7.47	7.68	7.87	8.03	8.18	8.31	8.44	8.55

9	.95	3.20	3.95	4.42	4.76	5.02	5.24	5.43	5.60	5.74	5.87	5.98	6.09	6.19	6.28
	.99	4.60	5.43	5.96	6.35	6.66	6.91	7.13	7.32	7.49	7.65	7.78	7.91	8.03	8.13
10	.95	3.15	3.88	4.33	4.65	4.91	5.12	5.30	5.46	5.60	5.72	5.83	5.93	6.03	6.11
	.99	4.48	5.27	5.77	6.14	6.43	6.67	6.87	7.05	7.21	7.36	7.48	7.60	7.71	7.81
11	.95	3.11	3.82	4.26	4.57	4.82	5.03	5.20	5.35	5.49	5.61	5.71	5.81	5.90	5.99
	.99	4.39	5.14	5.62	5.97	6.25	6.48	6.67	6.84	6.99	7.13	7.26	7.36	7.46	7.56
12	.95	3.08	3.77	4.20	4.51	4.75	4.95	5.12	5.27	5.40	5.51	5.62	5.71	5.80	5.88
	.99	4.32	5.04	5.50	5.84	6.10	6.32	6.51	6.67	6.81	6.94	7.06	7.17	7.26	7.36
13	.95	3.06	3.73	4.15	4.45	4.69	4.88	5.05	5.19	5.32	5.43	5.53	5.63	5.71	5.79
	.99	4.26	4.96	5.40	5.73	5.98	6.19	6.37	6.53	6.67	6.79	6.90	7.01	7.10	7.19
14	.95	3.03	3.70	4.11	4.41	4.64	4.83	4.99	5.13	5.25	5.36	5.46	5.55	5.64	5.72
	.99	4.21	4.89	5.32	5.63	5.88	6.08	6.26	6.41	6.54	6.66	6.77	6.87	6.96	7.05
16	.95	3.00	3.65	4.05	4.33	4.56	4.74	4.90	5.03	5.15	5.26	5.35	5.44	5.52	5.59
	.99	4.13	4.78	5.19	5.49	5.72	5.92	6.08	6.22	6.35	6.46	6.56	6.66	6.74	6.82
18	.95	2.97	3.61	4.00	4.28	4.49	4.67	4.82	4.96	5.07	5.17	5.27	5.35	5.43	5.50
	.99	4.07	4.70	5.09	5.38	5.60	5.79	5.94	6.08	6.20	6.31	6.41	6.50	6.58	6.65
20	.95	2.95	3.58	3.96	4.23	4.45	4.62	4.77	4.90	5.01	5.11	5.20	5.28	5.36	5.43
	.99	4.02	4.64	5.02	5.29	5.51	5.69	5.84	5.97	6.09	6.19	6.29	6.37	6.45	6.52

Table G (Continued)

df for error variance	$1 - \alpha$	r — number of steps between ordered means													
		1	3	4	5	6	7	8	9	10	11	12	13	14	15
24	.95	2.92	3.53	3.90	4.17	4.37	4.54	4.68	4.81	4.92	5.01	5.10	5.18	5.25	5.32
	.99	3.96	4.54	4.91	5.17	5.37	5.54	5.69	5.81	5.92	6.02	6.11	6.19	6.26	6.33
30	.95	2.89	3.49	3.84	4.10	4.30	4.46	4.60	4.72	4.83	4.92	5.00	5.08	5.15	5.21
	.99	3.89	4.45	4.80	5.05	5.24	5.40	5.54	5.56	5.76	5.85	5.93	6.01	6.08	6.14
40	.95	2.86	3.44	3.79	4.04	4.23	4.39	4.52	4.63	4.74	4.82	4.91	4.98	5.05	5.11
	.99	3.82	4.37	4.70	4.93	5.11	5.27	5.39	5.50	5.60	5.69	5.77	5.84	5.90	5.96
60	.95	2.83	3.40	3.74	3.98	4.16	4.31	4.44	4.55	4.65	4.73	4.81	4.88	4.94	5.00
	.99	3.76	4.28	4.60	4.82	4.99	5.13	5.25	5.36	5.45	5.53	5.60	5.67	5.73	5.79
120	.95	2.80	3.36	3.69	3.92	4.10	4.24	4.36	4.48	4.56	4.64	4.72	4.78	4.84	4.90
	.99	3.70	4.20	4.50	4.71	4.87	5.01	5.12	5.21	5.30	5.38	5.44	5.51	5.56	5.61
∞	.95	2.77	3.31	3.63	3.86	4.03	4.17	4.29	4.39	4.47	4.55	4.62	4.68	4.74	4.80
	.99	3.64	4.12	4.40	4.60	4.76	4.88	4.99	5.08	5.16	5.23	5.29	5.35	5.40	5.45

Source: Abridged from Table II.2 in *Probability Integrals of the Range and of the Studentized Range*, prepared by H. Leon Harter, Donald S. Clemm, and Eugene H. Guthrie. Wright Air Development Center Technical Report 58-484, vol. 2, 1959. Reproduced with permission of the authors.

Table H Distribution of the Rank Sum T' for the Mann-Whitney Test

The values of T'_α, $T'_{1-\alpha}$, and α are such that if the N_1 and N_2 observations are chosen at random from the same population the chance that the rank sum T' of the N_1 observations in the smaller sample is equal to or less than T'_α is α and the chance that T' is equal to or greater than $T'_{1-\alpha}$ is α. The sample sizes are shown in parentheses (N_1, N_2).

T'_α	$T'_{1-\alpha}$	α
(1,1)		
1	2	.500
(1,2)		
1	3	.333
2	2	.667
(1,3)		
1	4	.250
2	3	.500
(1,4)		
1	5	.200
2	4	.400
3	3	.600
(1,5)		
1	6	.167
2	5	.333
3	4	.500
(1,6)		
1	7	.143
2	6	.286
3	5	.428
4	4	.571

T'_α	$T'_{1-\alpha}$	α
(1,7)		
1	8	.125
2	7	.250
3	6	.375
4	5	.500
(1,8)		
1	9	.111
2	8	.222
3	7	.333
4	6	.444
5	5	.556
(1,9)		
1	10	.100
2	9	.200
3	8	.300
4	7	.400
5	6	.500
(1,10)		
1	11	.091
2	10	.182
3	9	.273

T'	$T'_{1-\alpha}$	α
(1,10) (cont.)		
4	8	.364
5	7	.455
6	6	.545
(2,2)		
3	7	.167
4	6	.333
5	5	.667
(2,3)		
3	9	.100
4	8	.200
5	7	.400
6	6	.600
(2,4)		
3	11	.067
4	10	.133
5	9	.267
6	8	.400
7	7	.600
(2,5)		
3	13	.047

T'	$T'_{1-\alpha}$	α
(2,5) (cont.)		
4	12	.095
5	11	.190
6	10	.286
7	9	.429
8	8	.571
(2,6)		
3	15	.036
4	14	.071
5	13	.143
6	12	.214
7	11	.321
8	10	.429
9	9	.571
(2,7)		
3	17	.028
4	16	.056
5	15	.111
6	14	.167
7	13	.250
8	12	.333

Table H (Continued)

T'_α	$T'_{1-\alpha}$	α	T'_α	$T'_{1-\alpha}$	α	T'_α	$T'_{1-\alpha}$	α	T'_α	$T'_{1-\alpha}$	α
(2,7) (cont.)			(3,5)			(3,9) (cont.)			(4,5) (cont.)		
9	11	.444	6	21	.018	9	30	.032	20	20	.548
10	10	.556	7	20	.036	10	29	.050	(4,6)		
(2,8)			8	19	.071	11	28	.073	10	34	.005
3	19	.022	9	18	.125	12	27	.105	11	33	.010
4	18	.044	10	17	.196	13	26	.141	12	32	.019
5	17	.089	11	16	.286	14	25	.186	13	31	.033
6	16	.133	12	15	.393	15	24	.241	14	30	.057
7	15	.200	13	14	.500	16	23	.300	15	29	.086
8	14	.267	(3,6)			17	22	.363	16	28	.129
9	13	.356	6	24	.012	18	21	.432	17	27	.176
10	12	.444	7	23	.024	19	20	.500	18	26	.238
11	11	.556	8	22	.048	(3,10)			19	25	.305
(2,9)			9	21	.083	6	36	.003	20	24	.381
3	21	.018	10	20	.131	7	35	.007	21	23	.457
4	20	.036	11	19	.190	8	34	.014	22	22	.545
5	19	.073	12	18	.274	9	33	.024	(4,7)		
6	18	.109	13	17	.357	10	32	.038	10	38	.003
7	17	.164	14	16	.452	11	31	.056	11	37	.006
8	16	.218	15	15	.548	12	30	.080	12	36	.012
9	15	.291	(3,7)			13	29	.108	13	35	.021
10	14	.364	6	27	.008	14	28	.143	14	34	.036
11	13	.455	7	26	.017	15	27	.185	15	33	.055
12	12	.545	8	25	.033	16	26	.234	16	32	.082

	(2,10)	
3	23	.015
4	22	.030
5	21	.061
6	20	.091
7	19	.136
8	18	.182
9	17	.242
10	16	.303
11	15	.379
12	14	.455
13	13	.545

	(3,3)	
6	15	.050
7	14	.100
8	13	.200
9	12	.350
10	11	.500

	(3,4)	
6	18	.028
7	17	.057
8	16	.114
9	15	.200
10	14	.314
11	13	.429
12	12	.571

9	24	.058
10	23	.092
11	22	.133
12	21	.192
13	20	.258
14	19	.333
15	18	.417
16	17	.500

	(3,8)	
6	30	.006
7	29	.012
8	28	.024
9	27	.042
10	26	.067
11	25	.097
12	24	.139
13	23	.188
14	22	.248
15	21	.315
16	20	.387
17	19	.461
18	18	.539

	(3,9)	
6	33	.005
7	32	.009
8	31	.018

17	25	.287
18	24	.346
19	23	.406
20	22	.469
21	21	.531

	(4,4)	
10	26	.014
11	25	.029
12	24	.057
13	23	.100
14	22	.171
15	21	.243
16	20	.343
17	19	.443
18	18	.557

	(4,5)	
10	30	.008
11	29	.016
12	28	.032
13	27	.056
14	26	.095
15	25	.143
16	24	.206
17	23	.278
18	22	.365
19	21	.452

17	31	.115
18	30	.158
19	29	.206
20	28	.264
21	27	.324
22	26	.394
23	25	.464
24	24	.538

	(4,8)	
10	42	.002
11	41	.004
12	40	.008
13	39	.014
14	38	.024
15	37	.036
16	36	.055
17	35	.077
18	34	.107
19	33	.141
20	32	.184
21	31	.230
22	30	.285
23	29	.341
24	28	.404
25	27	.467
26	26	.533

Table H (Continued)

T'_α	$T'_{1-\alpha}$	α	T'_α	$T'_{1-\alpha}$	α	T'	$T'_{1-\alpha}$	α	T'	$T'_{1-\alpha}$	α
	(4,9)			(5,5) (cont.)			(5,8) (cont.)			(5,10) (cont.)	
10	46	.001	22	33	.155	21	49	.023	24	56	.028
11	45	.003	23	32	.210	22	48	.033	25	55	.038
12	44	.006	24	31	.274	23	47	.047	26	54	.050
13	43	.010	25	30	.345	24	46	.064	27	53	.065
14	42	.017	26	29	.421	25	45	.085	28	52	.082
15	41	.025	27	28	.500	26	44	.111	29	51	.103
16	40	.038		(5,6)		27	43	.142	30	50	.127
17	39	.053	15	45	.002	28	42	.177	31	49	.155
18	38	.074	16	44	.004	29	41	.217	32	48	.185
19	37	.099	17	43	.009	30	40	.262	33	47	.220
20	36	.130	18	42	.015	31	39	.311	34	46	.257
21	35	.165	19	41	.026	32	38	.362	35	45	.297
22	34	.207	20	40	.041	33	37	.416	36	44	.339
23	33	.252	21	39	.063	34	36	.472	37	43	.384
24	32	.302	22	38	.089	35	35	.528	38	42	.430
25	31	.355	23	37	.123		(5,9)		39	41	.477
26	30	.413	24	36	.165	15	60	.000	40	40	.523
27	29	.470	25	35	.214	16	59	.001		(6,6)	
28	28	.530	26	34	.268	17	58	.002	21	57	.001
	(4,10)		27	33	.331	18	57	.003	22	56	.002
10	50	.001	28	32	.396	19	56	.006	23	55	.004
11	49	.002	29	31	.465	20	55	.009	24	54	.008
12	48	.004	30	30	.535	21	54	.014	25	53	.013

13	47	.007
14	46	.012
15	45	.018
16	44	.026
17	43	.038
18	42	.053
19	41	.071
20	40	.094
21	39	.120
22	38	.152
23	37	.187
24	36	.227
25	35	.270
26	34	.318
27	33	.367
28	32	.420
29	31	.473
30	30	.527

(5,5)

15	40	.004
16	39	.008
17	38	.016
18	37	.028
19	36	.048
20	35	.075
21	34	.111

(5,7)

15	50	.001
16	49	.003
17	48	.005
18	47	.009
19	46	.015
20	45	.024
21	44	.037
22	43	.053
23	42	.074
24	41	.101
25	40	.134
26	39	.172
27	38	.216
28	37	.265
29	36	.319
30	35	.378
31	34	.438
32	33	.500

(5,8)

15	55	.001
16	54	.002
17	53	.003
18	52	.005
19	51	.009
20	50	.015

22	53	.021
23	52	.030
24	51	.041
25	50	.056
26	49	.073
27	48	.095
28	47	.120
29	46	.149
30	45	.182
31	44	.219
32	43	.259
33	42	.303
34	41	.350
35	40	.399
36	39	.449
37	38	.500

(5,10)

15	65	.000
16	64	.001
17	63	.001
18	62	.002
19	61	.004
20	60	.006
21	59	.010
22	58	.014
23	57	.020

26	52	.021
27	51	.032
28	50	.047
29	49	.066
30	48	.090
31	47	.120
32	46	.155
33	45	.197
34	44	.242
35	43	.294
36	42	.350
37	41	.409
38	40	.469
39	39	.531

(6,7)

21	63	.001
22	62	.001
23	61	.002
24	60	.004
25	59	.007
26	58	.011
27	57	.017
28	56	.026
29	55	.037
30	54	.051
31	53	.069

Table H (Continued)

T'_α	$T'_{1-\alpha}$	α	T'_α	$T'_{1-\alpha}$	α	T'_α	$T'_{1-\alpha}$	α	T'_α	$T'_{1-\alpha}$	α
	(6,7) (cont.)			(6,9) (cont.)			(7,7) (cont.)			(7,8) (cont.)	
32	52	.090	33	63	.044	29	76	.001	53	59	.389
33	51	.117	34	62	.057	30	75	.001	54	58	.433
34	50	.147	35	61	.072	31	74	.002	55	57	.478
35	49	.183	36	60	.091	32	73	.003	56	56	.522
36	48	.223	37	59	.112	33	72	.006		(7,9)	
37	47	.267	38	58	.136	34	71	.009	28	91	.000
38	46	.314	39	57	.164	35	70	.013	29	90	.000
39	45	.365	40	56	.194	36	69	.019	30	89	.000
40	44	.418	41	55	.228	37	68	.027	31	88	.001
41	43	.473	42	54	.264	38	67	.036	32	87	.001
42	42	.527	43	53	.303	39	66	.049	33	86	.002
	(6,8)		44	52	.344	40	65	.064	34	85	.003
21	69	.000	45	51	.388	41	64	.082	35	84	.004
22	68	.001	46	50	.432	42	63	.104	36	83	.006
23	67	.001	47	49	.477	43	62	.130	37	82	.008
24	66	.002	48	48	.523	44	61	.159	38	81	.011
25	65	.004		(6,10)		45	60	.191	39	80	.016
26	64	.006	21	81	.000	46	59	.228	40	79	.021
27	63	.010	22	80	.000	47	58	.267	41	78	.027
28	62	.015	23	79	.000	48	57	.310	42	77	.036
29	61	.021	24	78	.001	49	56	.355	43	76	.045
30	60	.030	25	77	.001	50	55	.402	44	75	.057
31	59	.041	26	76	.002	51	54	.451	45	74	.071

32	58	.054
33	57	.071
34	56	.091
35	55	.114
36	54	.141
37	53	.172
38	52	.207
39	51	.245
40	50	.286
41	49	.331
42	48	.377
43	47	.426
44	46	.475
45	45	.525

(6,9)

21	75	.000
22	74	.000
23	73	.001
24	72	.001
25	71	.002
26	70	.004
27	69	.006
28	68	.009
29	67	.013
30	66	.018
31	65	.025
32	64	.033

27	75	.004
28	74	.005
29	73	.008
30	72	.011
31	71	.016
32	70	.021
33	69	.028
34	68	.036
35	67	.047
36	66	.059
37	65	.074
38	64	.090
39	63	.110
40	62	.132
41	61	.157
42	60	.184
43	59	.214
44	58	.246
45	57	.281
46	56	.318
47	55	.356
48	54	.396
49	53	.437
50	52	.479
51	51	.521

(7,7)

28	77	.000
52	53	.500

(7,8)

28	84	.000
29	83	.000
30	82	.001
31	81	.001
32	80	.002
33	79	.003
34	78	.005
35	77	.007
36	76	.010
37	75	.014
38	74	.020
39	73	.027
40	72	.036
41	71	.047
42	70	.060
43	69	.076
44	68	.095
45	67	.116
46	66	.140
47	65	.168
48	64	.198
49	63	.232
50	62	.268
51	61	.306
52	60	.347

46	73	.087
47	72	.105
48	71	.126
49	70	.150
50	69	.175
51	68	.204
52	67	.235
53	66	.268
54	65	.303
55	64	.340
56	63	.379
57	62	.419
58	61	.459
59	60	.500

(7,10)

28	98	.000
29	97	.000
30	96	.000
31	95	.000
32	94	.001
33	93	.001
34	92	.001
35	91	.002
36	90	.003
37	89	.005
38	88	.007
39	87	.009

Table H (Continued)

T'_α	$T'_{1-\alpha}$	α	T'_α	$T'_{1-\alpha}$	α	T'	$T'_{1-\alpha}$	α	T'	$T'_{1-\alpha}$	α
(7,10) (cont.)			(8,8) (cont.)			(8,10) (cont.)			(9,9) (cont.)		
40	86	.012	61	75	.253	46	106	.003	67	104	.057
41	85	.017	62	74	.287	47	105	.004	68	103	.068
42	84	.022	63	73	.323	48	104	.006	69	102	.081
43	83	.028	64	72	.360	49	103	.008	70	101	.095
44	82	.035	65	71	.399	50	102	.010	71	100	.111
45	81	.044	66	70	.439	51	101	.013	72	99	.129
46	80	.054	67	69	.480	52	100	.017	73	98	.149
47	79	.067	68	68	.520	53	99	.022	74	97	.170
48	78	.081	(8,9)			54	98	.027	75	96	.193
49	77	.097	36	108	.000	55	97	.034	76	95	.218
50	76	.115	40	104	.000	56	96	.042	77	94	.245
51	75	.135	41	103	.001	57	95	.051	78	93	.273
52	74	.157	42	102	.001	58	94	.061	79	92	.302
53	73	.182	43	101	.002	59	93	.073	80	91	.333
54	72	.209	44	100	.003	60	92	.086	81	90	.365
55	71	.237	45	99	.004	61	91	.102	82	89	.398
56	70	.268	46	98	.006	62	90	.118	83	88	.432
57	69	.300	47	97	.008	63	89	.137	84	87	.466
58	68	.335	48	96	.010	64	88	.158	85	86	.500
59	67	.370	49	95	.014	65	87	.180	(9,10)		
60	66	.406	50	94	.018	66	86	.204	45	135	.000
61	65	.443	51	93	.023	67	85	.230	52	128	.000
62	64	.481	52	92	.030	68	84	.257	53	127	.001

	(8,8)	
63	63	.519
36	100	.000
37	99	.000
38	98	.000
39	97	.001
40	96	.001
41	95	.001
42	94	.002
43	93	.003
44	92	.005
45	91	.007
46	90	.010
47	89	.014
48	88	.019
49	87	.025
50	86	.032
51	85	.041
52	84	.052
53	83	.065
54	82	.080
55	81	.097
56	80	.117
57	79	.139
58	78	.164
59	77	.191
60	76	.221

53	91	.037
54	90	.046
55	89	.057
56	88	.069
57	87	.084
58	86	.100
59	85	.118
60	84	.138
61	83	.161
62	82	.185
63	81	.212
64	80	.240
65	79	.271
66	78	.303
67	77	.336
68	76	.371
69	75	.407
70	74	.444
71	73	.481
72	72	.519

	(8,10)	
36	116	.000
41	111	.000
42	110	.001
43	109	.001
44	108	.002
45	107	.002

69	83	.286
70	82	.317
71	81	.348
72	80	.381
73	79	.414
74	78	.448
75	77	.483
76	76	.517

	(9,9)	
45	126	.000
50	121	.000
51	120	.001
52	119	.001
53	118	.001
54	117	.002
55	116	.003
56	115	.004
57	114	.005
58	113	.007
59	112	.009
60	111	.012
61	110	.016
62	109	.020
63	108	.025
64	107	.031
65	106	.039
66	105	.047

54	126	.001
55	125	.001
56	124	.002
57	123	.003
58	122	.004
59	121	.005
60	120	.007
61	119	.009
62	118	.011
63	117	.014
64	116	.017
65	115	.022
66	114	.027
67	113	.033
68	112	.039
69	111	.047
70	110	.056
71	109	.067
72	108	.078
73	107	.091
74	106	.106
75	105	.121
76	104	.139
77	103	.158
78	102	.178
79	101	.200
80	100	.223

Table H (Continued)

T'_α	$T'_{1-\alpha}$	α	T'_α	$T'_{1-\alpha}$	α	T'_α	$T'_{1-\alpha}$	α	T'_α	$T'_{1-\alpha}$	α
(9,10) (cont.)			(10,10) (cont.)			(10,10) (cont.)			(10,10) (cont.)		
81	99	.248	65	145	.001	79	131	.026	93	117	.197
82	98	.274	66	144	.001	80	130	.032	94	116	.218
83	97	.302	67	143	.001	81	129	.038	95	115	.241
84	96	.330	68	142	.002	82	128	.045	96	114	.264
85	95	.360	69	141	.003	83	127	.053	97	113	.289
86	94	.390	70	140	.003	84	126	.062	98	112	.315
87	93	.421	71	139	.004	85	125	.072	99	111	.342
88	92	.452	72	138	.006	86	124	.083	100	110	.370
89	91	.484	73	137	.007	87	123	.095	101	109	.398
90	90	.516	74	136	.009	88	122	.109	102	108	.427
(10,10)			75	135	.012	89	121	.124	103	107	.456
55	155	.000	76	134	.014	90	120	.140	104	106	.485
63	147	.000	77	133	.018	91	119	.157	105	105	.515
64	146	.001	78	132	.022	92	118	.176			

For sample sizes greater than 10 the chance that the statistic T' will be less than or equal to an integer k is given approximately by the area under the standard normal curve to the left of

$$z = \frac{k + \frac{1}{2} - N_1(N_1 + N_2 + 1)/2}{\sqrt{N_1 N_2 (N_1 + N_2 + 1)/12}}$$

Source: From W. J. Dixon and F. J. Massey, "Introduction to Statistical Analysis," 2d ed., McGraw-Hill Book Company, New York, 1957.

Table I Critical Values of Wilcoxon's *T* Statistic for the Matched-Pairs Signed-Ranks Test

Number of matched pairs	Level of significance for one-tailed test		
	.025	.01	.005
	Level of significance for two-tailed test		
	.05	.02	.01
6	1	—	—
7	2	0	—
8	4	2	0
9	6	3	2
10	8	5	3
11	11	7	5
12	14	10	7
13	17	13	10
14	21	16	13
15	25	20	16
16	30	24	19
17	35	28	23
18	40	33	28
19	46	38	32
20	52	43	37
21	59	49	43
22	66	56	49
23	73	62	55
24	81	69	61
25	90	77	68

Source: Adapted from Table 2 of F. Wilcoxon and Roberta A. Wilcox, *Some Rapid Approximate Statistical Procedures*, Lederle Laboratories, a division of American Cyanamid Company, Pearl River, N.Y., rev. ed., 1964.

332

TABLE J Table of Squares and Square Roots

Number	Square	Square root	Number	Square	Square root
1	1	1.000	36	12 96	6.000
2	4	1.414	37	13 69	6.083
3	9	1.732	38	14 44	6.164
4	16	2.000	39	15 21	6.245
5	25	2.236	40	16 00	6.325
6	36	2.449	41	16 81	6.403
7	49	2.646	42	17 64	6.481
8	64	2.828	43	18 49	6.557
9	81	3.000	44	19 36	6.633
10	1 00	3.162	45	20 25	6.708
11	1 21	3.317	46	21 16	6.782
12	1 44	3.464	47	22 09	6.856
13	1 69	3.606	48	23 04	6.928
14	1 96	3.742	49	24 01	7.000
15	2 25	3.873	50	25 00	7.071
16	2 56	4.000	51	26 01	7.141
17	2 89	4.123	52	27 04	7.211
18	3 24	4.243	53	28 09	7.280
19	3 61	4.359	54	29 16	7.348
20	4 00	4.472	55	30 25	7.416
21	4 41	4.583	56	31 36	7.483
22	4 84	4.690	57	32 49	7.550
23	5 29	4.796	58	33 64	7.616
24	5 76	4.899	59	34 81	7.681
25	6 25	5.000	60	36 00	7.746
26	6 76	5.099	61	37 21	7.810
27	7 29	5.196	62	38 44	7.874
28	7 84	5.292	63	39 69	7.937
29	8 41	5.385	64	40 96	8.000
30	9 00	5.477	65	42 25	8.062
31	9 61	5.568	66	43 56	8.124
32	10 24	5.657	67	44 89	8.185
33	10 89	5.745	68	46 24	8.246
34	11 56	5.831	69	47 61	8.307
35	12 25	5.916	70	49 00	8.367

Table J (Continued)

Number	Square	Square root	Number	Square	Square root
71	50 41	8.426	106	1 12 36	10.296
72	51 84	8.485	107	1 14 49	10.344
73	53 29	8.544	108	1 16 64	10.392
74	54 76	8.602	109	1 18 81	10.440
75	56 25	8.660	110	1 21 00	10.488
76	57 76	8.718	111	1 23 21	10.536
77	59 29	8.775	112	1 25 44	10.583
78	60 84	8.832	113	1 27 69	10.630
79	62 41	8.888	114	1 29 96	10.677
80	64 00	8.944	115	1 32 25	10.724
81	65 61	9.000	116	1 34 56	10.770
82	67 24	9.055	117	1 36 89	10.817
83	68 89	9.110	118	1 39 24	10.863
84	70 56	9.165	119	1 41 61	10.909
85	72 27	9.220	120	1 44 00	10.954
86	73 96	9.274	121	1 46 41	11.000
87	75 69	9.327	122	1 48 84	11.045
88	77 44	9.381	123	1 51 29	11.091
89	79 21	9.434	124	1 53 76	11.136
90	81 00	9.487	125	1 56 25	11.180
91	82 81	9.539	126	1 58 76	11.225
92	84 64	9.592	127	1 61 29	11.269
93	86 49	9.644	128	1 63 84	11.314
94	88 36	9.695	129	1 66 41	11.358
95	90 25	9.747	130	1 69 00	11.402
96	92 16	9.798	131	1 71 61	11.446
97	94 09	9.849	132	1 74 24	11.489
98	96 04	9.899	133	1 76 89	11.533
99	98 01	9.950	134	1 79 56	11.576
100	1 00 00	10.000	135	1 82 25	11.619
101	1 02 01	10.050	136	1 84 96	11.662
102	1 04 04	10.100	137	1 87 69	11.705
103	1 06 09	10.149	138	1 90 44	11.747
104	1 08 16	10.198	139	1 93 21	11.790
105	1 10 25	10.247	140	1 96 00	11.832

334

Table J (Continued)

Number	Square	Square root	Number	Square	Square root
141	1 98 81	11.874	176	3 09 76	13.266
142	2 01 64	11.916	177	3 13 29	13.304
143	2 04 49	11.958	178	3 16 84	13.342
144	2 07 36	12.000	179	3 20 41	13 379
145	2 10 25	12.042	180	3 24 00	13.416
146	2 13 16	12.083	181	3 27 61	13.454
147	2 16 09	12.124	182	3 31 24	13.491
148	2 19 04	12.166	183	3 34 89	13.528
149	2 22 01	12.207	184	3 38 56	13.565
150	2 25 00	12.247	185	3 42 25	13.601
151	2 28 01	12.288	186	3 45 96	13.638
152	2 31 04	12.329	187	3 49 69	13.675
153	2 34 09	12.369	188	3 53 44	13.711
154	2 37 16	12.410	189	3 57 21	13.748
155	2 40 25	12.450	190	3 61 00	13.784
156	2 43 36	12.490	191	3 64 81	13.820
157	2 46 49	12.530	192	3 68 64	13.856
158	2 49 64	12.570	193	3 72 49	13.892
159	2 52 81	12.610	194	3 76 36	13.928
160	2 56 00	12.649	195	3 80 25	13.964
161	2 59 21	12.689	196	3 84 16	14.000
162	2 62 44	12.728	197	3 88 09	14.036
163	2 65 69	12.767	198	3 92 04	14.071
164	2 68 96	12.806	199	3 96 01	14.107
165	2 72 25	12.845	200	4 00 00	14.142
166	2 75 56	12.884	201	4 04 01	14.177
167	2 78 89	12.923	202	4 08 04	14.213
168	2 82 24	12.961	203	4 12 09	14.248
169	2 85 61	13.000	204	4 16 16	14.283
170	2 89 00	13.038	205	4 20 25	14.318
171	2 92 41	13.077	206	4 24 36	14.353
172	2 95 84	13.115	207	4 28 49	14.387
173	2 99 29	13.153	208	4 32 64	14.422
174	3 02 76	13.191	209	4 36 81	14.457
175	3 06 25	13.229	210	4 41 00	14.491

Table J (Continued)

Number	Square	Square root	Number	Square	Square root
211	4 45 21	14.526	246	6 05 16	15.684
212	4 49 44	14.560	247	6 10 09	15.716
213	4 53 69	14.595	248	6 15 04	15.748
214	4 57 96	14.629	249	6 20 01	15.780
215	4 62 25	14.663	250	6 25 00	15.811
216	4 66 56	14.697	251	6 30 01	15.843
217	4 70 89	14.731	252	6 35 04	15.875
218	4 75 24	14.765	253	6 40 09	15.906
219	4 79 61	14.799	254	6 45 16	15.937
220	4 84 00	14.832	255	6 50 25	15.969
221	4 88 41	14.866	256	6 55 36	16.000
222	4 92 84	14.900	257	6 60 49	16.031
223	4 97 29	14.933	258	6 65 64	16.062
224	5 01 76	14.967	259	6 70 81	16.093
225	5 06 25	15.000	260	6 76 00	16.125
226	5 10 76	15.033	261	6 81 21	16.155
227	5 15 29	15.067	262	6 86 44	16.186
228	5 19 84	15.100	263	6 91 69	16.217
229	5 24 41	15.133	264	6 96 96	16.248
230	5 29 00	15.166	265	7 02 25	16.279
231	5 33 61	15.199	266	7 07 56	16.310
232	5 38 24	15.232	267	7 12 89	16.340
233	5 42 89	15.264	268	7 18 24	16.371
234	5 47 56	15.297	269	7 23 61	16.401
235	5 52 25	15 330	270	7 29 00	16.432
236	5 56 96	15.362	271	7 34 41	16.462
237	5 61 69	15.395	272	7 39 84	16.492
238	5 66 44	15.427	273	7 45 29	16.523
239	5 71 21	15.460	274	7 50 76	16.553
240	5 76 00	15.492	275	7 56 25	16.583
241	5 80 81	15.524	276	7 61 76	16.613
242	5 85 64	15.556	277	7 67 29	16.643
243	5 90 49	15.588	278	7 72 84	16.673
244	5 95 36	15.620	279	7 78 41	16.703
245	6 00 25	15.652	280	7 84 00	16.733

Table J (Continued)

Number	Square	Square root	Number	Square	Square root
281	7 89 61	16.763	316	9 98 56	17.776
282	7 95 24	16.793	317	10 04 89	17.804
283	8 00 89	16.823	318	10 11 24	17.833
284	8 06 56	16.852	319	10 17 61	17.861
285	8 12 25	16.882	320	10 24 00	17.889
286	8 17 96	16.912	321	10 30 41	17.916
287	8 23 69	16.941	322	10 36 84	17.944
288	8 29 44	16.971	323	10 43 29	17.972
289	8 35 21	17.000	324	10 49 76	18.000
290	8 41 00	17.029	325	10 56 25	18.028
291	8 46 81	17.059	326	10 62 76	18.055
292	8 52 64	17.088	327	10 69 29	18.083
293	8 58 49	17.117	328	10 75 84	18.111
294	8 64 36	17.146	329	10 82 41	18.138
295	8 70 25	17.176	330	10 89 00	18.166
296	8 76 16	17.205	331	10 95 61	18.193
297	8 82 09	17.234	332	11 02 24	18.221
298	8 88 04	17.263	333	11 08 89	18.248
299	8 94 01	17.292	334	11 15 56	18.276
300	9 00 00	17.321	335	11 22 25	18.303
301	9 06 01	17.349	336	11 28 96	18.330
302	9 12 04	17.378	337	11 35 69	18.358
303	9 18 09	17.407	338	11 42 44	18.385
304	9 24 16	17.436	339	11 49 21	18.412
305	9 30 25	17.464	340	11 56 00	18.439
306	9 36 36	17.493	341	11 62 81	18.466
307	9 42 49	17.521	342	11 69 64	18.493
308	9 48 64	17.550	343	11 76 49	18.520
309	9 54 81	17.578	344	11 83 36	18.547
310	9 61 00	17.607	345	11 90 25	18.574
311	9 67 21	17.635	346	11 97 16	18.601
312	9 73 44	17.664	347	12 04 09	18.628
313	9 79 69	17.692	348	12 11 04	18.655
314	9 85 96	17.720	349	12 18 01	18.682
315	9 92 25	17.748	350	12 25 00	18.708

Table J (Continued)

Number	Square	Square root	Number	Square	Square root
351	12 32 01	18.735	386	14 89 96	19.647
352	12 39 04	18.762	387	14 97 69	19.672
353	12 46 09	18.788	388	15 05 44	19.698
354	12 53 16	18.815	389	15 13 21	19.723
355	12 60 25	18.841	390	15 21 00	19.748
356	12 67 36	18.868	391	15 28 81	19.774
357	12 74 49	18.894	392	15 36 64	19.799
358	12 81 64	18.921	393	15 44 49	19.824
359	12 88 81	18.947	394	15 52 36	19.849
360	12 96 00	18.974	395	15 60 25	19.875
361	13 03 21	19.000	396	15 68 16	19.900
362	13 10 44	19.026	397	15 76 09	19.925
363	13 17 69	19.053	398	15 84 04	19.950
364	13 24 96	19.079	399	15 92 01	19.975
365	13 32 25	19.105	400	16 00 00	20.000
366	13 39 56	19.131	401	16 08 01	20.025
367	13 46 89	19.157	402	16 16 04	20.050
368	13 54 24	19.183	403	16 24 09	20.075
369	13 61 61	19.209	404	16 32 16	20.100
370	13 69 00	19.235	405	16 40 25	20.125
371	13 76 41	19.261	406	16 48 36	20.149
372	13 83 84	19.287	407	16 56 49	20.174
373	13 91 29	19.313	408	16 64 64	20.199
374	13 98 76	19.339	409	16 72 81	20.224
375	14 06 25	19.363	410	16 81 00	20.248
376	14 13 76	19.391	411	16 89 21	20.273
377	14 21 29	19.416	412	16 97 44	20.298
378	14 28 84	19.442	413	17 05 69	20.322
379	14 36 41	19.468	414	17 13 96	20.347
380	14 44 00	19.494	415	17 22 25	20.372
381	14 51 61	19.519	416	17 30 56	20.396
382	14 59 24	19.545	417	17 38 89	20.421
383	14 66 89	19.570	418	17 47 24	20.445
384	14 74 56	19.596	419	17 55 61	20.469
385	14 82 25	19.621	420	17 64 00	20.494

Table J (Continued)

Number	Square	Square root	Number	Square	Square root
421	17 72 41	20.518	456	20 79 36	21.354
422	17 80 84	20.543	457	20 88 49	21.378
423	17 89 29	20.567	458	20 97 64	21.401
424	17 97 76	20.591	459	21 06 81	21.424
425	18 06 25	20.616	460	21 16 00	21.448
426	18 14 76	20.640	461	21 25 21	21.471
427	18 23 29	20.664	462	21 34 44	21 494
428	18 31 84	20.688	463	21 43 69	21.517
429	18 40 41	20.712	464	21 52 96	21.541
430	18 49 00	20.736	465	21 62 25	21.564
431	18 57 61	20.761	466	21 71 56	21.587
432	18 66 24	20.785	467	21 80 89	21.610
433	18 74 89	20.809	468	21 90 24	21.633
434	18 83 56	20.833	469	21 99 61	21.656
435	18 92 25	20.857	470	22 09 00	21.679
436	19 00 96	20.881	471	22 18 41	21.703
437	19 09 69	20.905	472	22 27 84	21.726
438	19 18 44	20.928	473	22 37 29	21.749
439	19 27 21	20.952	474	22 46 76	21.772
440	19 36 00	20.976	475	22 56 25	21.794
441	19 44 81	21.000	476	22 65 76	21.817
442	19 53 64	21.024	477	22 75 29	21.840
443	19 62 49	21.048	478	22 84 84	21.863
444	19 71 36	21.071	479	22 94 41	21.886
445	19 80 25	21.095	480	23 04 00	21.909
446	19 89 16	21.119	481	23 13 61	21.932
447	19 98 09	21.142	482	23 23 24	21.954
448	20 07 04	21.166	483	23 32 89	21.977
449	20 16 01	21.190	484	23 42 56	22.000
450	20 25 00	21.213	485	23 52 25	22.023
451	20 34 01	21.237	486	23 61 96	22.045
452	20 43 04	21.260	487	23 71 69	22.068
453	20 52 09	21.284	488	23 81 44	22.091
454	20 61 16	21.307	489	23 91 21	22.113
455	20 70 25	21 331	490	24 01 00	22.136

Table J (Continued)

Number	Square	Square root	Number	Square	Square root
491	24 10 81	22.159	526	27 66 76	22.935
492	24 20 64	22.181	527	27 77 29	22.956
493	24 30 49	22.204	528	27 87 84	22.978
494	24 40 36	22.226	529	27 98 41	23.000
495	24 50 25	22.249	530	28 09 00	23.022
496	24 60 16	22.271	531	28 19 61	23.043
497	24 70 09	22.293	532	28 30 24	23.065
498	24 80 04	22.316	533	28 40 89	23.087
499	24 90 01	22.338	534	28 51 56	23.108
500	25 00 00	22.361	535	28 62 25	23.130
501	25 10 01	22.383	536	28 72 96	23.152
502	25 20 04	22.405	537	28 83 69	23.173
503	25 30 09	22 428	538	28 94 44	23.195
504	25 40 16	22.450	539	29 05 21	23.216
505	25 50 25	22.472	540	29 16 00	23.238
506	25 60 36	22.494	541	29 26 81	23.259
507	25 70 49	22.517	542	29 37 64	23.281
508	25 80 64	22.539	543	29 48 49	23.302
509	25 90 81	22.561	544	29 59 36	23.324
510	26 01 00	22.583	545	29 70 25	23.345
511	26 11 21	22.605	546	29 81 16	23.367
512	26 21 44	22.627	547	29 92 09	23.388
513	26 31 69	22.650	548	30 03 04	23.409
514	26 41 96	22.672	549	30 14 01	23.431
515	26 52 25	22.694	550	30 25 00	23.452
516	26 62 56	22.716	551	30 36 01	23.473
517	26 72 89	22.738	552	30 47 04	23.495
518	26 83 24	22.760	553	30 58 09	23.516
519	26 93 61	22.782	554	30 69 16	23.537
520	27 04 00	22.804	555	30 80 25	23.558
521	27 14 41	22.825	556	30 91 36	23.580
522	27 24 84	22.847	557	31 02 49	23.601
523	27 35 29	22.869	558	31 13 64	23.622
524	27 45 76	22.891	559	31 24 81	23.643
525	27 56 25	22.913	560	31 36 00	23.664

Table J (Continued)

Number	Square	Square root	Number	Square	Square root
561	31 47 21	23.685	596	35 52 16	24.413
562	31 58 44	23.707	597	35 64 09	24.434
563	31 69 69	23.728	598	35 76 04	24.454
564	31 80 96	23.749	599	35 88 01	24.474
565	31 92 25	23.770	600	36 00 00	24.495
566	32 03 56	23.791	601	36 12 01	24.515
567	32 14 89	23.812	602	36 24 04	24.536
568	32 26 24	23.833	603	36 36 09	24.556
569	32 37 61	23.854	604	36 48 16	24.576
570	32 49 00	23.875	605	36 60 25	24.597
571	32 60 41	23.896	606	36 72 36	24.617
572	32 71 84	23.917	607	36 84 49	24.637
573	32 83 29	23.937	608	36 96 64	24.658
574	32 94 76	23.958	609	37 08 81	24.678
575	33 06 25	23.979	610	37 21 00	24.698
576	33 17 76	24.000	611	37 33 21	24.718
577	33 29 29	24.021	612	37 45 44	24.739
578	33 40 84	24.042	613	37 57 69	24.759
579	33 52 41	24.062	614	37 69 96	24.779
580	33 64 00	24.083	615	37 82 25	24.799
581	33 75 61	24.104	616	37 94 56	24.819
582	33 87 24	24.125	617	38 06 89	24.839
583	33 98 89	24.145	618	38 19 24	24.860
584	34 10 56	24.166	619	38 31 61	24.880
585	34 22 25	24.187	620	38 44 00	24.900
586	34 33 96	24.207	621	38 56 41	24.920
587	34 45 69	24.228	622	38 68 84	24.940
588	34 57 44	24.249	623	38 81 29	24.960
589	34 69 21	24.269	624	38 93 76	24.980
590	34 81 00	24.290	625	39 06 25	25.000
591	34 92 81	24.310	626	39 18 76	25.020
592	35 04 64	24.331	627	39 31 29	25.040
593	35 16 49	24.352	628	39 43 84	25.060
594	35 28 36	24.372	629	39 51 41	25.080
595	35 40 25	24.393	630	39 69 00	25.100

Table J (Continued)

Number	Square	Square root	Number	Square	Square root
631	39 81 61	25.120	666	44 35 56	25.807
632	39 94 24	25.140	667	44 48 89	25.826
633	40 06 89	25.159	668	44 62 24	25.846
634	40 19 56	25.179	669	44 75 61	25.865
635	40 32 25	25.199	670	44 89 00	25.884
636	40 44 96	25.219	671	45 02 41	25.904
637	40 57 69	25.239	672	45 15 84	25.923
638	40 70 44	25.259	673	45.29 29	25.942
639	40 83 21	25.278	674	45 42 76	25.962
640	40 96 00	25.298	675	45 56 25	25.981
641	41 08 81	25 318	676	45 69 76	26.000
642	41 21 64	25.338	677	45 83 29	26.019
643	41 34 49	25.357	678	45 96 84	26.038
644	41 47 36	25.377	679	46 10 41	26.058
645	41 60 25	25.397	680	46 24 00	26.077
646	41 73 16	25.417	681	46 37 61	26.096
647	41 86 09	25.436	682	46 51 24	26.115
648	41 99 04	25.456	683	46 64 89	26.134
649	42 12 01	25.475	684	46 78 56	26.153
650	42 25 00	25.495	685	46 92 25	26.173
651	42 38 01	25.515	686	47 05 96	26.192
652	42 51 04	25.534	687	47 19 69	26.211
653	42 64 09	25.554	688	47 33 44	26.230
654	42 77 16	25.573	689	47 47 21	26.249
655	42 90 25	25.593	690	47 61 00	26.268
656	43 03 36	25.612	691	47 74 81	26.287
657	43 16 49	25.632	692	47 88 64	26.306
658	43 29 64	25.652	693	48 02 49	26.325
659	43 42 81	25.671	694	48 16 36	26.344
660	43 56 00	25.690	695	48 30 25	26.363
661	43 69 21	25.710	696	48 44 16	26.382
662	43 82 44	25.729	697	48 58 09	26.401
663	43 95 69	25.749	698	48 72 04	26.420
664	44 08 96	25.768	699	48 86 01	26.439
665	44 22 25	25.788	700	49 00 00	26.458

Table J (Continued)

Number	Square	Square root	Number	Square	Square root
701	49 14 01	26.476	736	54 16 96	27.129
702	49 28 04	26.495	737	54 31 69	27.148
703	49 42 09	26.514	738	54 46 44	27.166
704	49 56 16	26.533	739	54 61 21	27.185
705	49 70 25	26.552	740	54 76 00	27.203
706	49 84 36	26.571	741	54 90 81	27.221
707	49 98 49	26.589	742	55 05 64	27.240
708	50 12 64	26.608	743	55 20 49	27.258
709	50 26 81	26.627	744	55 35 36	27.276
710	50 41 00	26.646	745	55 50 25	27.295
711	50 55 21	26.665	746	55 65 16	27.313
712	50 69 44	26.683	747	55 80 09	27.331
713	50 83 69	26.702	748	55 95 04	27.350
714	50 97 96	26.721	749	56 10 01	27.368
715	51 12 25	26.739	750	56 25 00	27.386
716	51 26 56	26.758	751	56 40 01	27.404
717	51 40 89	26.777	752	56 55 04	27.423
718	51 55 24	26.796	753	56 70 09	27.441
719	51 69 61	26.814	754	56 85 16	27.459
720	51 84 00	26.833	755	57 00 25	27.477
721	51 98 41	26.851	756	57 15 36	27.495
722	52 12 84	26.870	757	57 30 49	27.514
723	52 27 29	26.889	758	57 45 64	27.532
724	52 41 76	26.907	759	57 60 81	27.550
725	52 56 25	26.926	760	57 76 00	27.568
726	52 70 76	26.944	761	57 91 21	27.586
727	52 85 29	26.963	762	58 06 44	27.604
728	52 99 04	26.981	763	58 21 69	27.622
729	53 14 41	27.000	764	58 36 96	27.641
730	53 29 00	27.019	765	58 52 25	27.659
731	53 43 61	27.037	766	58 67 56	27.677
732	53 58 24	27.055	767	58 82 89	27.695
733	53 72 89	27.074	768	58 98 24	27.713
734	53 87 56	27.092	769	59 13 61	27.731
735	54 02 25	27.111	770	59 29 00	27.749

Table J (Continued)

Number	Square	Square root	Number	Square	Square root
771	59 44 41	27.767	806	64 96 36	28.390
772	59 59 84	27.785	807	65 12 49	28.408
773	59 75 29	27.803	808	65 28 64	28.425
774	59 90 76	27.821	809	65 44 81	28.443
775	60 06 25	27.839	810	65 61 00	28.460
776	60 21 76	27.857	811	65 77 21	28.478
777	60 37 29	27.875	812	65 93 44	28.496
778	60 52 84	27.893	813	66 09 69	28.513
779	60 68 41	27.911	814	66 25 96	28.531
780	60 84 00	27.928	815	66 42 25	28.548
781	60 99 61	27.946	816	66 58 56	28.566
782	61 15 24	27.964	817	66 74 89	28.583
783	61 30 89	27.982	818	66 91 24	28.601
784	61 46 56	28.000	819	67 07 61	28.618
785	61 62 25	28.018	820	67 24 00	28.636
786	61 77 96	28.036	821	67 40 41	28.653
787	61 93 69	28.054	822	67 56 84	28.671
788	62 09 44	28.071	823	67 73 29	28.688
789	62 25 21	28.089	824	67 89 76	28.705
790	62 41 00	28.107	825	68 06 25	28.723
791	62 56 81	28.125	826	68 22 76	28.740
792	62 72 64	28.142	827	68 39 29	28.758
793	62 88 49	28.160	828	68 55 84	28.775
794	63 04 36	28.178	829	68 72 41	28.792
795	63 20 25	28.196	830	68 89 00	28.810
796	63 36 16	28.213	831	69 05 61	28.827
797	63 52 09	28.231	832	69 22 24	28.844
798	63 68 04	28.249	833	69 38 89	28.862
799	63 84 01	28.267	834	69 55 56	28.879
800	64 00 00	28.284	835	69 72 25	28.896
801	64 16 01	28.302	836	69 88 96	28.914
802	64 32 04	28.320	837	70 05 69	28.931
803	64 48 09	28.337	838	70 22 44	28.948
804	64 64 16	28.355	839	70 39 21	28.965
805	64 80 25	28.373	840	70 56 00	28.983

Table J (Continued)

Number	Square	Square root	Number	Square	Square root
841	70 72 81	29.000	876	76 73 76	29.597
842	70 89 64	29.017	877	76 91 29	29.614
843	71 06 49	29.034	878	77 08 84	29.631
844	71 23 36	29 052	879	77 26 41	29.648
845	71 40 25	29.069	880	77 44 00	29.665
846	71 57 16	29.086	881	77 61 61	29.682
847	71 74 09	29.103	882	77 79 24	29.698
848	71 91 04	29.120	883	77 96 89	29.715
849	72 08 01	29.138	884	78 14 56	29.732
850	72 25 00	29.155	885	78 32 25	29.749
851	72 42 01	29.172	886	78 49 96	29.766
852	72 59 04	29.189	887	78 67 69	29.783
853	72 76 09	29.206	888	78 85 44	29.799
854	72 93 16	29.223	889	79 03 21	29.816
855	73 10 25	29.240	890	79 21 00	29.833
856	73 27 36	29.257	891	79 38 81	29.850
857	73 44 49	29.275	892	79 56 64	29.866
858	73 61 64	29.292	893	79 74 49	29.883
859	73 78 81	29.309	894	79 92 36	29.900
860	73 96 00	29.326	895	80 10 25	29.916
861	74 13 21	29.343	896	80 28 16	29.933
862	74 30 44	29.360	897	80 46 09	29.950
863	74 47 69	29.377	898	80 64 04	29.967
864	74 64 96	29.394	899	80 82 0˙	29.983
865	74 82 25	29.411	900	81 00 00	30.000
866	74 99 56	29.428	901	81 18 01	30.017
867	75 16 89	29.445	902	81 36 04	30.033
868	75 34 24	29.462	903	81 54 09	30.050
869	75 51 61	29.479	904	81 72 16	30.067
870	75 69 00	29.496	905	81 90 25	30.083
871	75 86 41	29.513	906	82 08 36	30.100
872	76 03 84	29.530	907	82 26 49	30 116
873	76 21 29	29.547	908	82 44 64	30.133
874	76 38 76	29.563	909	82 62 81	30.150
875	76 56 25	29.580	910	82 81 00	30.166

Table J (Continued)

Number	Square	Square root	Number	Square	Square root
911	82 99 21	30.183	946	89 49 16	30.757
912	83 17 44	30.199	947	89 68 09	30.773
913	83 35 69	30 216	948	89 87 04	30.790
914	83 53 96	30.232	949	90 06 01	30.806
915	83 72 25	30.249	950	90 25 00	30.822
916	83 90 56	30.265	951	90 44 01	30.838
917	84 08 89	30.282	952	90 63 04	30.854
918	84 27 24	30.299	953	90 82 09	30.871
919	84 45 61	30.315	954	91 01 16	30.887
920	84 64 00	30.332	955	91 20 25	30.903
921	84 82 41	30.348	956	91 39 36	30.919
922	85 00 84	30.364	957	91 58 49	30.935
923	85 19 29	30.381	958	91 77 64	30.952
924	85 37 76	30.397	959	91 96 81	30.968
925	85 56 25	30.414	960	92 16 00	30.984
926	85 74 76	30.430	961	92 35 21	31.000
927	85 93 29	30.447	962	92 54 44	31.016
928	86 11 84	30.463	963	92 73 69	31.032
929	86 30 41	30.480	964	92 92 96	31.048
930	86 49 00	30.496	965	93 12 25	31.064
931	86 67 61	30.512	966	93 31 56	31.081
932	86 86 24	30.529	967	93 50 89	31.097
933	87 04 89	30.545	968	93 70 24	31.113
934	87 23 56	30.561	969	93 89 61	31.129
935	87 42 25	30.578	970	94 09 00	31.145
936	87 60 96	30.594	971	94 28 41	31.161
937	87 79 69	30.610	972	94 47 84	31.177
938	87 98 44	30.627	973	94 67 29	31.193
939	88 17 21	30.643	974	94 86 76	31.209
940	88 36 00	30.659	975	95 06 25	31.225
941	88 54 81	30.676	976	95 25 76	31.241
942	88 73 64	30.692	977	95 45 29	31.257
943	88 92 49	30.708	978	95 64 84	31.273
944	89 11 36	30.725	979	95 84 41	31.289
945	89 30 25	30.741	980	96 04 00	31.305

Table J (Continued)

Number	Square	Square root	Number	Square	Square root
981	96 23 61	31.321	991	98 20 81	31.480
982	96 43 24	31.337	992	98 40 64	31.496
983	96 62 89	31.353	993	98 60 49	31.512
984	96 82 56	31.369	994	98 80 36	31.528
985	97 02 25	31.385	995	99 00 25	31.544
986	97 21 96	31.401	996	99 20 16	31.559
987	97 41 69	31.417	997	99 40 09	31.575
988	97 61 44	31.432	998	99 60 04	31.591
989	97 81 21	31.448	999	99 80 01	31.607
990	98 01 00	31.464	1000	100 00 00	31.623

Source: From Table II in E. L. Lindquist, *First Course in Statistics*, rev. ed., Boston: Houghton Mifflin Company.

references

Adamson, J. 1960. *Born Free*. New York: Pantheon Books.

Brady, J. V. 1964. Ulcers in "executive" monkeys. In S. Coopersmith, *Frontiers of Psychological Research*. San Francisco: Freeman.

Bruning, J. L., & Kintz, B. L. 1968. *Computational Handbook of Statistics*. Glenview, Illinois: Scott, Foresman.

Bruner, J. S., & Postman, L. 1949. On the perception of incongruity: A paradigm. *Journal of Personality*, **18**:206–223.

Bruner, J. S., & Minturn, A. L. 1955. Perceptual identification and perceptual organization. *Journal of General Psychology*, **53**:21–28.

Dobzhansky, T. 1951. *Genetics and the Origin of Species*. New York: Columbia University Press.

Edgington, E. S. 1964. Tabulation of inferential statistics used in psychological journals. *American Psychologist*, **19**:202–203.

Ferguson, G. A. 1971. *Statistical Analysis in Psychology and Education*. New York: McGraw-Hill.

Guilford, J. P. 1965. *Fundamental Statistics in Psychology and Education*. New York: McGraw-Hill.

Hanson, N. R. 1958. *Patterns of Discovery*. Cambridge: Cambridge University Press.

Kerlinger, F. N. 1964. *Foundations of Behavioral Research*. New York: Holt, Rinehart and Winston.

Kuhn, T. S. 1970. *The Structure of Scientific Revolutions*. Chicago: University of Chicago Press.

Lindsay, P. H., & Norman, D. A. 1972. *Human Information Processing*. New York: Academic Press.

Marascuilo, L. A. 1971. *Statistical Methods for Behavioral Science Research*. New York: McGraw-Hill.

Myers, J. L. 1966. *Fundamentals of Experimental Design*. Boston: Allyn and Bacon.

Nagel, E. 1961. *The Structure of Science*. New York: Harcourt, Brace, & World.

Overmier, J. B., & Seligman, M. E. 1967. Effects of inescapable shock upon subsequent escape and avoidance responding. *Journal of Comparative and Physiological Psychology*, **63**:28–33.

Rosenthal, R. 1966. *Experimenter Effect in Behavioral Research*. New York: Appleton-Century-Crofts.

Scott, J. B. 1968. *Early Experience and the Organization of Behavior*. Belmont (Calif.): Wadsworth.

Segal, S. 1956. *Nonparametric Statistics*. New York: McGraw Hill.

Short, D. J., & Woodnott, D. P. (eds.). 1969. *The I.T.A. Manual of Laboratory Animal Practice and Techniques*. London: Lockwood.

Spence, K. W., & Taylor, J. A. 1951. Anxiety and strength of the UCS as determiners of the amount of eyelid conditioning. *Journal of Experimental Psychology*, **41**:183–188.

Taylor, J. A. 1953. A personality scale of manifest anxiety. *Journal of Abnormal and Social Psychology*, **48**:285–290.

Weil, A. T., Zinberg, N. E., & Nelson, J. 1968. Clinical and psychological effects of marijuana in man. *Science*, **162**:1234–1242.

Winer, B. J. 1971. *Statistical Principles in Experimental Design*. New York: McGraw-Hill.

index